ICONS OF WORLD SPORT

Copyright © 2008 Roving Eye Publishing Group
PO Box 433 Springwood NSW 2777 Australia
Email: publishing@rovingeye.com

Cover & Book Design by Glen Hannah (Goonga Design)
Editor: Rod Nicholson
Managing Editor: Glen Hannah
Publisher: Melissa Whitelaw

ISBN 13: 978-0-9804495-3-2

The National Library of Australia Cataloguing-in-Publication:
 1. Don Bradman 2. Cricket captain/player - Australia - Biography.
Editor: Rod Nicholson (Series : Icons Of World Sport). Dewey: 796.358092

Printed in Australia by BPA Print Group - Melbourne, Australia - 2008.

Table Of Contents

A National Icon

It is right and fitting that Australians celebrate the centenary of the birth of Sir Donald Bradman. He was central to the establishment of a national identity, a role model as a superior sportsman and citizen whose deeds engendered pride and passion within a nation that needed inspiration during a period of depression and between World Wars.

Bradman's impact on cricket is undeniable. His extraordinary feats will testify to that so long as the game exists. Simply, he was the best.

More, his impact on the national psyche cannot be under-estimated. A young man from the bush went to England in 1930 and with unprecedented performances almost single-handedly won back the coveted Ashes against all odds. He was young (21), good-looking, respectful, eager and modest. His efforts focused the nation's mind and freed Australians from the mindset that they were somehow a poor colonial outpost. In this way he helped the nation to identify itself squarely and proudly as Australians.

Respect for him transcended the sporting arena. Shortly before he retired from cricket he became a much admired speaker who was witty, intelligent and insightful and who held very high principles. He believed in respect for one's parents, a high sense of duty to one's roles as a parent, husband, worker, sportsman or cricket administrator. Despite the incessant adulation he received throughout his entire life Bradman remained unswervingly true to these values.

It says much about the man that 60 years after he retired as the greatest batsman the game has even seen that he was regarded fondly - with almost reverence - by millions around the world, regardless of age or nationality.

To emphasise this, consider that The International Who's Who selected Bradman as one of only two Australians among the top 100 people who had done the most to shape the 20th century. The other was Rupert Murdoch.

And Bradman was one of only three athletes selected in that illustrious group, the other two being boxer Muhammad Ali and soccer player Pele.

The Australian Confederation of Sport voted Bradman the greatest male athlete of the past 200 years in 1988; the World Confederation of Sport nominated Bradman among the top ten sports people of the 20th century; the Sport Australia Hall of Fame named him the 'Male Athlete of the Century' in 1999; Sports Illustrated magazine ranked him the No. 1 Australian athlete of the 20th Century and Wisden Cricket Almanack, in a unanimous decision among the 100 judges, voted Bradman the greatest cricketer of the 20th century in 2000.

Such are some of the accolades that have been bestowed on him since 1949 when King George VI made him the only Australian cricketer to be knighted.

And it was extended further in 2000. The Bradman Foundation successfully secured the support of the Federal Government in protecting the Bradman name from indiscriminate commercial usages.

The Corporations Amendments Regulations 2000 made it illegal for any company to suggest a link to "Sir Donald Bradman" where such a link did not in fact exist - a protection that placed Bradman on a par with members of the royal family and the Anzacs.

This book pays tribute to The Don in his centenary year. The scrapbook traces his life from humble, almost frugal upbringing in Bowral under the watchful eye of his parents who largely shaped his character, to his death in 2001 that stopped a nation.

It tracks his cricket career - his feats that include an extraordinary Test average of 99.94, his dominance of the game for 20 years that ended with the most famous "duck" in Test history.

This tremendous contribution to cricket administration, often under-played, is examined and highlighted by previously unseen letters.

His devotion to wife Jessie, his vintage days when bridge replaced cricket and golf as his main pastimes, and his lifelong habit of replying to thousands of letters are also highlighted.

Bradman had the ability to mingle with royalty and ragamuffin alike. He touched, directly or indirectly, millions of people during his life.

We have sought out a host of them to pay homage to the man who former Prime Minister John Howard describes as Australia's first and greatest celebrity.

This book contains personal tributes, written specifically for this publication, from former Prime Ministers Bob Hawke and John Howard, old friends and foes Sir Alec Bedser, Arthur Morris, Neil Harvey and Sam Loxton, and international legends Sir Garfield Sobers, Sunil Gavaskar, Graeme Pollock, and Sir Richard Hadlee.

Former Australian captains Richie Benaud and Mark Taylor share their anecdotes, while media guru Sir Michael Parkinson, along with Australasian financial whiz Sir Ron Brierley also have their say.

Two of Bradman's favourites, Shane Warne and Sachin Tendulkar, head a list of modern day champions, along with Australian captain Ricky Ponting and Brett Lee, Michael Clarke and Michael Hussey as well as Chairman of the ICC cricket committee Sir Clive Lloyd.

Administrators including International Cricket Council former chairman Malcolm Gray, current ICC chief referee Ranjan Madugalle, Cricket Australia's chief executive James Sutherland and former Test umpire Col Egar pay tribute. So too do Pakistan champ Imran Khan, former England skipper Tony Greig, former Australian team manager Bill Jacobs, friend and bridge partner Mrs Judy Gribble and Bradman Foundation curator David Wells.

Those paying homage have personal stories to relate, moments they will cherish with the great man forever. Millions around the world will reflect on Don Bradman this year. He deserves this ultimate tribute.

Rod Nicholson

Rod Nicholson - Editor

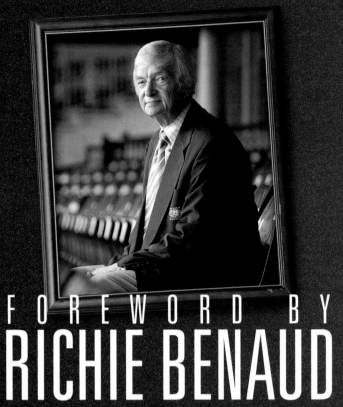

FOREWORD BY
RICHIE BENAUD

(Former Australian captain and patron of the Bradman Foundation)

Speaking or writing? Which aspect of Bradman would you prefer; to hear him speak in some unusual context or read something he has written on the game? Some might have preferred to see him bat, make a hundred, play a short dynamic innings to twist a game Australia's way, even to win it. Bradman was the best example of how Australian cricket provides opportunity for all. Eighty-five years ago, a youngster living in a country town wanting to play Sheffield Shield could travel to the city, play on a Saturday afternoon, then complete the match the following Saturday. Cricket in Australia still gives that kind of opportunity to youngsters, though in a more modern sophisticated manner.

On the question of speaking and writing, I was able in later years to listen to Bradman and to read what he had written and there are two occasions that stand out. First there was the time of the Tied Test at the Gabba in Brisbane. It was 8th of December, 1960 on the evening of the practice day prior to the start of the most famous Test of all. There was a good chance I wouldn't play in that game against Frank Worrell's team.

New South Wales had just completed a Sheffield Shield match against Victoria at the MCG, I had spent the Sunday rest day, Monday and Tuesday in bed with what was diagnosed as very severe tonsillitis. We arrived in Brisbane late on the Wednesday and on the Thursday I went through one hell of a fitness test under the watchful eyes of Jack Ryder, Dudley Seddon and Sir Donald Bradman. Somehow I passed it, then Sir Donald asked if he could come to our team meeting that evening to have a quick chat to the team. No inkling what it was about. I said I would go and ask the boys if that unusual request was OK and I went back to him and said, "7.30pm in my room at Lennon's."

His talk was short and to the point. He was carrying a message from the selectors that this could be a wonderful year of cricket and that this Australian team in 1960-61 could lead the way to one of the most attractive cricket series seen in Australia. "The selectors will look in kindly fashion on players who play aggressively and are clearly thinking about those who pay their money at the turnstiles." It followed that they would be looking in unkindly fashion on those who allowed the game to be unattractive for the cricket follower!

The second occasion was the written word in Wisden of 1986 where he drew the comparison between Test cricket and limited-overs internationals. 'Whither cricket now?' was brilliantly constructed and in the course of it he said he confessed to a love for both types of games. He added that limited-overs cricket rids the game of the unutterable bore who thinks occupancy of the crease and his own personal aggrandisement are all that matter. He stressed the fielding improvement and the fact that it is not necessarily true the one-day game has brought in its wake a decline in batting technique. He said this may have some validity but people get confused between a normal mode of play and the essential improvisation needed to circumvent defensive fields.

Twenty-two years ago he was writing about television and instant replays, suggesting, long before anyone else, that umpires when in doubt about a decision could seek arbitration from 'the box' for run-outs, stumpings, disputed catches and boundary decisions. He was well ahead of his time concluding that cricket had its problems for a century past. "Things have not changed much. Problems are still there - they are just different. It remains for players and administrators to accept the challenge to keep cricket alive and vibrant and not to shrink from the decisions needed to ensure that end."

Brilliant speaking and thinking.

INTRODUCTION BY
JOHN HOWARD
(Former Prime Minister of Australia)

I took a lot of stick from certain commentators, whenever I described Don Bradman as the greatest living Australian. To some it was incomprehensible that a sportsman could ever be so described; to others, who might admit that possibility, the fact that I would give that description to someone then approaching 90 years of age was an example of hopeless nostalgia for a bygone age.

Neither criticism properly comprehended the lasting impact Sir Donald Bradman had had on the Australian psyche. His influence went way beyond the indisputable fact that he has been the greatest cricketer the world has ever seen. Bradman was also Australia's first great celebrity.

Moreover, he acquired his iconic status at a time when Australia was going through the pain of the Great Depression. His remarkable cricketing prowess was a happy diversion for many Australians from the economic, family and social worries of the time.

He fitted the Australian narrative very well. He was born in the bush, at Cootamundra, and when he grew up in Bowral it was also seen by many as part of the bush. He then came to the big city to make his future.

Elsewhere in this book Bradman's remarkable cricketing career will be chronicled in detail and I will not impinge on the contribution of others. A measure of his dominance is that his fame continued to grow long after he stopped playing. Only a small percentage of Australians alive today would have seen him play, yet his place in the esteem and affection of Australians is unquestioned.

By coincidence, President George W Bush rang me the day after Don Bradman had died. It was to talk about political issues and it was only a few weeks after he had become President. In the conversation he mentioned The Don's death and what a remarkable person he had been. We were, at that time, on quite formal terms and I said, "Mr President, I can honestly say that Babe Ruth was the Don Bradman of America". It was a cheeky Australian way of saying that we thought he was the best and that the appropriate comparison was others to Bradman, not Bradman to others.

Prior to becoming Prime Minister I saw Sir Donald from time to time. As Prime Minister I tried to call on him every six months or so, seeing it as very much one of my responsibilities (and a very enjoyable one at that) on behalf of the nation to this remarkable man. Dropping in to see him and talking about any manner of subjects at his Adelaide home was, on every occasion, a huge privilege.

My wife and I especially recall visiting Sir Donald and Lady Jessie Bradman at their home, appropriately after stumps, during an Australia Day Test Match in Adelaide in January 1997. This was before, sadly, the pressure of the international cricket calendar had taken this wonderful event from cricket-loving South Australians. The four of us had a marvellous talk over a glass of champagne in the garden of their home about cricket and national and world affairs with Don reminiscing about past Australian political figures and their involvement with cricket.

Bradman was a very self-confident person. He was publicly quite modest. In private he had great certitude of opinion. There was no ambiguity in any of his views. If he had an opinion on a subject it was a very clear cut one.

He was an extremely sharp and hugely interesting conversationalist on issues that went far beyond cricket. He never tired of talking cricket but he was easily engaged on other subjects which affected our nation. He never gave me the impression of someone who believed that everything done in his day had been the only way of doing it.

His attitude towards One Day Cricket was an example. Although he was a traditionalist he recognised that limited overs cricket had brought a new dimension to the game.

Good sportsmanship was a given in Don Bradman's character. He played the game in a hard but fair manner. I can still remember as a very young boy reading of things that Don Bradman said about sportsmanship. They have stayed with me to this day.

I saw Don Bradman play only once. That was in his last match at the Sydney Cricket Ground in the Kippax/Oldfield Testimonial Match. I would have been nine years of age and my father took me to see the game. That was fifty-nine years ago and I have never forgotten the experience.

It was my privilege in August of 2000 to deliver the first Bradman Oration at the Melbourne Club. The former Chairman of the Australian Cricket Board, Bob Parrish, and the late Kerry Packer were both there. As readers of this book will know, those two men had been fierce rivals more than thirty years earlier over the future of cricket. I am told that at that dinner, in honour of Don Bradman, they shook hands and conversed after years of not talking to each other.

If, as I believe, that story is true there is a wonderful symbolism in a dinner honouring Sir Donald Bradman being the place at which some old cricketing differences were put to rest.

SHANE WARNE

(Champion leg-spinner who retired with a world record 708 wickets at an average of 25.41 and 3154 runs and 125 catches in 145 Tests)

Sir Donald Bradman is to me Australia's greatest ever sportsman, so to be invited to his home to chat for a couple of hours on his 90th birthday was a real thrill.

I went along with India's batting maestro Sachin Tendulkar and Sir Donald paid us both tremendous compliments - as if being in his home on such an important day wasn't a big enough compliment.

He said Sachin reminded him so much of himself as a batsman, and he told me he liked the way I bowled and how attacking I was. He said I reminded him so much of Bill O'Reilly. That was a fantastic compliment because Sir Donald always maintained O'Reilly was the best bowler he ever saw.

O'Reilly had one great experience I never did. He bowled to The Don.

I'd have loved to have bowled at him, as I am sure any bowler who has played international cricket would. He would certainly have smashed me all around the park but it would have been great to have bowled against the best batsman of all time.

One thing I did learn from Sir Donald Bradman: I answer my own fan mail. He did it all his life, on his trusty old typewriter. He would go to the Adelaide Oval every Friday and reply to all the fans around the world.

I take pride in doing it as well. I reply to requests for autographs on posters, birthday cards and letters in general. I help school children with question and answer assignments and projects.

I think back and consider how much pressure he must have been under as a national hero, with autograph hunters virtually chasing him everywhere he went. I think, perhaps, that people of his era had more manners. These days it is not so easy: as a whole the public is fantastic but there seems to be one lout in every crowd who spoils the link between the player and the public.

And I look back on that day at his home and realise how contemporary he had remained. He loved attacking and entertaining cricket, and both Sachin and I were chuffed that he thought so much of our styles that he sought our company on his 90th birthday.

Sachin and I naturally were inquisitive. We asked him what he thought of the game today, and Sachin was particularly interested in how he prepared for his big day at the cricket.

He explained that he went to work. That was hard to comprehend: leaving an office and going to play in a Test match.

I used to sleep as long as I could, have a shower, put on my gear, grab a piece of toast and get to the ground. I rested as much as I could before play. And the legendary Don Bradman went to work and did his job before going to the ground!

He told us he thought the fielding of the modern generation, particularly the out-fielding, throwing and the way players threw themselves around was fantastic and a vast improvement on his playing days.

I have always had a great admiration for Sir Donald Bradman. Cricket is played in so many countries around the world and for an Australian to be regarded as the best ever in the game's history is something special.

I am not big on statistics but when you consider Sir Donald has an average 40 per cent better than any other player, and a phenomenal innings to hundred ratio of 1 in 3, it is hard to get your head around such figures.

I get on very well with Arthur Morris and to hear him talk about Sir Donald, how he used to play and how he went about things, is enthralling.

It is common that as the years go by stories get exaggerated. A dashing century somehow takes fewer deliveries or the tough circumstances of a match-winning knock becomes almost an impossible feat.

Yet I don't think anything was exaggerated about Sir Donald's cricket or the way he played. He did score all those runs at a really fast rate, he did set all those records. And he did win games off his own bat.

And he changed the game forever. He did not accumulate runs, he amassed them in an attacking and entertaining way that set the tone and standard for all to follow. No wonder the public loved him and flocked to see him play.

The opposition from England had to come up with Bodyline to curb him, which is the ultimate compliment. Fancy having to devise a plan for a player because he was just too good to tackle in the normal way. I respect Douglas Jardine for coming up with such a plan. The English restricted him and won the series.

That they could cut his average in half was a coup - but he still averaged better than most do under normal circumstances!

I still marvel at how Sir Donald was regarded 60 years after his last game. It is a true test of his character and says so much about how he played the game, and the spirit in which he played, and how he carried himself for the rest of his life.

I judge cricketers by the way they play: how they are capable of changing a game and how people fear playing against them. I can tell you that while Mark Waugh's statistics may not look stunning, lots of opponents feared bowling to him, and the public loved watching him, bat, bowl and field.

You can only imagine how the opposing bowlers must have dreaded being given the ball when Bradman was taking strike.

But gee, I would have loved to have done it just for a few overs.

Stand in The Room Where The Don was Born

← **BRADMAN'S BIRTHPLACE**

Australian Cricketing Legend, Sir Donald Bradman,
was born on this site, 89 Adams Street, Cootamundra
on 27th. August 1908. The Cottage has been restored and
contains Memorabilia depicting the life and exploits of
One of Australia's Greatest Sporting Heroes.

MEMORABILIA COTTAGE →

Memorabilia Cottage contains a nostalgic collection of
historical curios and bric-a-brac, from Australia's past.

OPEN 9 a.m. - 5 p.m. DAILY.

COOTAMUNDRA SHIRE COUNCIL

BRADMAN'S BIRTHPLACE

CRICKETING LEGEND,
SIR DONALD BRADMAN, A.C.,
WAS BORN IN THIS COTTAGE
AT 89 ADAMS STREET, COOTAMUNDRA
ON THE 27TH AUGUST, 1908.

THE COTTAGE WAS RESTORED BY
COOTAMUNDRA SHIRE COUNCIL IN RECOGNITION OF
SIR DONALD'S CONTRIBUTION
TO AUSTRALIA'S SPORTING HERITAGE.

OFFICIALLY OPENED
BY
MR. ALAN K. DAVIDSON, A.M., M.B.E.,
PRESIDENT, NEW SOUTH WALES CRICKET ASSOCIATION

23RD OCTOBER, 1992

Form No. 5.
NO. OF CERTIFICATE 6

Registered
1908 BIRTHS in the District of Gundagai at Cootamundra
In the State of New South Wales.
Registered by Lachlan Wentworth Broughton District Registrar.

17 AUG 1978

Column		
1	Number in Register ...	423
2	Child— When and where born ...	27th August, 1908,- Cootamundra.
3	Name, and whether present or not	Donald George Not present.
4	Sex	Male.
5	Parents— Father— Name and Surname, rank or profession of the father, age and birthplace	George Bradman, Farmer, 32 years, Jindalee, N.S. Wales.
6	When and where married, previous issue living and deceased.	16 December, 1893, Cootamundra, N.S. Wales. Islet N. 14 years , Lillian M. 9, Elizabeth M. 7, Victor C. 3. Living. None dead.
7	Mother— Name and maiden surname of the mother, age and birthplace.	Emily Whatman, 36 years, Glengarry, N.S. Wales.
8	Informant— Signature, description, and residence of informant.	G. Bradman, father, Yeo Yeo.
9	Witnesses— Accoucheur, Nurse, or names of witnesses.	Dr. H.M. Anderson, Nurse Scholtz, Miss Scholtz.
10	Registrar— Signature of District Registrar, date, and where registered.	L.W. Broughton, 8th September, 1908, Cootamundra.
11	Name, if added after registry of birth.	

I, William Swift Bromhead do hereby
certify that the above is a true copy of the particulars in an entry in a Register of Births kept at
the District Registry Office at SOUTH WALES Cootamundra and extracted
this 29th day of September, 1924.

REGISTER OF BIRTHS, DEATHS
AND MAR...
DISTRICT OF GUNDAGAI
AT COOTAMUNDRA
District Registrar

Bradman's birthplace at Cootamundra.

The Bradman story began when Don was born at a nursing home at 89 Adams Street, Cootamundra, 320km south-west of Sydney, on August 27th, 1908. Delivered by local "Granny" Scholz, he was the youngest of five children to George and Emily Bradman, following sisters Islet, Lilian and May, and brother Victor.

When Don was two years of age, not long after the earliest portrait shown here, the family moved to a weatherboard house in Shepherd St, Bowral.

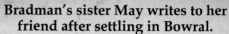

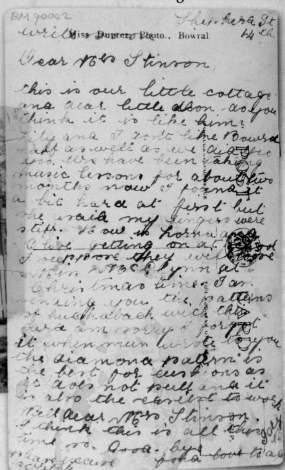

Don Bradman's early life was that of a country kid growing up in tough financial times that had engulfed the world. He was born in the western NSW town of Cootamundra on 27 August 1908, the fifth child of George and Emily Bradman. He was the youngest of the Bradman children, following sisters Islet, Lilian and Elizabeth (May) and brother Victor.

His father, who was born in 1876 and died in 1961, married Emily (1871-1944) in 1893 at Cootamundra. George was a farmer when he married and they lived on a property of 542 acres, seven miles from Cootamundra and three miles from Jindalee in NSW.

They sold the farm in 1906, and moved to the small nearby locality of Yeo Yeo, where they lived in a slab hut on a property. In the 1970s the house was moved to the museum in Temora. All that remains on-site today is a single brick chimney, although this is on a large private property and not available for public viewing.

The first four children were schooled at a now defunct Yeo Yeo Public School before the family moved to Bowral in 1911 when Don was only two and a half years old.

In Bowral, the Bradman family first lived in a still surviving weatherboard house in Shepherd Street, before moving to a new brick house that George built in 1924 in Glebe Street. This house survives today and is owned by the Bradman Foundation.

Don Bradman with dog "Teddy". Shepherd Street, Bowral, c.1917.

"At the age of eight or nine he was a very fair bat." (George Bradman, Don's father).

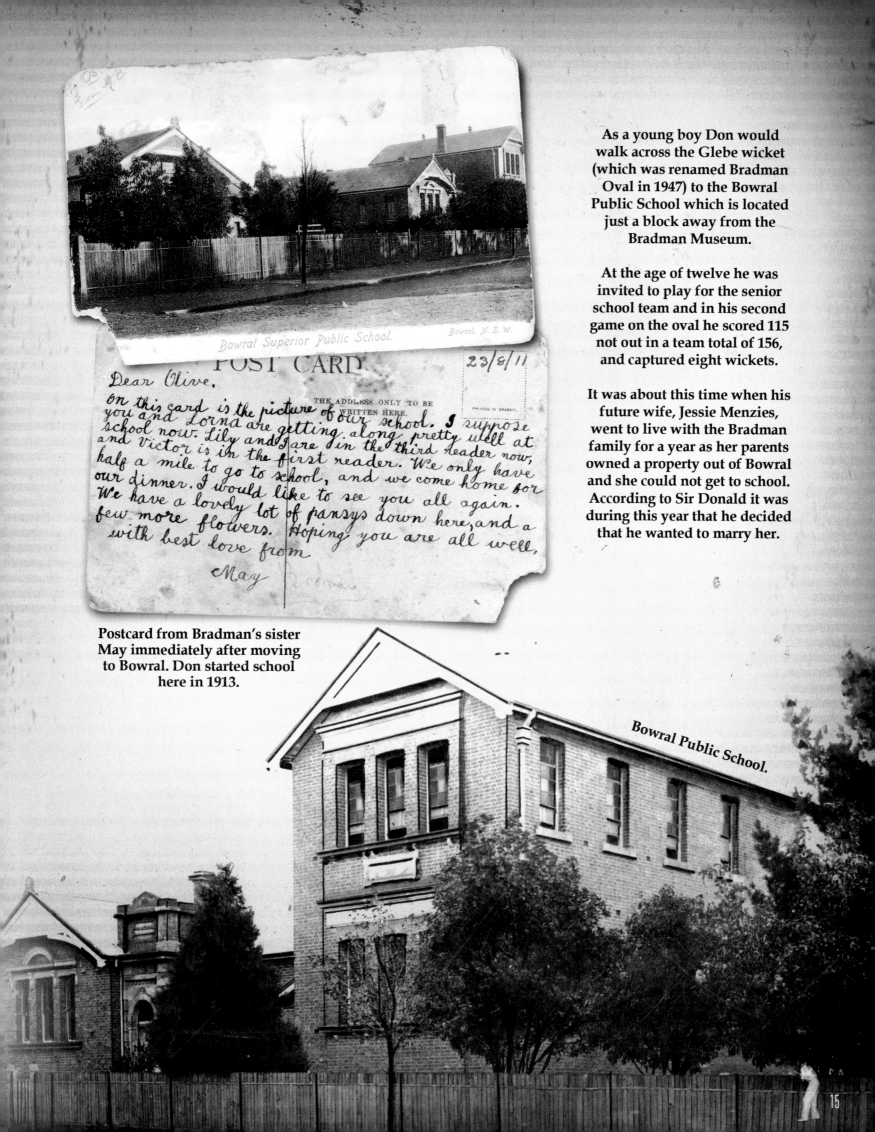

Bowral Superior Public School.   Bowral. N.S.W.

POST CARD

Dear Olive,

23/8/11

THE ADDRESS ONLY TO BE
WRITTEN HERE.

PRINTED IN SAXONY.

On this card is the picture of our school. I suppose
you and Lorna are getting along pretty well at
school now. Lily and I are in the third reader now,
and Victor is in the first reader. We only have
half a mile to go to school, and we come home for
our dinner. I would like to see you all again.
We have a lovely lot of pansys down here, and a
few more flowers. Hoping you are all well,
with best love from
May

Postcard from Bradman's sister
May immediately after moving
to Bowral. Don started school
here in 1913.

As a young boy Don would
walk across the Glebe wicket
(which was renamed Bradman
Oval in 1947) to the Bowral
Public School which is located
just a block away from the
Bradman Museum.

At the age of twelve he was
invited to play for the senior
school team and in his second
game on the oval he scored 115
not out in a team total of 156,
and captured eight wickets.

It was about this time when his
future wife, Jessie Menzies,
went to live with the Bradman
family for a year as her parents
owned a property out of Bowral
and she could not get to school.
According to Sir Donald it was
during this year that he decided
that he wanted to marry her.

Bowral Public School.

Bradman honoured his mother and father while they were alive, often returning to Bowral to visit them. While overseas playing cricket, regular correspondence was maintained between he and his parents and it is clear that both of them had a very strong and enduring influence over their son. Certainly Bradman's lifelong values of duty, honesty, diligence and accepting responsibility, were shaped by both George and Emily Bradman.

George and Emily Bradman.

Bradman's parents were also no doubt proud of their son's achievements, but his successes on the field were considered secondary to how he conducted himself. Emily once replied to a cricket fan who'd written to her congratulating her on his cricket performances '...he's always been a good-living boy'.

The main street of Bowral, Bong Bong St., as Bradman knew it in the early 1920s.

Kissed His Mother

She sat on the porch in the sunshine
As I went down the street
A woman whose hair was silver,
But whose face was blossom sweet
Making me think of a garden
When, in spite of the frost & snow
Of bleak November weather
Late, fragrant lilies blow

I heard a footstep behind me
And the sound of a merry laugh
And I knew the heart it came from
Would be like a comforting staff
In the time & the hour of trouble
Hopeful, and brave, and strong
One of the hearts to lean on,
When we think all things go wrong

I turned at the click of the gate latch
And met his manly look
A face like his gives me pleasure
Like the page of a pleasant book
It told of a steadfast purpose
Of a brave and daring will

A face with a promise in it,
That God grant, the years fulfil

He went up the pathway, singing;
I saw the woman's eyes
Grow bright with a wordless welcome,
As sunshine warms the skies
"Back again sweetheart mother,"
He cried, & bent to kiss
The loving face that was lifted
For what some mothers miss

That boy will do to depend on.
I hold that this is true —
From lads in love with their mothers
Our bravest heroes grew
Earth's grandest hearts have been loving hearts
Since time & earth began
And the boy who kisses his mother
Is every inch a man

My thoughts are yours to day dear
My loving wishes too
And so I send you greetings
Affection warm & true

This verse was on
the card I sent to
Don for his Birthday
in England August 27
1934

Emily Whatman, Don's mother, who was born in Mittagong, was the sixth of nine children. Her father was William Whatman and her mother Sophia Cupitt. Emily met George Bradman when visiting Cootamundra and the couple were married in 1893. Five years George's senior, Emily found being a farmer's wife challenging, having to battle the deprivations of the Australian bush with five young children.

Don Bradman dearly loved both his parents, but had a special fondness for Emily. The Bradman Museum has copies of many of her writings including a journal, which she is understood to have compiled between 1912 to well into the 1930s. This journal contains all manner of 'cure alls' for minor ailments and remedies on topics as broad as how to deal with indigestion, thinning hair, scaly skin, rheumatism, tired eyes, circulation and dental care. There are even recipes for making soap, liniment and a 'pick me up' tonic.

The book is clearly a place of reflection for Emily and prayers and religious verse are commonplace. Her neat hand cites numerous wise sayings which dot the pages and it is clear that she found them of comfort in how she lived and raised her family. There are many references to motherhood, and a dim view of alcohol: 'He who learns strong drink to despise will find himself healthy, wealthy and wise'.

Or a persistent theme of hard work, application and toil: 'What glory has ever been rendered manifest except through suffering'. Music is also an obvious interest with many songs and verses featured.

The other role of the book was to track the progress of her children. For example Emily has recorded when Don started primary school (13/9/1913), when he sang at the Kangaloon concert (24/8/1920), when he first went to Sydney (1920), when he first played competitive tennis aged 10 years and ten months, and even when he contracted the measles on 19 May 1915.

Don went to Sydney for the first
time June midwinter holidays
with Miss Chalker 1920

Don sang in Kangaloon Concert 24th August 1920
3 days before he was 12 year old
Islet married 16th December 1919

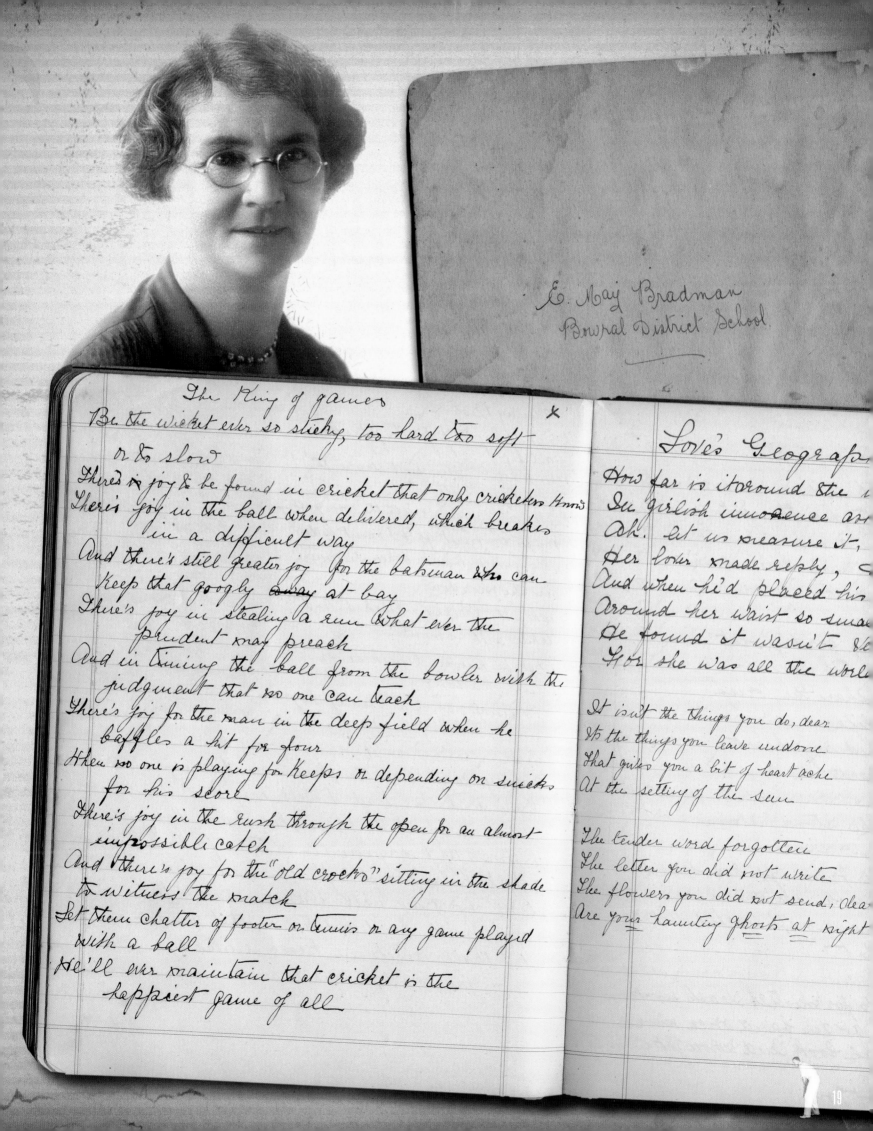

E. May Bradman
Bowral District School.

The King of games

But the wicket ever so sticky, too hard too soft
   or to slow
There's joy to be found in cricket that only cricketers know
There's joy in the ball when delivered, which breaks
   in a difficult way
And there's still greater joy for the batsman who can
   keep that googly away at bay
There's joy in stealing a run what ever the
   prudent may preach
And in timing the ball from the bowler with the
   judgment that no one can teach
There's joy for the man in the deep field when he
   baffles a hit for four
When no one is playing for keeps or depending on snicks
   for his score
There's joy in the rush through the open for an almost
   impossible catch
And there's joy for the "old crocks" sitting in the shade
to witness the match
Let them chatter of footer or tennis or any game played
   with a ball
He'll ever maintain that cricket is the
   happiest game of all

Love's Geograp

How far is it around the
In girlish innocence a
Ah. let us measure it,
Her lover made reply,
And when he'd placed his
Around her waist so sma
He found it wasn't
For she was all the worl

It isn't the things you do, dear
It's the things you leave undone
That gives you a bit of heart ache
At the setting of the sun

The tender word forgotten
The letter you did not write
The flowers you did not send, dea
Are your haunting ghosts at night

George Bradman (fourth from right in back row) playing for Bowral circa 1912.

George Bradman (front right) outside his employer's building.

Don's father was originally a farmer but turned his hand to being a fencer and a carpenter when he arrived in Bowral. He worked for many years for a local timber and joinery works, Alf Stephens & Son, and erected some magnificent fences in the locale.

The fence below at Bowral was built by George and was commonly referred to as 'Bradman's Fence'.

Aside from school and backyard cricket, the young Don was a busy boy, with piano lessons, choir practice, golf caddie jobs and helping his father. As a teenager, he played rugby, tennis and athletics as well as cricket.

December 1922, Bradman in back row fourth from left.

Bradman in back row second from right.

Due to the lack of a senior high school in the Southern Highlands Bradman left school at 14 at the end of 1922 and proceeded to earn a living to help sustain the family. He believed his career would be as a house painter, but took a position with Mr Percy Westbrook as a clerk in a Bowral Real Estate Agency. Mr Westbrook played an important role in Don's early career by allowing him the time to play cricket in Sydney when the offer came in 1926.

Don Bradman remembered this at a function in Bowral in 1930: "After leaving school I spent five years with Mr Westbrook before going to Sydney. Everything lay in his hands, but at great inconvenience he let me go to Sydney. It was due to him that I got my chance in big cricket".

Don was an active sporting youngster. There was no organised sport or coaching at school, and Don didn't have any children to play with in the neighbourhood, so he developed a ball game in his backyard.

DON BRADMAN

This unusual game involved throwing a golf ball at the round brick base of a water tank, and then hitting the ball with a cricket stump. This was not an easy game when the ball would fly off in all directions. Without knowing it, he was developing his precise co-ordination and skill which would serve him so well later as an international cricketer.

"I can understand how it must have developed the co-ordination of brain, eye and muscle which was to serve me so well in matches later on." (Bradman on his childhood golf ball/cricket stump game)

SIR GARFIELD SOBERS

(Champion all-rounder named as one of the top five cricketers of the 20th century. The West Indian captain scored 8032 runs at 57.78, captured 235 wickets at 34.03 and took 109 catches in 93 Tests)

SIR Donald Bradman was an influential man. In fact, he was the only person who could have talked me into being captain the Rest Of The World team that played Australia in 1971/72 after the apartheid issue forced the cancellation of the South Africa visit.

At the time I was taking a break from international cricket and had a contract to play for South Australia in the Sheffield Shield competition, which suited me just fine. Then Don approached me about leading the Rest Of The World combination but I told him I wasn't too keen.

However I had too much respect for him and I simply couldn't say no when he said: `You are the only one who can do it. I would appreciate it if you would come and do me this favour."

I did it just for him - nobody else could have got me to do it.

And I am glad I did. I met Dennis Lillee at his best after he came back from injury and some other wonderful cricketers during that series.

And I scored 254 at the MCG, an innings that Sir Donald said was the best innings he had ever seen. I was proud to hear that, but as he was a good friend maybe he was a bit biased!

I had nothing but admiration for Sir Don. When I was growing up in Barbados, Don Bradman's name was often mentioned. People talked about other Australian players too - Lindsay Hassett, Ray Lindwall and Keith Miller, Neil Harvey and Arthur Morris. But Bradman was always the man, the one who dominated everyone's thoughts.

I was born in 1936 so I was only 12 when Don made his farewell 1948 tour of England, when he was at the end of his career. But I read lots of books on him, and heard lots of people talking about his accomplishments.

I got to know him when I played for South Australia for three seasons from 1961/62 to 1963/64 when South Australia won the Sheffield Shield in my final year.

I realised then the amount of respect he had and the amount of work he had done for Australian and South Australian cricket.

He was the kind of man you looked up to and he commanded a very prominent profile. People always talked about him in the highest regard and with great respect. He was a great man, and I was lucky to get to know him.

I spent a couple of nights at his house for dinner and we discussed cricket.

I still remember an amazing thing. It was in 1962 and we were discussing deliveries going down the leg side. Don suggested they should be called wides because they deprived batsmen from playing shots. Cricket authorities have introduced the exact rule that he was promoting 46 years earlier!

I argued that it would be unfair for a spin bowler or swing bowler to pitch outside off stump and have the ability to move the ball far enough for it to go down the leg side, only for it to be called a wide. Don said: "That's why I cannot argue with you!" because he recognised that I had a point, which I maintain today despite the introduction of the rule.

But it just showed that he was such a forward-thinker, a man before his time in many ways. I was amazed by the sports he was so good at. Besides his extraordinary cricket skills, he was good at tennis and squash and golf. I played golf with him and I was never in his league, despite our age difference. He used to say he knew I would out-drive him but that he would have the better of me when we got closer to the cup. And he was right. His short game and irons into the greens were marvelous and he beat me every time.

Don always knew how to get the best out of people. When I played for South Australia I had a habit of taking a nap in the rooms during games. If South Australia was in trouble Don would come into the rooms and wake me up and say: "You have to get me some runs." And if I was lucky enough to get a score, he would come back and say: "I knew you would not let me down."

He loved the game, the challenge. And he surprised me one day when I was at Adelaide Oval to pack my gear for a trip to Queensland. I heard someone hitting balls in the practice nets. I asked one of my teammates, Duncan Sharpe, who it was and he said it was the Knight.

He was preparing to play a game, I think in Canberra, and I went and watched the great man. I could see his class even at the age of about 60. He stroked the ball beautifully.

You could only imagine what he was like at his peak!

At the age of twelve Bradman was invited to play for the senior school team and in his second game he scored 115 not out in a team total of 156, and captured eight wickets.

On weekends Don acted as scorer for the Bowral team which included his father as umpire, brother and two uncles. One day the team was short a player and he was sent in at the fall of the eighth wicket, and scored an unbeaten 37. For the return innings the following Saturday he scored 29 not out. As a reward for his fine effort a Bowral team member gave him his first cricket bat (pictured here to the left). Don's father had to saw three inches off the bat to suit the young Don. He later used this bat in his first full season in the senior men's team. This prize possession is now on display in the Bradman Museum.

Don begged his father to take him to the Sydney Cricket Ground in February 1921 to watch his first Test match, the fifth of the series between England and Australia. The two day excursion so impressed Don he vowed to his father that he would never be satisfied until he played cricket on that ground.

Don Bradman

At the age of 17, he had developed into a serious cricketer for the Bowral team. He continued to make high scores, take wickets and hold catches, making an enormous impact in the Berrima District competition. His mother promised him a new bat if he made a century in the final between Bowral and Moss Vale. Rising to the occasion in the match held over five consecutive Saturdays, the dashing teenager amassed 300 runs, breaking another record in the Berrima District final. He joked with his mother that perhaps his score deserved three bats but he gratefully received the one.

Bowral and Mittagong teams, Glebe Park, 1925. Bradman is in the second row wearing a cap. On his right is his uncle and team captain, Dick Whatman. His father is standing in the back row, far right.

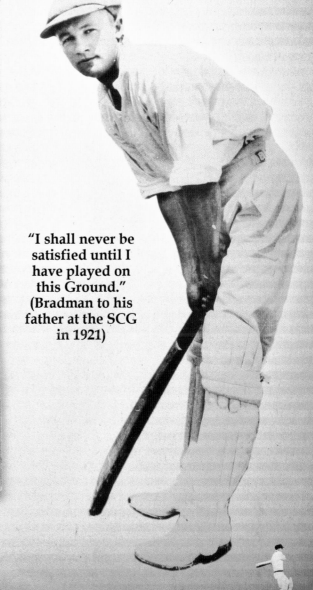

"I shall never be satisfied until I have played on this Ground." (Bradman to his father at the SCG in 1921)

In October 1926, the NSW selectors invited him to a cricket trial in Sydney at the SCG. The selectors were mostly looking for promising young bowlers, however the press of the day were to report "...the practice produced a batsman, and a batsman from the country too." Because Don was used to playing country cricket on concrete and dirt pitches, his footwork was considered to be slow. He quickly adjusted to the grass wickets.

SOUTHERN COUNTRY WEEK TEAM

NEW SOUTH WALES CRICKET ASSOCIATION

Address all Communications
to The Secretary.

Telephone: B.3541.

HH/IM

254a GEORGE STREET,
SYDNEY.

5th October, 1926.

D. Bradman, Esq.,
C/o A. Stephens, Esq.,
Boolwey Street,
BOWRAL.

Dear Sir:

The State Selectors have had under consideration your record in cricket in the past season, and in view of such record they particularly desire to see you in action.

For this purpose I would like you to attend practice at the Sydney Cricket Ground on Monday next, 11th instant. Practice commences at 4 p.m. and continues through out the afternoon. Should you be able to attend as requested, please let me know in order that I may inform the Selectors who will be on the watch for you and in order that I may advise you as to the further particulars. My Association is prepared to pay your fare from Bowral and return and should you deem it necessary to remain in Sydney overnight you will be reimbursed to the extent of your accommodation.

I sincerely trust that you will give this matter the consideration its importance warrants and hope that you will realise that this is an opportunity which should not be missed. If you will be able to attend, let me know immediately and state the time you hope to arrive in Sydney. Should you find it impossible to attend on the 11th, please inform me if any other Monday in the near future would be suitable, and I will have arrangements made accordingly.

Yours faithfully,

SECRETARY.

1318 RUNS

AVERAGE OF OVER 100

BOY OF 17

DISTRICT RECORD OF 300

BOWRAL, Monday.

That the district record score of 300 by Don Bradman, a lad of 17, in Bowral's final competition match against Moss Vale, was no fluke is shown by the young cricketer's other performances during the season.

In the club's competition matches he played 12 innings (three not out), for 985 runs, an average of 109.4.

In addition to winning the batting average, he was second in bowling with an average of 8.1 for 35 wickets;

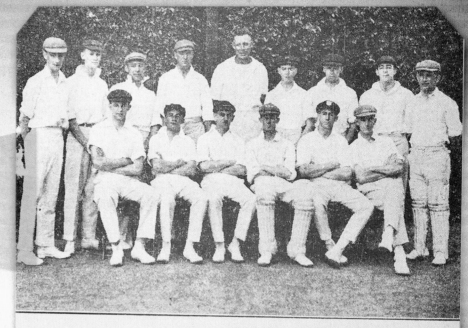

THE POSSIBLES.

Back row (reading from left to right): J. Fisher (Balmain), S. King (Petersham), J. Foskett (Glebe), D. Mullarkey (St. George), C. Nicholls (Cumberland), J. Carter (Randwick), A. McGrath (North Sydney), G. Amos (Marrickville), R. Loder (Northern District).

Front row: F. Jordan (Glebe), D. Bradman (Bowral), R. E. Gostelow (Paddington), H. C. Steele (Marrickville), captain, H. Waghorn (St. George), A. Hall (Cumberland).

D. BRADMAN
N.S.W.

DON. BRADMAN.

BOWRAL'S MOST FAMOUS CRICKETER.

After achieving a splendid cricket record in his native town, Donald has gone to Sydney, where he plays with St. George. Good judges in the metropolis say Don. will soon take his place in interstate contests. Our photo. by courtesy of the Telegraph Pictorial.

Soon after the trial, he was invited to play for the Southern team in a Country Cricket Week in Sydney. During that week he agreed to play for the St George Cricket Club if they paid his train fare from Bowral. Each Saturday, Don had to get up out of bed before 5am to catch the train from Bowral to Sydney, often not getting home until midnight.

Don Bradman

he won the trophy for most catches, 16, and the trophy for best fielding. Including non-competition matches, he played 21 innings, eight not out, for 1318, average 101.3, took 51 wickets at an average of 7.8, and held 26 catches.

His best batting performances were 300 against Moss Vale in the final match for the Mack Cup, 234 against Wingello (premiers 1924-25), 120 against Bundanoon in the semi-final for the cup, and 105 against Bowral R.

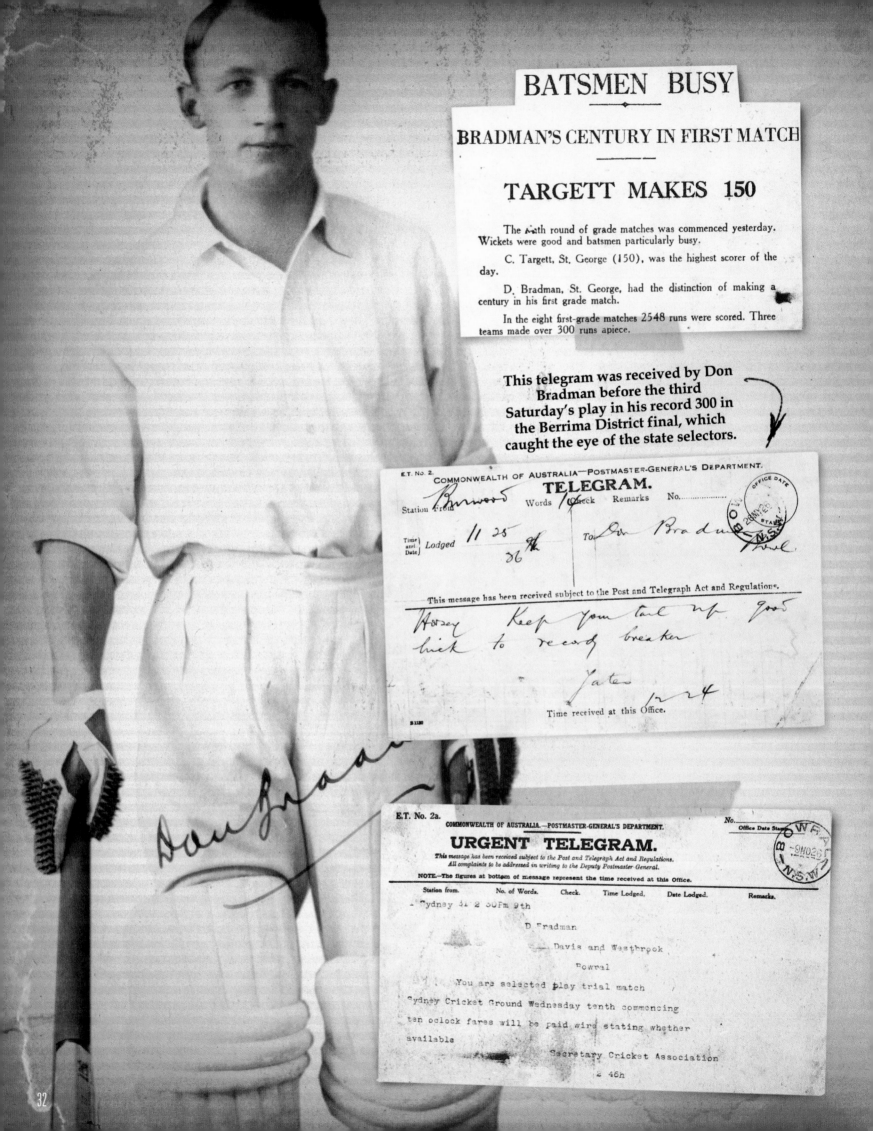

BATSMEN BUSY

BRADMAN'S CENTURY IN FIRST MATCH

TARGETT MAKES 150

The fifth round of grade matches was commenced yesterday. Wickets were good and batsmen particularly busy.

C. Targett, St. George (150), was the highest scorer of the day.

D. Bradman, St. George, had the distinction of making a century in his first grade match.

In the eight first-grade matches 2548 runs were scored. Three teams made over 300 runs apiece.

This telegram was received by Don Bradman before the third Saturday's play in his record 300 in the Berrima District final, which caught the eye of the state selectors.

E.T. No. 2.
COMMONWEALTH OF AUSTRALIA—POSTMASTER-GENERAL'S DEPARTMENT.

TELEGRAM.

Station From Burwood Words / Check Remarks No.

Time and Date Lodged 11 25 86th To Don Bradman Bowral

This message has been received subject to the Post and Telegraph Act and Regulations.

Horsey Keep your tail up good luck to record breaker

Yates

Time received at this Office.

E.T. No. 2a.
COMMONWEALTH OF AUSTRALIA.—POSTMASTER-GENERAL'S DEPARTMENT. No.
Office Date Stamp

URGENT TELEGRAM.

This message has been received subject to the Post and Telegraph Act and Regulations.
All complaints to be addressed in writing to the Deputy Postmaster-General.

NOTE.—The figures at bottom of message represent the time received at this Office.

Station from.	No. of Words.	Check.	Time Lodged.	Date Lodged.	Remarks.

Sydney 41 2 30Pm 9th

D. Bradman

Davis and Westbrook

Bowral

You are selected play trial match Sydney Cricket Ground Wednesday tenth commencing ten oclock fares will be paid wire stating whether available

Secretary Cricket Association

2 46h

BARRIER DISTRICT CRICKET LEAGUE

❊

Visit of N.S.W.

**Sheffield Shield
Team**

❊

December 13th and 14th
1927

Nicholls & Sons Print, Broken Hill.

B. H. Team.	N. S. W. Team
J. W. Salter CAPTAIN	A. Kippax CAPTAIN
B. Chandler VICE-CAPT.	A. A. Mailey
C. G. Davison	W. A. Oldfield
S. Arnold	D. Bradman
E. J. Carragher	A. Jackson
C. J. Mitchell	R. McNamee
L. Rook	G. Morgan
C. Hill	N. E. Phillips
A. F. Pincombe	A. Scanes
J. Lyons	F. Jordan
W. English	S. Everett
F. Gulliford (12th)	Dr. B. F. McADAM MANAGER

The Visitors have been extended the privilege of honorary members of the "Broken Hill Club."

⊁⊱ ITINERARY. ⊰⊀

Arrival of Visitors, Dec. 13th   8.30 a.m.

Civic Reception   ...   10.30 a.m.

Official Luncheon, Grand Hotel   12 noon

Visit to Surface of South Mine   2 p.m.

Practice at Jubilee   ...   4 p.m.

Visit Underground South, North
and Zinc Corp.   8 p.m.

Wed., December 14th—Cricket

10.30 a.m. to 12.45 p.m.

2.0 p.m. to 6.0 p.m.

Farewell Sulphide Street   8 p.m.

33

NSW CRICKET ASSOCIATION
SOUTHERN TOUR - DECEMBER 1927

BACK ROW: N. Phillips, F. Jordan, A. Scanes, S. Everett, T.J.E. Andrews, D.G. Bradman, A. Jackson, W.A. Oldfield.
FRONT ROW: G. Morgan, A.F. Kippax (Captain), Dr. F.V. McAdam (Manager), R. McNamee, A. Mailey.

Bradman first represented NSW on the southern tour in December of 1927.
He proudly wore the team blazer (left) en route to Melbourne.

egins With a Century

Donald Bradman, the 19-year-old boy from Bowral, made a very fine start for New South Wales with his 118 at Adelaide in his first Shield match. He is the seventh New South Wales batsman to begin with a century against South Australia, the others being L. S. Poidevin, E. F. Waddy, A. Diamond, J. Boyle, H. O. Rock and L. T. Gwynne. For South Australia, L. T. Gun is the only one to accomplish the feat. Bradman's batting appears to have impressed the Adelaide people, and he showed in the match against Victoria that he is a lad likely to make runs in dashing style. The confidence he showed in going out to Blackie's tempting ones and driving them hard greatly pleased the crowd. Bradman looks like a boy who will go far in the game.

In December 1927, now aged 19, Bradman stepped into first-class cricket when selected to play Sheffield Shield for New South Wales. On the tour of the southern states - his first venture outside Sydney and its environs, he travelled on the new railway line to Broken Hill before going on to Adelaide. The players wore sandshoes in the match against Broken Hill which was played on a hard sun-baked red dirt pitch. To add to the challenge, a dust storm hit the game.

TEL. KOGARAH 31

ALL COMMUNICATIONS TO
BE ADDRESSED TO THE
TOWN CLERK

MUNICIPALITY OF HURSTVILLE

IN REPLY PLEASE
QUOTE Nº G.I.DK.

Council Chambers,
Hurstville

9th. December 1927.

D. Bradman, Esq.,
¢/- N.S.W. Cricket Association,
254, George Street,
SYDNEY.

Dear Sir,

At the meeting of my Council held last evening, attention was directed to the fact that two members of the St. George District Cricket Club had conferred upon them the very great honor of being selected to represent this State against Victoria and South Australia in the forthcoming "Sheffield Shield" Cricket matches, and as one of those selected, I was directed to convey to you the hearty congratulations of the Council, and the hope that when the occasion arises, you will indeed prove a very worthy representative, and thus justify the confidence reposed in you by the selectors.

Yours faithfully,

Town Clerk.

BRADMAN 118 NSW v SA

He began his own historic batting career when he scored 118 in the first innings for NSW against South Australia in his first-class debut. Now known as 'The Boy from Bowral', he became the 20th Australian to score a century on debut.

BRADMAN'S BRILLIANT DEBUT

DON BRADMAN, ST. GEORGE COLT.

Made a century in his first match in the Sheffield Shield. A product of Bowral he is short, quick on his feet drives crisply, fields smartly, and has a fine temperament for big cricket.

The young cricketer returned home to Bowral after playing in Melbourne to a proud welcome. The Bowral community loved their hero, now affectionately calling him 'Our Don'.

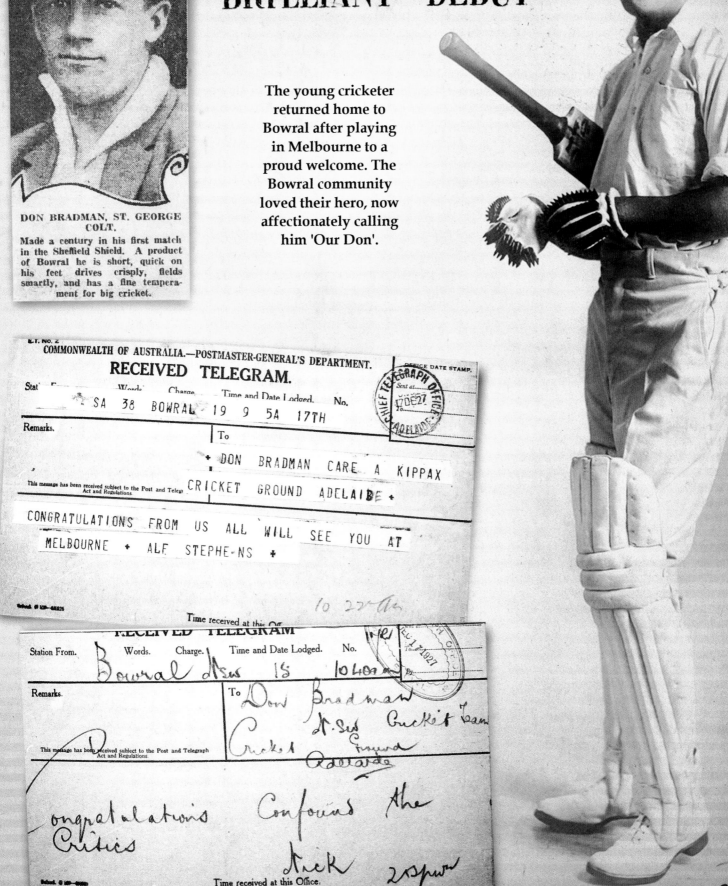

E.T. No. 2

COMMONWEALTH OF AUSTRALIA.—POSTMASTER-GENERAL'S DEPARTMENT.

RECEIVED TELEGRAM.

Stat... F...	Words	Charge	Time and Date Lodged	No.
SA 38		BOWRAL 19 9 5A 17TH	

Remarks.

To

+ DON BRADMAN CARE A KIPPAX

CRICKET GROUND ADELAIDE +

This message has been received subject to the Post and Teleg Act and Regulations

CONGRATULATIONS FROM US ALL WILL SEE YOU AT

MELBOURNE + ALF STEPHE-NS +

RECEIVED TELEGRAM

Station From.	Words.	Charge.	Time and Date Lodged.	No.
Bowral NSW	15		10 40 a m	

Remarks.

To Don Bradman
N Sw Cricket team
Cricket Ground
Adelaide

Congratulations Confound the Critics

Nick 20 p w n

Time received at this Office.

37

MATCH BETWE...

and

at NSW

ADELAIDE

on

1ST.

Innings of

Date	Time In	Score	Adjm.	Score	Time Out	Total		Name	Runs as Score...
16.12.27	11·35			11	11·51	15	1	G. Morgan	11341
16.12.27	11·35	59	1·5	112	3·26	224	2	N. Phillips	112414211121114123114121441132111112221122211
16.12.27	11·58	48	1·5	58	2·19	137	3	T.J.E. Andrews	112221311122114411111411121242
	2·21			10.55		511	4	A. Kippax	12221114421411142142141112221212114111241
	3·6	24	40·44	44	40·44	298	5	A. Scanes	114211212133114213311131
	3·28			12	3·33	250	6	W.A. Oldfield	21111222
	3·55	9	40·44	118	1·3	519	7	D. Bradman	44111424111321141111422112111112112111
	4·13			1	4·40	306	8	F. Jordan	1
	5·10			5	6·0	400	9	L. Everett	2111
	12·57			0	12·59	514	10	A. Mailey	0
	1·1					519	11	R. McNamee	1

		1	2	3	4	5
Fall of Wickets	...	15	137	224	250	298
Batsman Out	...	Morgan	Andrews	Phillips	Oldfield	Scan...
" Not Out	...	Phillips 4	Phillips 67	Scanes 9	Scanes 22	Bradman...

Don Bradman made an instant impact in first-class cricket, scoring 118 on debut for NSW against South Australia, the first of his 117 first-class centuries.

	How Out	Bowled	Tot
2	4	2	4	1	1	3 /	Bowled	Scott	11
	Bowled	Whitfield	112
	ct. Williams	Grimmett	58
3	3	1	3	1	1	4	1	1	4	1	4	1	4	4	Ct. Alexander	Williams	143
	ct. Williams	Schneider	44
2	4	2	1	1	4	1	1	2	2	1	1	3	4 /	ct. A. Hack	Grimmett	12
	ct. Williams	Scott	118
	L. B. W.	Scott	1
	st. A. Hack	Grimmett	5
	Bowled	Scott	0
	Not Out		1
	Byes 2		2
	Leg Byes //// 2		5
	Wides 1		1
	No Balls ///// 1		6

6	7	8	9	10		
306	400	511	514	519	TOTAL	519
adman 3	Everett	Kippax	Bailey	Bradman		
	Bradman 16	Bradman 111	Bradman 114	McKenzie 1		

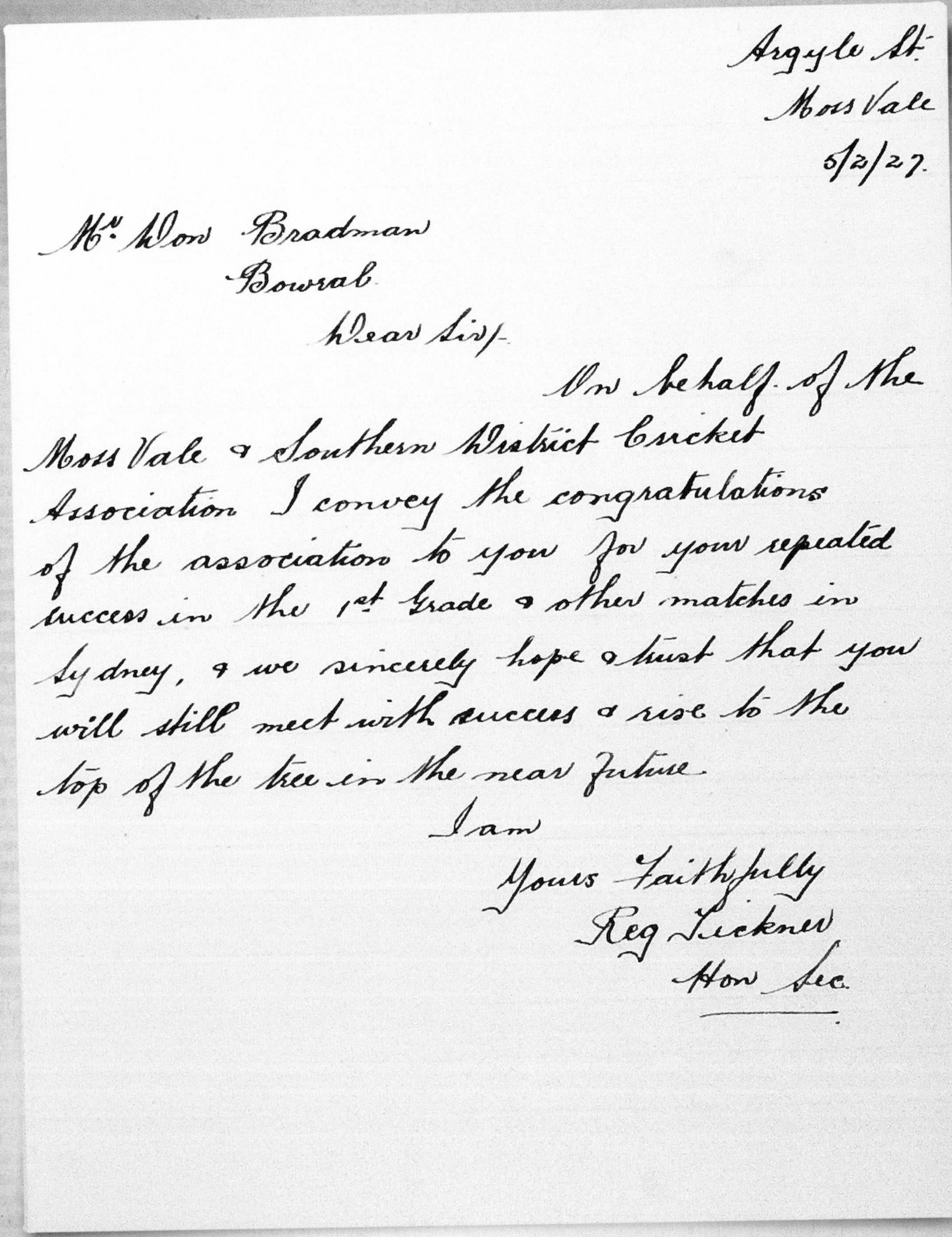

Argyle St.
Moss Vale
5/2/27.

Mr. Don Bradman
Bowral.

Dear Sir,

On behalf of the
Moss Vale & Southern District Cricket
Association I convey the congratulations
of the association to you for your repeated
success in the 1st Grade & other matches in
Sydney, & we sincerely hope & trust that you
will still meet with success & rise to the
top of the tree in the near future.

I am
Yours faithfully
Reg Lickner
Hon Sec.

**Bradman was the pride of Bowral and the entire district by
1927, as shown by this letter of praise and encouragement
10 months before his first-class debut century.**

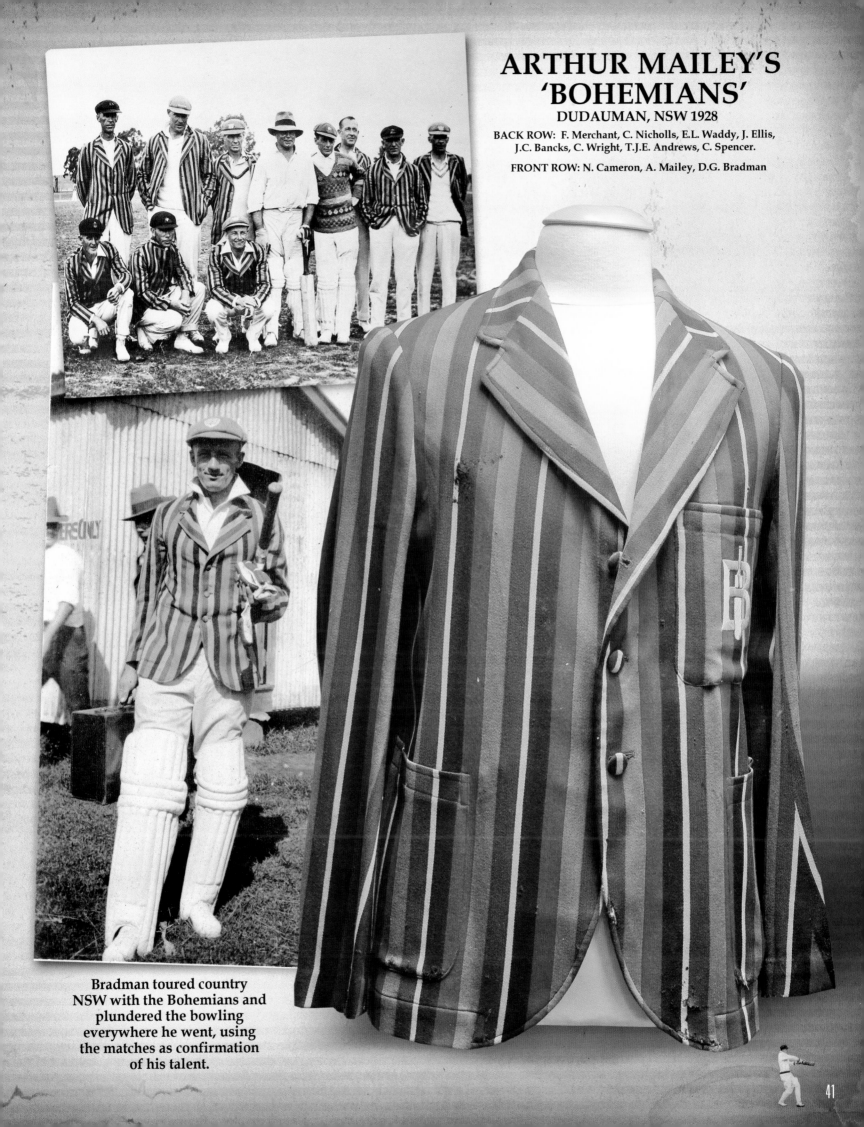

ARTHUR MAILEY'S 'BOHEMIANS'

DUDAUMAN, NSW 1928

BACK ROW: F. Merchant, C. Nicholls, E.L. Waddy, J. Ellis, J.C. Bancks, C. Wright, T.J.E. Andrews, C. Spencer.

FRONT ROW: N. Cameron, A. Mailey, D.G. Bradman

Bradman toured country NSW with the Bohemians and plundered the bowling everywhere he went, using the matches as confirmation of his talent.

BRADMAN'S CLASS

POTENTIAL TEST PLAYER

DONS SHARE HONORS

(By W. H. Ponsford)

We found ourselves in an impossible position when the last phases were entered upon this morning. Victoria's chance of retrieving the game definitely passed yesterday afternoon when the golden opportunity of running young Don Bradman out was not availed of. That was the turning point, as Bradman gave us another three hours of his company.

Yesterday was a triumph for the two Dons, Blackie and Bradman. It was a coincidence that the honors of the day were shared by these two players, who are the oldest and youngest who took part in the match.

Although not yet stroke-perfect, Bradman has all the attributes of a potential test match player and, had our bowlers been able to get rid of him after the sensational dismissal of Andrews, Jackson and Morgan, there is no saying how the match would have ended, especially as we scored well this morning and the wicket was as good as ever.

FINE TEMPERAMENT

It spoke volumes for the temperament of Bradman when it is recalled that he had to face Blackie when the hat-trick was a possibility, as Jackson and Morgan had been got rid of with successive deliveries. Bradman's century was all the more praiseworthy as he had to face Blackie, who bowled in his very best form. Blackie's sustained and successful effort with the ball in N.S.W.'s second innings completely satisfied players and spectators alike that he is the best medium-paced bowler at the present time.

Charles Bannerman, the first man to make a century in Test cricket, (165 not out for Australia at Melbourne in the 1876/77 season) gives Bradman some advice.

DON BRADMAN.

Who saved N.S.W. in the match against Victoria at a time when matters were looking serious for the home State. He scored 134 (not out) in the second innings. A biographical sketch of this skilful young player will appear next week.

DON BRADMAN–WONDER CRICKETER OF 1928

Eight Years Ago "Smith's Weekly" Picked the Hero of To-day

MARKED HIM AT THE AGE OF 12 FOR PRESENT HONORS

BY J. MATHERS.

ABOUT eight years ago, a sub-editor of "Smith's Weekly," with a humorous flair for writing head-lines, unsuspectingly predicted the greatness of an obscure little lad who was subsequently to write his name in the highest company of International cricket.

The little chap was playing in the school yard when he hit a ball that balanced on the top of a post, then ran along the edge of a paling fence, and performed a few more tricks before it ultimately came to rest on the ground.

The incident was published exclusively in "Smith's" in a par which referred to him as "A crack bat." Don Bradman was the lad.

To-day he is THE crack bat.

"I've still got that cutting from 'Smith's,'" proudly admitted Bradman the other evening during the course of a chat over the dinner table.

"And, although many nice things have been written about me, that first paragraph still takes the bun."

The following season, 1928/1929, Bradman was one of the most talked about cricketers in Australia and was selected to make his Test debut in the first Test ever held in Brisbane.

Bradman returning to the pavilion after being bowled.

Bradman relaxing in Rockdale at the home of St George Cricket Club's secretary, Frank Cush, circa 1928/29.

Bowral Honors Her Cricket Hero.

PRESENTATION OF GOLD WATCH AND CHAIN TO DON BRADMAN.

INTERSTATE PLAYERS LAUD THE BOWRAL BOY.

There was an exceptionally large attendance at the Reception and Dance given in Bowral on Friday night in honor of Don. Bradman and the visiting St. George players. Such a tribute of respect and admiration has rarely been paid to a resident in these districts and Don might have been pardoned had he shown some little sign of swelled head. But his greetings of old friends and his reply to the speeches made in his praise was marked by a modesty of demeanor that explains the rapid progress he has made in the affections of his new associates in the game. For the most notable feature of the speeches of the visitors, from Richardson downwards, was the evident pleasure they had in praising their new associate. As Mr. Westbrook said, Don Bradman had endeared himself to the public not only by his masterly cricket but by his character, which was the same in private life as on the cricket field.

Mayor Stephens has every reason to feel satisfied with the success of his first official effort to promote sport and sociability in Bowral. Everyone was in the happiest mood and the reception was one of the most successful functions ever held in the town—a success which was repeated on Loseby Park the following day.

After dancing had been indulged in for some time to the strains of Mr. Beavan's orchestra, Mr. Mailey and other visiting and local cricketers were invited to take seats on the platform. The Mayor then introduced local players to the visitors, after which he proceeded with the presentation. He said there was no need to tell them that they had met primarily to do honor to Don Bradman. They had also to extend to Mr. Mailey and the visitors from St. George a very hearty welcome. Mr. Kippax was being married that night and some of their expected visitors were at the wedding, but they would be along on Saturday. When he (the Mayor) first got the idea of opening the turf wicket in Loseby Park, he asked Don Bradman to bring along a team. Don was too modest to do that, but he interested Mr. Jones in the project and on Saturday, Bowral would have a red letter day in cricket. The occasion was a fitting one to show Don that his services to N.S.W. cricket and to Bowral were appreciated in the town in which he had first won his laurels. It was no mean achievement for a country boy to go to Sydney and in his first season win second place in the Sheffield Shield averages and second place in first grade averages in Sydney. The great wish of his Bowral admirers was to see him in an Australian team. (Applause).

Mr. P. A. Westbrook said he was a little nervous in the presence of Mr. Mailey who not only played good cricket but made good humorous pictures. He did not think they should wait till a man was dead before they told him how they admired his good qualities. Rather would be endorse the sentiment of the legend which greeted the return of a wanderer to his own land, "We love you and we tell you so." Whether it was keeping books, playing tennis, driving a car or wielding a bat, the smartest man of his age known to the speaker was Don Bradman. To keep up his wicket when others had fallen disastrously was the supreme test of a cricketer and that their young guest had done. He was undoubtedly one of the greatest cricketers in the State. They were proud of the illustrious deeds performed by the incomparable boy from Bowral. (Applause).

Mr. Mailey did not claim to be a wonderful judge of cricket, but one of the best innings he had ever seen was Don Bradman's knock at Adelaide. He was undoubtedly a coming international. Not only was Don a fine cricketer, but he was a good sportsman. They were lucky to have produced so fine a chap as Don.

The Mayor presented Bradman with a handsome gold watch and chain saying that he would live long to wear them and go far in the cricket world.

Mr. Bradman, who was received with "For He's a Jolly Good Fellow," was evidently overcome by the extreme cordiality of his reception. He said that after the glowing remarks of the chairman he found difficulty in putting his feelings into words. In the first place there were several people he had to thank for whatever success he had made. Mr. Stephens had got him the chance to have a knock in Sydney. Mr. Jones and Mr. Cush had given him his next chance for if he hadn't got into St. George he could not have gone further. Then, when that was achieved, Mr. Westbrook had given him time off, for without that it would have been impossible for him to retain his place in his Club. Cricket was a wonderful character builder and he had met some of the finest of men amongst his cricket associates. He thanked them all from the bottom of his heart and hoped he would never do anything to make them regret they had given him their present.

An excellent supper was served by the ladies.

Colts Don Bradman and Archie Jackson, who makes their debut against England at the Sydney Cricket Ground in the England v N.S.W. game.

Bradman Should Play In First Test Match

GATES OF FAME ARE NOW OPEN TO HIM

Bowral Lad Has Century Habit Well Developed

ROMANCE OF CRICKET FIELD

(By A. G. MOYES.)

BRADMAN'S DOUBLE.

CENTURY IN EACH INNINGS.

NEW SOUTH WALES WINS.

PLAYER'S CIGARETTES

D.G. BRADMAN
NEW SOUTH WALES

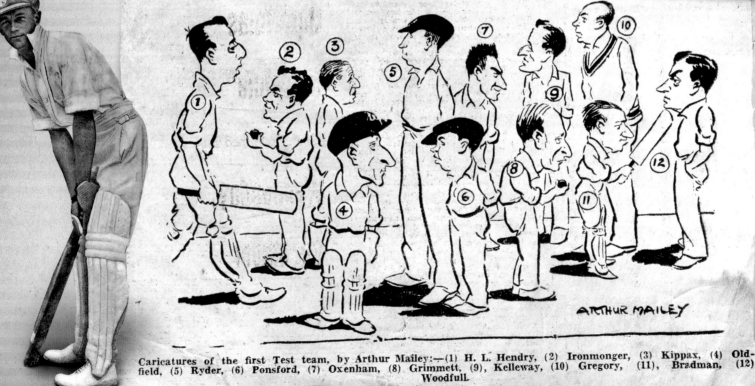

AUSTRALIA'S CHOSEN.

ARTHUR MAILEY

Caricatures of the first Test team, by Arthur Mailey:—(1) H. L. Hendry, (2) Ironmonger, (3) Kippax, (4) Oldfield, (5) Ryder, (6) Ponsford, (7) Oxenham, (8) Grimmett, (9) Kelleway, (10) Gregory, (11) Bradman, (12) Woodfull.

THE AUSTRALIAN BOARD OF CONTROL
— FOR —
INTERNATIONAL CRICKET.

W. H. JEANES
SECRETARY

WHJ/IV

TELEGRAMS AND CABLES:
"CRICKET" ADELAIDE

Manufactures Building.

Pirie Street.

Adelaide 20th November, 192 8
(SOUTH AUSTRALIA)

CIRCULAR TO TEST MATCH PLAYERS
- - - - - - -

Dear Sir, -

I have pleasure in advising that you have
been selected as one of the twelve players from whom the team
to play against England in the First Test Match at Brisbane,
commencing November 30th, will be chosen.   Will you please
arrive in Brisbane on Tuesday the 27th inst.

If you apply to the Secretary of your State
Association he will make you an advance to cover your travelling
expenses.

The allowance to each player will be £30 for
the match, together with railway fares and sleepers and 30/-
per day (Sundays included) whilst absent from his home State to
cover personal expenses.

Players must supply their own board and
lodging.

Yours faithfully,

W H Jeanes

Secretary.

On a sticky wicket, Australia
lost the Test with Bradman
scoring only 18 and one.
Bradman later wrote, "...it was
a great disappointment to
bat on a sticky wicket in our
second innings, (the first time
I had ever seen one), and find
I knew absolutely nothing
about that kind of wicket."

He was made 12th man for the
second Test in Sydney - the
only time he was not included
in the Australian XI for the
next 20 years.

Bradman received this
telegram, followed by
the confirming letter
above, to advise of his
Test debut selection on
November 20, 1928.

COMMONWEALTH OF AUSTRALIA.—POSTMASTER-GENERAL'S DEPARTMENT.

RECEIVED TELEGRAM.

The first line of this Telegram contains the following particulars in the order named.

STATION FROM.   WORDS.   TIME AND DATE LODGED.   No.

Stock Exchange Adelaide 25 10 45

Remarks

To
Bradman
c/ CKt Assn
Sydney

This message has been received subject to the Post and Telegraph
Act and Regulations.
The time received at this Office is shown at the foot of the Form.
Sch. C 999/1987.—Z9-10.

Confirm your selection in twelve
from whom first test team will be
chosen necessary arrive. Brisbane
twentyseventh letter following
Jeanes

45

DON BRADMAN

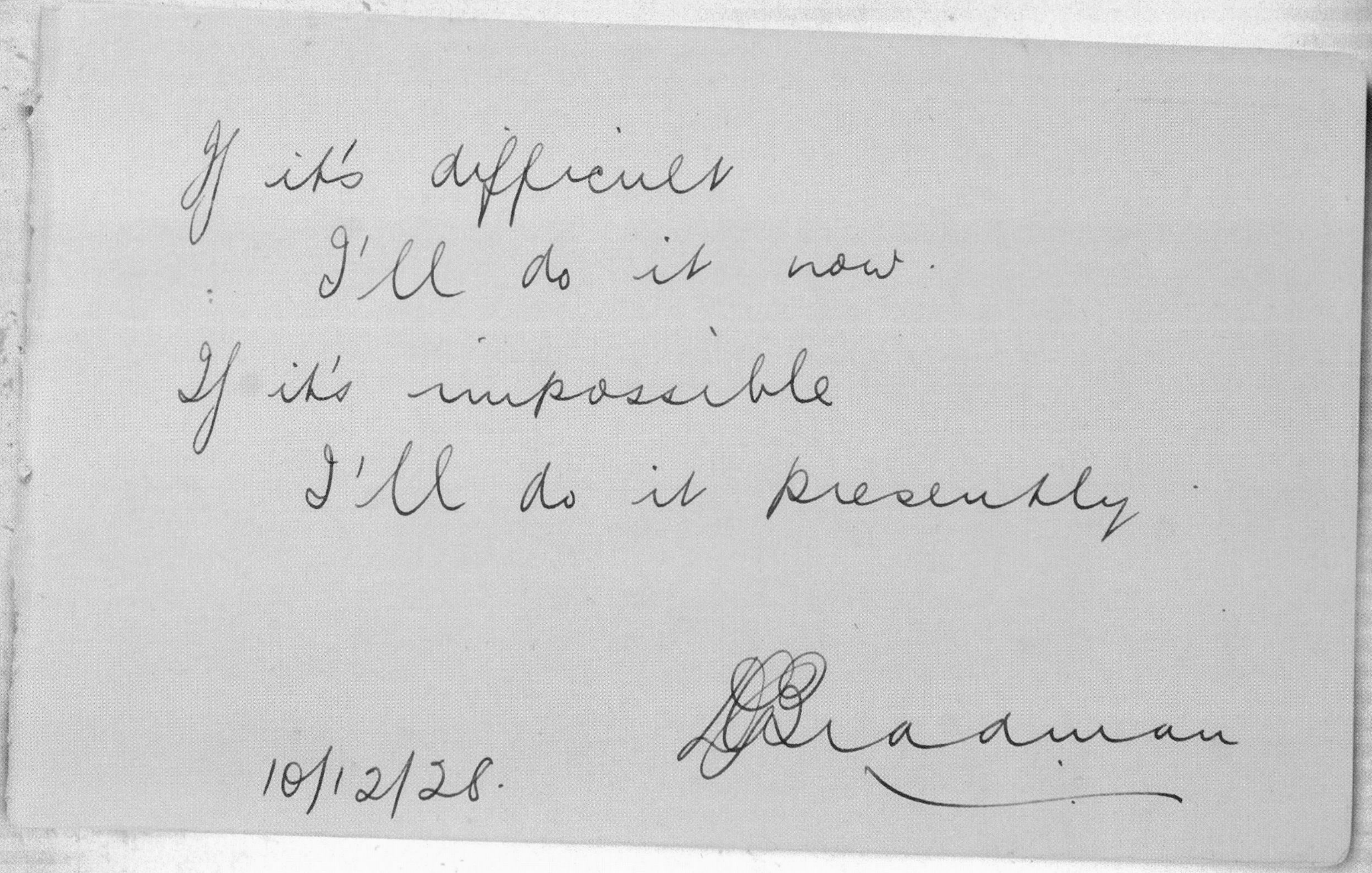

If it's difficult
I'll do it now.
If it's impossible
I'll do it presently.

Bradman

10/12/28.

David Gilbert, former Australian fast bowler and for the past seven years the Chief Executive of Cricket New South Wales, helped secure this revealing note penned by Bradman in 1928.

Gilbert, who has been on the board of the Bradman Foundation since 2005, was told of the pending sale of the letter by his brother Mark, who for the past decade has delved into cricket memorabilia.

"It was being auctioned in England and I informed the Bradman Foundation and they were lucky enough to buy it in mid 2008," Gilbert said. "It is difficult to believe that a 20-year-old could write such a note, especially as he had played only one Test at the time. It just shows the confidence of Bradman in his own ability."

Indeed it was audacious as he wrote it on December 10, 1928, soon after scoring only 18 and 1 on his Test debut in Brisbane against England.

He was not playing cricket on this day, which was before he played for NSW against Victoria from December 22 when he scored 1 and 71 not out.

He certainly was showing no signs of lacking confidence as most would at that early stage of their international career. He was made 12th man for the 2nd Test, which began on December 14 - the only time he was left out of the Test line-up in a 20 year international career.

Gilbert had this note enlarged and placed over the NSW/Australia team dressing room door and it will be the last thing a player will see before walking onto the Sydney Cricket Ground.

"It should be inspirational," Gilbert said. "I have a real passion for cricket history and someone as prestigious as Bradman is the pinnacle. It will be great for the players to see this sign as they walk out to play, remembering what Bradman said he would do - and then did."

Bradman Leaps to Fame

BRADMAN'S CENTURY
STIRRED TO FRENZY
40,000 OUTSIDE "NEWS"

YESTERDAY'S CENTURY
WAS GREAT FEAT
He and Woodfull Carried Australia to Dominating Position

AMAZING SCENES

ENGLISH BOWLING MASTERED.
Fighting Century by Woodfull.

OUR MAGNETIC BOARD
MADE HISTORY

'AS ONE COLT TO ANOTHER" --- BRADMAN SHOWS "HOW"

VAST CROWD MAD WITH DELIGHT

THE scene in Hyde Park last night, in front of the "News" magnetic cricket scoring board, when Bradman got his century, was without parallel in Sydney as a demonstration.

There were easily 40,000 people present. The demonstration was as great as that when Charlie Macartney played, Leeds in 1926, what has been generally acclaimed as the most remarkable innings in Test cricket.

It is understood that a competitor, staggered by the success and the popularity of the "News" magnetic board, put a check on it, without, however, being able to pierce the armory of the "News" enterprise.

HERO WORSHIP ON THE CRICKET FIELD.—Don Bradman, with his 340 not out in the Sheffield Shield match between New South Wales and Victoria, has scored 1207 in first-class matches this season, broken the individual score record for New South Wales, and put up an aggregate only 39 short of Trumper's total in first-class matches for a season.—The boy in the picture copies the style of his obliging hero and has visions of "doing it himself" some day.

Donald Bradman
A MAKER OF CENTURIES

Written by C. R. BRADISH
Illustrated by L. F. REYNOLDS

Bradman forced his way into the 3rd Test at Melbourne and scored 79 and 112 and emphasised his form with 340 not out for NSW against Victoria in Sydney - becoming the youngest to score more than 300 in a first-class innings.

He ended his first Ashes series with 123 and 37 not out in the 5th Test in Melbourne.

Bat used by Bradman in scoring his first Test century for Australia against England at the Melbourne Cricket Ground, 2nd January 1929.

HOW YOUNGSTERS BATTLED FOR THEIR COUNTRY

BRADMAN AND a'BECKETT, AGED 41 BETWEEN THEM, SHOW ENGLAND GREAT CRICKET

Don Bradman— Young Breaker of Cricket Records

Bradman rebounded with a brilliant 112 in the second innings of the third Test in Melbourne and his future at the highest level was secured.

Youngest Batsman to Score More Than 300 in Innings

By E. H. M. BAILLIE

Don Bradman wearing the honor cap and badge which were presented to him by Mr. J.J. Giltinan to commemorate his 340 not out against Victoria.

Mr. Giltinan, in association with Victor Trumper, was one of the men responsible for the establishment of Rugby League football in New South Wales.

OUR FAMOUS PAIR: Bradman and a'Beckett coming in for luncheon at Melbourne on Monday.

During 1928/29 he scored a record 1690 first-class runs, averaging 148.33 in the Sheffield Shield competition. His score of 340 not out against Victoria was the highest individual score ever made on the Sydney Cricket Ground. Also, he joined an elite group when he scored a century in each innings - 131 and 133 not out against Queensland at Brisbane.

Don Bradman's Chanceless World's Record Innings of 452

Bradman made international headlines during 1929/30 when, at the age of 21, he broke the world record for the highest score in first-class cricket. His 452 not out came for NSW against Queensland at Sydney in January of 1930. Bradman's innings took only 415 minutes and passed the previous best by Bill Ponsford, who took 621 minutes to reach his score of 437.

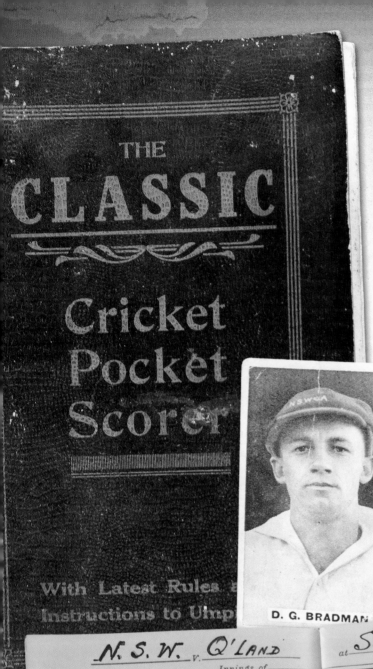

THE CLASSIC Cricket Pocket Scorer

With Latest Rules and Instructions to Umpires

D. G. BRADMAN

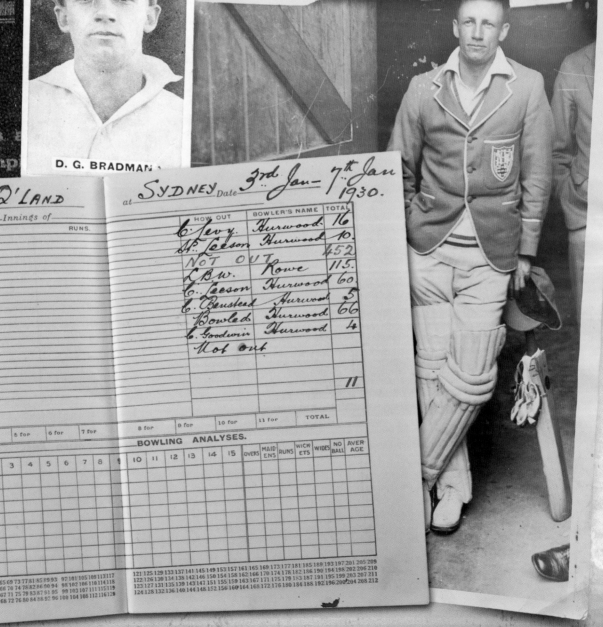

N.S.W. v. Q'LAND at SYDNEY Date 3rd Jan — 7th Jan 1930.

Batsmen		How Out	Bowler's Name	Total
1 Andrews. C.		C. Levy.	Hurwood	16
2 Fairfax. A.		St. Leeson	Hurwood	10
3 BRADMAN. D.G		NOT OUT		452
4 Kippax A.		L.B.W.	Rowe	115
5 McCabe S.		C. Leeson	Hurwood	60
6 Marks. A.		C. Benstead	Hurwood	5
7 Allsop A.		Bowled	Hurwood	66
8 Everett S.		C. Goodwin	Hurwood	4
9 Davidson A.		Not out		

Bradman was now called the 'run-making machine' and was carried from the field by some of the Queensland players. His domestic season yielded 1586 runs at an average of 113.28.

452

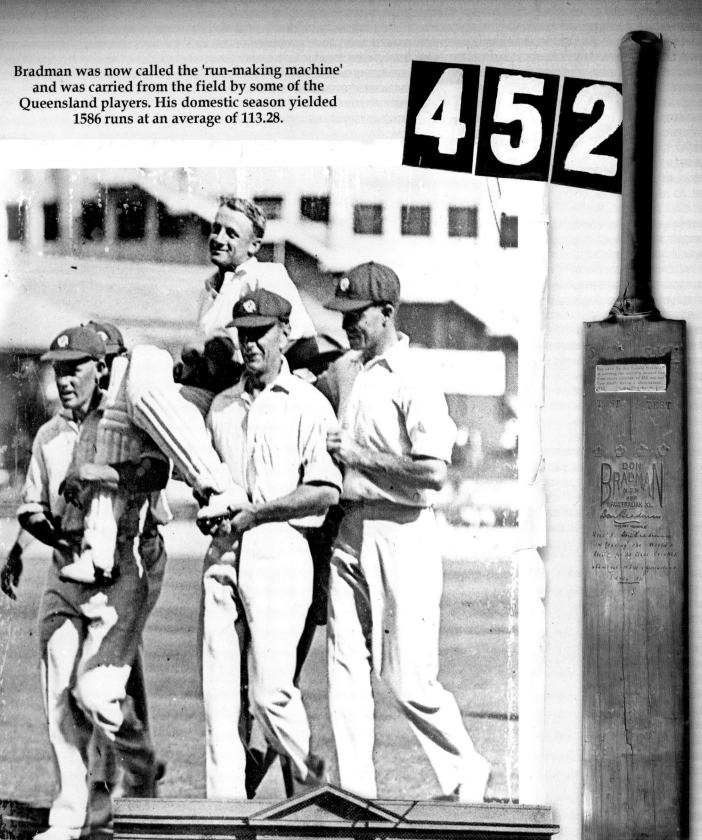

Scoreboard at Sydney Cricket Ground.

HOW BRADMAN SCORED HIS RUNS

APART from his first half-century, which occupied 54 minutes, Don Bradman scored all the fifties in his mammoth score under even time.

The rate of scoring was as follows:—

50 in 54 minutes.
100 in 103 minutes.
150 in 140 minutes.
200 in 185 minutes.
250 in 230 minutes.
300 in 288 minutes.
350 in 333 minutes.
440 in 377 minutes.
450 in 414 minutes.
452 in 415 minutes.

BOWLER	WATS	RUNS
GOODWIN		1
LEVY		20
O'CONNOR		
COUCH		40
ROWE	1	143
THOMPSON		90
BREW		61
BENSTEAD		70
HURWOOD	6	179
THURLOW	1	47

N.S.W. 1ST INS 235

QUEENS⁰ 1ST INS 227

BATSMEN		
BRADMAN	452	
DAVIDSON	22	
8 FOR 761		

BATSMEN	OUT	FOFW
ANDREWS	16	22
FAIRFAX	10	33
KIPPAX	115	305
McCABE	60	461
MARKS	5	469
ALLSOPP	66	649
EVERETT	4	669
SUNDRIES	11	

Bat used by Bradman in scoring the then world-record first-class cricket score of 452 not out for NSW, against QLD at the Sydney Cricket Ground, January 1930.

WONDERFUL DON

The young giant, Don Bradman, as pictured by Hector Morrison.

Bradman received a Cup for his record breaking effort and was flooded with congratulatory telegrams.

"FOR MUM," SAYS DON

Famous Cricket Colt Leaves Trophy at Home

"There's a spot in me heart
That no colleen may own."

HANDED a handsome rose bowl in recognition of his world's record score of 452 not out against Queensland, Don Bradman, at last night's dinner to the N.S.W. members of the Australian Eleven, explained why he had selected such a present.

"There is someone who will treasure this bowl more than I do," he said.

"I refer to my mother. The rose bowl is for her."

Don Bradman Gives Amazing Display to Break Ponsford's World Record

DON BRADMAN THE WONDER CRICKETER OF THE SEASON

PAST 437

COLT'S GREAT OVATION

TERRIFIC HITTING

PLAYER'S CIGARETTES

W. H. PONSFORD (VICTORIA)

RECEIVED TELEGRAM
URGENT RATE

Congratulations great feat player your ability deserves the honor. Ponsford

Bradman's world record score put him on a pedestal - earning praise from the man who set all the standards before him, Bill Ponsford.

No. 9 — D. G. Bradman

Bradman, naturally enough, was made captain of the 'NSW Team Of The Century' as painted by Dave Thomas in 2007.

MATCH BETWEEN

NEW. SOUTH. WALES. and QUEENSLAND

at SYDNEY. CRICKET. GROUND. on JANUARY. 3·4·6+7ᵗʰ 1930

SECOND. Innings of NEW. SOUTH. WALES.

BRADMAN 438 WORLD'S RECORD in 406 M.

	Date	Time In	Score	Adjm.	Score	Time Out	Total		Name	Runs as Scored.	How Out	Bowled	Total
	4·1·30	2·0		–	33	2·41	41ᴹ	1	FAIRFAX. A.	12⎪⎪⎪⎪⎪⎪⎪	Sᵗ LEESON.	HURWOOD	10
	4·1·30	2·0		–	22	2·26	26ᴹ	2	ANDREWS. C	1⎪22⎪2⎪⎪1⎪4 4+⎪⎪+⎪2⎪⎪3⎪⎪2⎪⎪⎪2⎪⎪ ...	C LEVY.	HURWOOD	16
	4·1·30 2·38 6·1·30 2·32 4·1·30		+0 -2 -1·16 +20	107 323 355 109	3·59	45ᴹ	3	BRADMAN. D.	32⎪124⎪4⎪2⎪24⎪242⎪452⎪⎪ ...	NOT	OUT	452
			–	305	5·23	43ᴹ	4	KIPPAX. A.	32⎪4⎪2222⎪2⎪⎪23⎪ ...	L. B. W	ROWE	115
	4·1·30 5·30 6·1·30	305 368		6·1 +61	368 461	12·20	81ᴹ	5	McCABE. S.	⎪⎪⎪⎪⎪44⎪4⎪4⎪⎪⎪⎪1⎪2⎪4	C LEESON	HURWOOD	60
	6·1·30 12·22	461		–	469	12·26	10ᴹ	6	MARKS. A	14	C BENSTEAD	HURWOOD	5
	6·1·30 12·32 2·3	469		1·16 –	551 649	2·54	93ᴹ	7	ALLSOPP A.	⎪⎪⎪3⎪33⎪⎪12⎪⎪ ...	BOWLED	HURWOOD	66
	6·1·30 2·50	649			669	5·9	13ᴹ	8	EVERETT. S.	31	C GOODWIN	HURWOOD	4
	6·1·30 5·11	669			761	3·54	43ᴹ	9	DAVIDSON. H	12⎪12⎪13⎪4⎪3	C + B	V GOODWIN	22
								10	BURT. S				
								11	CHILVERS. H.				

PARTNERSHIPS
KIPPAX. 50=35ᴹ
+BRADMAN.
100= 57ᴹ
150= 84ᴹ
200= 109ᴹ
250= 128ᴹ
272= 145ᴹ
BRADMAN + McCABE
100= 51ᴹ
130= 76ᴹ
150= 84ᴹ
BRADMAN + ALLSOPP
100= 57ᴹ
130= 70ᴹ
180= 93ᴹ

BRADMAN 50= 51ᴹ
100= 130ᴹ
130= 138ᴹ
200= 185ᴹ
KIPPAX 50= 70ᴹ
100= 137ᴹ
BRADMAN 250= 232ᴹ
200= 288ᴹ
300= 333ᴹ
400= 370ᴹ
McCABE 50= 63ᴹ
ALLSOPP 50= 67ᴹ
BRADMAN 450=
414ᴹ

INNINGS 443ᴹ

		Byes ⎪⎪2⎪⎪	6
		Leg Byes ⎪	1
		Wides ⎪⎪	2
		No Balls ⎪⎪	2

	1	2	3	4	5	6	7	8	9	10	8 WKS
Fall of Wickets ...	22	33	305	461	469	649	669	761			FOR TOTAL 761
Batsman Out ...	ANDREWS	FAIRFAX	KIPPAX	McCABE	MARKS	ALLSOPP	EVERETT	DAVIDSON.			CLOSED
" Not Out ...	FAIRFAX. 6	BRADMAN. 7	BRADMAN 16	BRADMAN 24	BRADMAN 36	BRADMAN 36	BRADMAN 38	BRADMAN 452			

"It was one of those occasions when everything went right. The wicket was true and firm, the outfield in good condition and the weather warm but not unduly hot...Apart from achieving a performance of this kind, I am gratified that the runs were made at speed and in a manner which clearly showed that I was attacking the bowling throughout the innings and not playing defensive cricket for selfish reasons."
(Bradman on scoring 452 not out, January 1930)

BOB HAWKE

(Former Australian Prime Minister)

To be born in 1929, a son of the manse, with an early passion for cricket meant that you had two Gods; that of your father and Donald George Bradman. The first was somewhat difficult to come to grips with, but Bradman regularly delivered you with glorious evidence of his omnipatience.

I was too young to realise in those dark and life-devastating days of the Great Depression that there was indeed a god-like dimension to the Don in that he provided a sense of joy and fulfilled hopes that took people beyond the burdens of their everyday life. Nor was this a god with feet of clay, but rather one whose twinkling feet and incomparable eye enabled him to match whatever was bowled up against him. Where happiness was in short supply he consistently brightened the lives of all Australians.

I was fortunate enough to see my second god in action. On his way to England in 1948, Bradman led the mighty Invincibles against a West Australian Eleven in Perth. I watched every ball of that match which was remarkable for two features involving Bradman. The first was the inevitable Bradman century executed with the customary trademarks of speed, elegance and innovative shot-making – a very good bowling attack had no answer to his genius.

The second showed Bradman the teacher. During the West Australian innings, their all-rounder, Basil Rigg, was battling against Keith Miller. He played a glorious cover drive to the boundary which seemed to upset Keith no end. Keith went back a little further on his mark and delivered a ferocious bouncer which Basil attempted, unsuccessfully, to hook. In those days there were no protective helmets and Basil was comprehensively pole-axed. After some time, during which Keith lay spread out on his back, Basil was assisted from the field. Towards the end of the innings, Basil left the dressing room to come out and resume his knock. Bradman met him at the gate, took his bat and, as they walked together towards the wicket, Bradman methodically demonstrated how the hook should be played. I might add that Miller wouldn't have won a popularity contest at the ground when he came on to bowl and let fly with another bouncer at Basil.

My first personal encounter with Don came twenty-three years later at his home in Adelaide in 1971. Earlier that year, as President of the ACTU, I had led the protests against the Springbok rugby tourists chosen on the apartheid policy of no non-white selections. The tour and the protests aroused considerable passion and a degree of violence. As Chairman of the Australian Cricket Board, Bradman was concerned about the implications for the South African cricket tour of Australia scheduled for the summer of 1971-72.

Don called me one day asking whether I would come and see him to discuss the matter, stipulating that our meeting should be entirely without publicity. I flew to Adelaide and got a cab to his home in Kensington where I was warmly welcomed by Don and his absolutely delightful wife, Jessie.

Don asked me if I would like a drink and I said a beer would be very acceptable. He came back with a bottle and mentioned that he had won it at cricket. When I observed it must be bloody well brewed by now he laughingly explained. He had recently been to a dinner at the South Australian Brewery and the CEO had ribbed Don about the fact that he had got a low score in the just televised computerised cricket match between an all time Australian and Rest of the World teams. Don said: "I bet him I would get a double century in the second innings – I did and this is part of his payment on the bet".

In this congenial setting we got down to business. Don went straight to the point, explaining that he held a firm view that politics should not be allowed to interfere with sport and espoused the hope that the tour would not be disrupted by protests. I responded to him directly: "Don, we didn't introduce politics into sport, it was the highest political authority in South Africa – the government – which instructed the sporting bodies, both rugby and cricket in this year, that a player could not be selected, however good he may be, if he was a non-white. It is they who introduced politics – the morally objectionable politics of apartheid – into sport, and that is and should be seen by your Board to be unacceptable."

Don was quiet for a few moments and then he looked me directly in the eye and said: "Bob, I can find no answer to that proposition." After a while, as I prepared to leave, we shook hands, and I had a feeling of confidence in this god of my childhood. The Board called off the tour and there was never another apartheid based sporting visit to this country; another entry into the debt of gratitude owed by Australians to Don Bradman.

A light note on which to finish. During my prime ministership, there was a dinner in Sydney honouring Don and I was sitting with him and Jessie and a number of others at the main table. At one stage I said across the table to Jessie: "Jessie, this bloke sitting next to me is not only, by far, the greatest cricketer the world has ever seen, he excelled at tennis squash, golf, billiards and with little formal education became an eminently successful stockbroker, businessman and administrator - tell me Jessie, is there anything the man couldn't do well."

Don's shrewd eyes seemed a little apprehensive I thought as he awaited the reply from his devoted wife of so many years. In turn her eyes twinkled as she paused and then said: "Yes, Bob, there is – he was hopeless at odd jobs. If there was a puncture in his bicycle tyre he would get someone else to fix it."

Everyone laughed and Don looked relieved. I observed that this proved he was an expert at delegation and so should it stand. We can't contemplate weakness in our gods and so huge has been the impact of this boyhood god of mine upon our nation that for me he remains an unstained treasure.

AUSTRALIAN XI
ENGLISH TOUR
1930

With the compliments of the
ORIENT LINE

The Australian Cricketers in England, 1930

Back Row (Left to Right)—S. J. McCabe, E. L. a'Beckett, P. M. Hornibrook, W. L. Kelly (manager), T. W. Wall, A. Hurwood, T. Howard (treasurer).
Middle Row—A. F. Kippax, A. Fairfax, V. Y. Richardson (vice-captain), W. M. Woodfull (captain), W. H. Ponsford, D. G. Bradman, A. Jackson.
Front Row—C. W. Walker, C. V. Grimmett, W. A. Oldfield.

We are indebted for this photograph to the Jaeger Co. Ltd., who fitted out the team with the "jogs" shown in the picture.

Wednesday, February 5, 1930

Australian Cricketers' Tour, 1930—The Selected Team

TEST MATCHES—OPENING DATES.
June 13 (Nottingham); June 27 (Lord's);
July 11 (Leeds); July 25 (Manchester);
August 16 (The Oval).

D. G. BRADMAN, N.S.W.—Batsman.
A. FAIRFAX, N.S.W.—All-rounder.
A. HURWOOD, Queensland—Bowler.
S. McCABE, N.S.W.—All-rounder.
P. M. HORNIBROOK, Queensland—Bowler.
A. JACKSON, N.S.W.—Batsman.

W. H. PONSFORD, Victoria—Batsman.
E. L. a'BECKETT, Victoria—All-rounder.
V. RICHARDSON, S.A.—Batsman (Vice-Capt.).
W. M. WOODFULL, Victoria — Batsman (Captain).
T. M. WALL, South Australia—Fast Bowler.
C. V. GRIMMETT, South Australia—Slow Bowler.
A. F. KIPPAX, N.S.W.—Batsman.

W. A. OLDFIELD, N.S.W.—1st Wicket-keeper.
C. W. WALKER, S.A.—2nd Wicket-keeper.

Programme:
April 30, May 1 and 2, v. Worcestershire, at Worcester.
May 3, 5, and 6, v. Leicestershire, at Leicester.
May 7, 8, and 9, v. Essex, at Leyton.
May 10, 12, and 13, v. Yorkshire, at Sheffield.
May 14, 15, and 16, v. Lancashire, at Liverpool.
May 17, 19, and 20, v. M.C.C., at Lord's.
May 21, 22, and 23, v. Derbyshire, at Chesterfield.
May 24, 26, and 27, v. Surrey, at The Oval.
May 28, 29, and 30, v. Oxford University, at Oxford.
May 31, June 2 and 3, v. Hampshire, at Southampton.
June 4, 5, and 6, v. Middlesex, at Lord's.
June 7, 9, and 10, v. Cambridge University, at Cambridge.
June 13, 14, 16, and 17, FIRST TEST, at Nottingham.
June 18, 19, and 20, v. Surrey, at The Oval.
June 21, 23, and 24, v. Lancashire, at Manchester.
June 27, 28, 30, and July 1, SECOND TEST, at Lord's.
July 2, 3, and 4, v. Yorkshire, at Bradford.
July 5, 7, and 8, v. Notts, at Nottingham.
July 11, 12, 14, and 15, THIRD TEST, at Leeds.
July 16 and 17, v. Scotland, at Glasgow.
July 18, 19, and 21, v. Scotland, at Edinburgh.
July 22 and 23, v. Durham, at Sunderland.
July 25, 26, 28, and 29, FOURTH TEST, at Manchester.
July 30 and 31, v. Somerset, at Taunton.
August 2, 4, and 5, v. Glamorgan, at Swansea.
August 6, 7, and 8, v. Warwickshire, at Birmingham.
August 9, 11, and 12, v. Northamptonshire, at Northampton.
August 16, etc., FIFTH TEST, at The Oval.
August 23, 25, and 26, v. Gloucestershire, at Bristol.
August 27, 28, and 29, v. Kent, at Canterbury.
August 30, September 1 and 2, v. Sussex, at Brighton.
August 30, September 4, and 5, v. South of England XI., at Folkestone.
September 6 and 8, v. Club Cricket Conference.
September 10, 11, and 12, v. an English XI., at Scarborough.

The cricket world was agog when Bradman ventured to England in 1930 to stamp his authority and unique talents on the game. From the moment he stepped to the crease, he set unprecedented standards that took both England and world cricket by storm.

He began with 236 in his first match in England, at Worcester, making him the youngest overseas player to score a double century in England.

Then he unleashed his unquenchable run-making genius on the England bowlers.

He scored eight and 131 in the opening Test at Nottingham which England won by 93 runs. He followed up with a flawless 254 and one at Lord's as Australia's seven wicket win squared the series.

The Test was drawn, as was the fourth at Manchester when no play was possible on the last day. Bradman scored 14 in his only innings.

The series decider was at The Oval and was a timeless Test which ran six days before Australia triumphed by an innings and 39 runs to regain the Ashes on foreign soil.

Bradman's 232 was the decisive innings of the match and he was the decisive player in the series success, He amassed a Test aggregate of 974 runs at an average of 139.14 - all this when still only 21 at the time.

D. G. BRADMAN
(NEW SOUTH WALES)

Born 27th August, 1908. Brilliant and enterprising batsman, and prolific rungetter. In 1928-9 season scored 1690, and in 1929-30, 1400 runs, the former being record aggregate for Australia. In the match between N.S.W. and Queensland at Sydney in January, 1930, made world's record of 452 not out. Change bowler and excellent outfield.

A. G. FAIRFAX
(NEW SOUTH WALES)

Born 16th June, 1906. Good all-rounder. His first representative match was with the Colts v. Queensland in October, 1928. Played in fifth Test Match v. Chapman's XI, March 1929, making 65 runs at critical time, this being his only innings; also bowled and fielded well. Good wet wicket batsman and bowler. Much is expected of him in England.

C. V. GRIMMETT
(SOUTH AUSTRALIA)

Born 25th December, 1892. Best slow bowler in Australia. In fifth Test Match in 1925 made sensational debut, taking 5 for 45 in first innings and 6 for 36 in the second. With last Australian XI in England, was one of the mainstays of the bowling, taking 120 wickets. In 1929-30 season took 63 wickets in first-class cricket at average of 26.58. Good in-field.

AUSTRALIA and W...

Worcester on ... Apr...

FIRST Innings of Austr...

at

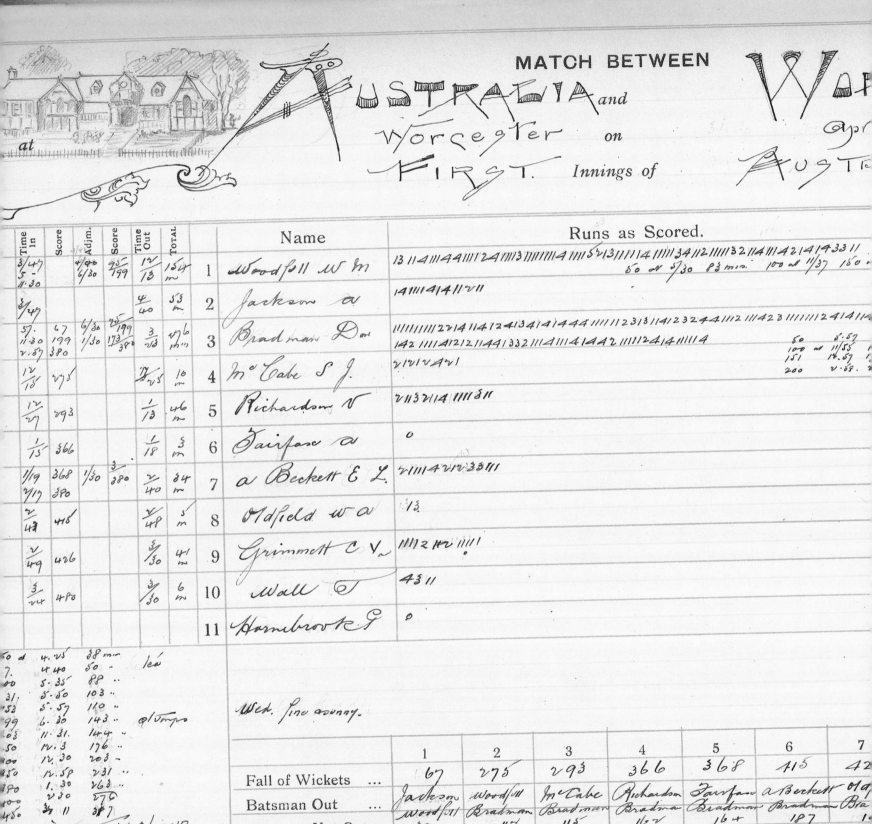

Time In	Score	Adjm.	Score	Time Out	Total		Name	Runs as Scored.
3/47 5. 11.30	4/46 6/30	95 199	12 13	154 m	1	Woodfull W M	13 114 114 44 1124 113 11114 111 5 13 11114 1111 34 112 111132 114 42141433 11
								50 at 5/30 83 min. 100 at 11/37 150 at
3/47			4 40	53 m	2	Jackson a	14 111 14 14 11 211
5. 11.30 v.57	67 199 380	6/30 1/30	25 199 173 380	3 v.13	176 m	3	Bradman Don	11111111 22 14 114 124 134 14 144 11111 23 13 114 123 24 4 112 111 423 1111111 124 14 114 142 1111 41 212 11 441 332 114 111 41 44 2 11111 24 14 11111 4
								50 5.57 100 at 11/55 151 12.57 200 v.33.
12 18	275		12 25	10 m	4	McCabe S J	2 1v1v 4v1
12 27	293		1 13	46 m	5	Richardson V	2 113 2 114 1111 311
1 15	366		1 18	3 m	6	Fairfax a	0
1/19 2/17	368 380	1/30	3 380	v 40	84 m	7	a Beckett E L	2 1111 4 2 1v v 33 111
v 43	415		v 48	5 m	8	Oldfield W a	13
v 49	426		3 30	41 m	9	Grimmett C V	11112 1v 2 11111
3 v14	480		3 30	6 m	10	Wall T	43 11
					11	Hornibrook G	0

50 d	4.25	38 min	Tea
7.	4 40	50 "	
00	5.35	88 "	
31	5.50	103 "	
53	5.57	110 "	
99	6.30	143 "	Stumps
03	11.31	144 "	
50	12.3	176 "	
00	12.30	203 "	
50	12.58	231 "	
80	1.30	263 "	
00	v 30	276 "	
450	3, 11	387 "	
		336 min	

Wed. fine & sunny.

	1	2	3	4	5	6	7
Fall of Wickets ...	67	275	293	366	368	415	42
Batsman Out ...	Jackson Woodfull	Woodfull Bradman	McCabe Bradman	Richardson Bradman	Fairfax Bradman	a Beckett Bradman	Old Bra
" Not Out...	39	114	115	162	164	187	1

Bradman took England by storm on is first tour of 1930. He started with 236 against Worcester, which was to begin a love-affair with the traditional opening first-class match.

He toured four times and scored a century every start to the tour, three of which were double-centuries.

...ESTER

..may. 1st & 2nd 1930

...IANS.

How Out	Bowled	Total
Bowled	Brook	133
c Walters sq leg	Brook	24
c Walters sq leg	Brook	236
c Root mid on	Brook	15
Run out off hand ball by bowler		24
c Root slip	Jackson	0
c Gilbert mid on	Root	24
c Jewell mid on	Root	4
not out		15
Not Out		9

Gilbert mid off.

Byes 31				4
Leg Byes 2				2
Wides 1				1
No Balls 1			Innings Close	1
8	9	10	TOTAL	492
480				
Bradman				
Grimmett				

AUTOGRAPHED SKETCHES
of the
1930
AUSTRALIAN CRICKETERS

PRICE 6D.

1930
BUSSEY
CRICKETERS
DIARY
AND
COMPANION

POST CARD

BRITISH MADE

...respondence

Address only

THE AUSTRALIAN TEST TEAM. 1930.
Left to right—Back Row:— S. McCABE, A. HURWOOD, T. WALL, P. M. HORNIBROOK, E. L. A'BECKETT, A. KIPPAX, C. V. GRIMMETT, W. A. OLDFIELD
Left to right—Front Row:— D. G. BRADMAN, W. H. PONSFORD, V. Y. RICHARDSON, W. M. WOODFULL, C. W. WALKER, A. JACKSON, A. FAIRFAX.
PUBLISHED BY J. SMITH, BOOKSTALL, LORDS.

BRADMAN 340

William Sykes bat used by Bradman in scoring 340 not out for NSW v VIC 25th January, 1929. At the time the highest score made at the SCG.

In May 1930 Don Bradman became the first Australian player to score 1000 runs in first-class cricket before the end of May in an English season. This is the bat with which he achieved this remarkable feat.

1000

This bat was used by Bradman to score a record Test match score of 223 against the West Indies at the Exhibition Ground in Brisbane, January 1931.

Bat used by Bradman to make a record Test match score of 226 against South Africa at the Brisbane Cricket Ground, November 1931.

DON BRADMAN – The Greatest Cricke[ter]

THE 1930 AUSTRALIAN XI

AND OTHER CARICATURES

BY ARTHUR MAILEY

Record Breaker Bradman
Adds Another To His List

BRADMAN
IN CRICKET'S HALL OF FAME

TRIUMPH WITH ONLY SECOND TO SPARE

MAGNIFICENT DON

From Our Special "Rep." with Team.

LONDON, Sunday.

Triumphantly and sensationally has Don Bradman entered the inner portals of the Hall of Cricket Fame.

ONE thousand runs in May, and one more to spare! A feat unequalled by any other Australian cricketer.

And how dramatically did he reach his magnificent 1001 at the very moment when rain ended May's cricket!

Don Bradman
DRINKS TEA
to celebrate his triumph

DON BRADMAN, the young Australian Cricketer, the world's wonder wielder of the willow—the batsman who makes hundreds as easily as the ordinary batsman makes tens—Don drinks tea to celebrate his triumphs and revive his flagging energy after a spell at the wickets or in the field.

B.170

Press Report from S.M. Herald, May 26, '30

after his grand display, Bradman modestly travelled home in a tube train, but took a long while to reach the station through the crowds of admirers, especially boys, some of whom fought to catch the same train, refusing to leave the carriage until the hero appeared at St. Pancras. Then Bradman, who drinks tea for breakfast, lunch, and dinner, celebrated his triumph in the same beverage before going to the theatre, where Fender entertained the Australian and Surrey teams. The young record-breaker is a bundle of energy, and seemed as fit as ever after batting nearly five hours. Though he was flagging somewhat towards the end, he was quite willing to attempt a fifth run for Fairfax's one big hit, but his cautious partner sent him back.

Bradman and Ponsford opened the Australian innings during which Bradman completed his 1000th run before the end of May.

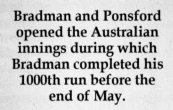

Woodfull leads the Australians onto the field for the opening match against Worcester.

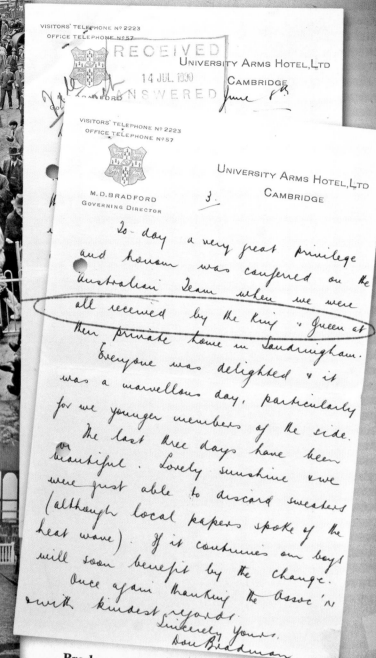

VISITORS' TELEPHONE Nº 2223
OFFICE TELEPHONE Nº 57

M. D. BRADFORD
GOVERNING DIRECTOR

UNIVERSITY ARMS HOTEL, LTD
CAMBRIDGE

3.

To-day a very great privilege and honour was conferred on the Australian Team when we were all received by the King & Queen at their private home in Sandringham.

Everyone was delighted & it was a marvellous day, particularly for we younger members of the side.

The last three days have been beautiful. Lovely sunshine & we were just able to discard sweaters (although local papers spoke of the heat wave). If it continues our boys will soon benefit by the change.

Once again thanking the Assoc'n with kindest regards

Sincerely yours,
Don Bradman

Bradman was a prolific letter writer. He clearly was delighted to report that he and the rest of the team were received by the King and Queen at their private house in Sandringham.

Don Bradman Follows Up His 236

With 185 Not Out At Leicester.

Bradman Bats 10 Hours For Once Out

A packed Lord's came to see Bradman score 254 - many waited through the night to be guaranteed a seat.

Lord's M C C Ground

"Bradman's Innings Will Live In History"

BRADMAN, GENIUS INCARNATE

AFLAME WITH FIRST CRICKET INSTINCT

CRICKET HISTORY.

BRADMAN THE MIGHTY

BRILLIANT FIGHTING EFFORT TO GIVE HIS TEAM VICTORY

Don Bradman Again To The Rescue

CENTURY IN FIRST TEST GAME
IN ENGLAND

BRADMAN BROKE RECORD AFTER RECORD

OUR FLASHING BATSMEN RAISED MAMMOTH SCORE IN WHIRLWIND STYLE

INNINGS CLOSED WITH TOTAL 729

Date	Time In	Score	Adjm.	Score	Time Out	Total		Name
	11.35 2.20 4.50	96 444	1.30 4.30	96 105 444	6 2.13	343 m	1	Woodfull W.
	11.35 2.20	96	1.30	59 46	3 27	172 min	2	Ponsford W.
	3.29 4.50 11.3 2.17	162 444 404 544	4.30 6.30 11.30	54 155 231 544	2 48	341 min	3	Bradman Don
	6.25 11.3 2.17	393 404 545	6.30 1.80	404 Frnr	2 55	193 min	4	Kippax A
	7.50	585			3 41	51 m	5	McCabe S.
	2.87	588			3 21	25 m	6	Richardson V
	3.25	643			4 30	65 m	7	Oldfield w a.
	3.43	671			4 30	47 m	8	Fairfax a
							9	
							10	
							11	

50 ad	12.48	73 min	lunch
96	1.30	115 "	
100	2.28	123 "	
150	3.15	170 "	
200	3.45	200 "	
244	4.30	235 "	Tea 10 minutes delay
250	4.35	246 "	
300	5.25	270 "	
350	5.57	302 "	
400	6.27	332 "	
404	6.30	335 "	stumps
425	11.37	372 "	
450	11.57	392 "	
500	12.54	449 "	lunch
544	1.30	488 "	
550	2.21	489 "	
600	3.2	530 "	
651	3.26	554 "	
700	4.7	597 "	Total time 615 minutes.
729	4.30	615 "	

Sat. beautiful fine day big crowds

Fall of Wickets ...

Batsman Out ...

" Not Out...

"There is not much personal satisfaction in making a hundred and being missed several times. Any artist must surely aim at perfection. This was the nearest that I could ever hope to get to such a goal," he said after scoring what he considered his best innings.

AUSTRALIA'S WONDERFUL DAY AT LORD'S

Mammoth Score in Second Test---254 by Bradman

AUSTRALIA—First Innings

W. M. Woodfull, st Duckworth, b Robins	155
W. H. Ponsford, c Hammond, b White	81
D. G. Bradman, c Chapman, b White	254
A. F. Kippax, b White	83
S. J. M'Cabe, c Woolley, b Hammond	44
V. Y. Richardson, c Hobbs, b Tate	30
W. A. Oldfield, not out	43
A. Fairfax, not out	20
Byes 6, leg-byes 8, wides 5	19
Six wickets for	729

Fall of wickets: 162, 393, 585, 587, 643, 672.

MATCH BETWEEN

ᴀᴜꜱᴛʀᴀʟɪᴀ and **ENGLAND.**

on JUNE. 27. 28. 1930

Innings of **AUSTRALIA** 2ᵈˢ

Runs as Scored.	How Out	Bowled	Total
150 at 6·13 318 minutes 100 at 4/23 228 minutes 50 at 2/50 145 .			
/////////// 3 2 1 2 / 4 // 2 4 // 3 // 2 2 2 2 / 2 / 2 // 3 / 4 4 / 3 / 4 2 // 2 / 3 // 4 // // 4 // // 4 3 //	st Duckworth.	Robins	155
/////// 2 / 3 /// / 2 / /	c Hammond slips	White	81
/ 4 // 2 // / 4 / 4 // / 2 // 2 // 4 4 4 // // / 2 // // // 3 // / / 3			
5 0 at 1/20 105 min.			
/ 4 4 / 4 / 4 / 2 /// 4 2 /// 2 ///////// 4 / 4 / / // / 4 4 4 ///// 4 2 // / 2 // / 4 4 / 4 / ///// 4 // 4 / 3 / 2 2 2 // 2 ///// 4 / 3	c Chapman mid off	White	254
4 2 /// 4 /// 4 // 2 / 4 // 2 3 2 2 / / / 2 / 2 // // //// 4 / 2 /// 4 // 4 /////// 4 / 4 50 at 4/15 46 min 100 at 7/35 106 min, 150 at 6/22 153 min , 173 at 11/42 207 mm, 200 at 17/16 236 mm, 250 at 2/4			
2 // 2 /////// 5 // / 2 // / 4 2 2 // / // 2 ///// 4 // 4 /// 4 // 2 /// 2 // 2	Bowled	White	83
5 0 at 11/38 123 min.			
3 4 4 / 4 / 4 / 4 4 4 /	c Woolley mid on	Hammond	44
2 2 6 / / 2 / 4 /	c Hobbs point	Tate	30
/ 4 3 2 / / 4 // 4 2 4 // 2 / 2	Not out		43
/ 4 2 2 2 ///	Not Out.		20

H.M. King George visited the match at. 3/15 to 3/45
met the teams on the field. fine sight.
Woodfull & Ponsford batting.

Partnerships   Woodfull & Bradman   100   13   66 minutes
                                      150   5/33   104 " "
                                      200   6/4   138 " "
                                      231   6/23   154 " "
                Bradman & Kippax   100   17/37   102 " "
                                    192   7+8   183 minutes.

	How Out	Bowled	Total
Byes /4/3			6
Leg Byes /// 8 ///			8
Wides / 4			5
No Balls			

	2	3	4	5	6	7	8	9	10	TOTAL
162	393	585	588	643	672					729
...ford	Woodfull	Bradman	Kippax	Richardson	McCabe					
...dfull	Bradman	Kippax	McCabe	McCabe	Oldfield					
78	151	81	1	25	9					

Bradman so totally dominated this Test that England, red hot favourites to retain the Ashes, suddenly realised a kid from country New South Wales could defeat the might of All England. Bradman regarded this innings as the pinnacle of his batting genius.

MATCH BETWEEN

AUSTRALIA and **ENG...**

at *Headingley Leeds* on

FIRST Innings of *Eng...*

Date	Time In	Score	Adjm.	Score	Time Out	Total		Name	Runs as Scored.	
	11/30		1/30	136	3/5	167 min	1	Woodfull W.	142 11112 1111114 11112 1134 1134 111	300 287 251
	2/18	136							50 at 3/4. 166 min.	200 150
	11/30				11/39	7	2	Jackson a.	1	100 50 at 11...
	11/38	2	1.30	105 136			3	Bradman Don	242 11442 14 1432 1 44 11444 2 14 111 21 124 112 144 121	
	2.18	136	4.30	170 305	11/39	383 min			41111 213 242 41141 4 1 1142 4211 2244 1111 4111111 4 11 431114 142 11143 1221	
	4.50	305	6.30	30						
	11—	458		309 458						
	3/7	194	4/30	53 305	6/10	163 m	4	Kippax a.	1141 11214 4 11112 1114 1111112 13 11111 2212 14 11111 4212	
	4/50	305							50 at 5/25 118 min	
Sat.	6/11	423	6/30	1m 458	11/20	39 m	5	McCabe S.	1441224444	
	11—	458								
	11/21	484			11/25	4 min	6	Richardson V.	1	
	11/27	491			12/20	53 m	7	a. Beckett E.L.	24121444124	
	11/40	508			12.	20 m	8	Oldfield W.A.	11	
	12/2	519			12/42	40 m	9	Grimmett C.V.	12 1113 6 6 111	
	12/22	544			12/37	15 m	10	Wall T.	111	
	12/39	565			12/42	3 m	11	Hornebrook P.	1	

50	12.43	53 min	
100	12.53	83 min	
186	1.30	120	lunch
151	2.27	129	
200	3.15	177	
250	3.52	214	
300	4.26	248	tea.
305	4.30	252	
352	5.21	283	
400	5.55	317	
450	6.25	347	
458	6.30	352	stumps
500	11.34	386	
560	12.29	441	

Total Time 454 minutes

Australia won toss, batted.
Friday. Fine & cool. big attendance.
Saty. fine warm. Bradman served highest Test match score record 288 Beat R.E...
Ponsford & Fairfax sick list.

Umpires Bestwick & C...
Scorers. Ferguson & Br...

	1	2	3	4	5	6
Fall of Wickets ...	2	194	423	486	491	50...
Batsman Out ...	Jackson	Woodfull	Kippax	McCabe	Richardson	Brad...
" Not Out...	Woodfull 1	Bradman 147	Bradman 293	Bradman 319	Bradman 323	a Bec...

100 partnership Woodfull & Bradman 77 min/s
100 " — Bradman & Kippax 79 "
229

Bradman scored a (then) world Test record of 334 in the first innings at Leeds, scored in only 383 minutes with 46 boundaries. During the innings he passed 1000 runs in Tests - in only his seventh Test. He was unbeaten on 309 at stumps on the opening day in a superb batting exhibition, a feat that earned him the award for the best individual sporting performance by an Australian male athlete in the Sport Australia Bicentenary awards in 1988.

CLAND

July 11. 12. 14. 15. 1930

LIA. 11th

	How Out	Bowled	Total	
836	Bowled	Hammond	50	
314"	c Larwood sq leg.	Tate	1	
274"				
172"				
99'				
49 min				
42 1111	/414 1141124443 111 41244 c Duckworth wkt.	Tate	334	a Catch at Wkt when 273
112 113				
	c Chapman point	Tate	77	
	Bowled	Larwood	30	
	c Larwood sq leg.	Tate	1	
	c Chapman mid off	Geary	29	
	c Hobbs c point	Tate	2	
	c Duckworth wkt	Tyldesley	24	
	Bowled	Tyldesley	3.	
	Not Out.		1	
	Byes 14		5	
4	Leg Byes 1141 11		8	
287.	Wides 1		1	
	No Balls			

	7	8	9	10		
	519	544	565	566	TOTAL	
	dfield a Beckett	Wall	Grimmett			566
	a Beckett Grimmett 10	Grimmett 6	Hornibrook 44	1		

6 pm
10 "

An Avalanche of Fours.

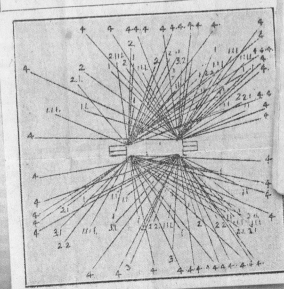

Writing in the Bradman Albums he said:
"In a long career there are many outstanding memories but I suppose the opening day of the Third Test at Leeds must rank as the greatest in my cricketing life. To break the world's record Test score was exciting. To do so against Australia's oldest and strongest rival was satisfying. More than anything else, however, was the knowledge that I had scored the runs at such a fast rate and therefore provided entertainment for the spectators".

BOUNDARY MAKERS IN ACTION

FRANK WOOLLEY of Kent, is coming to the end of his Test match career, but before the start of the present season he had played in 29 games against Australia. Tall and slim, he is a most entertaining left-handed bat and still a useful change bowler.

KUMAR SHRI DULEEPSINHJI is a nephew of the great 'Ranji,' and also plays for Sussex. With keen eyes and a supple wrist is a sheer delight to watch. Scored 173 in his first Test at Lords.

FEARLESS FIGHTERS

A right-hand, medium-pace bowler, HURWOOD, the sun-tanned Queenslander, is respected by all batsmen. The running off-breaks he delivers are a constant puzzle to his opponents.

DON BRADMAN, the wonder bat from New South Wales. Only 21, he has seen some great cricket matches, and has scored 452 not out, creating a new world's record.

Don Bradman (portrait above), the twenty-one-year-old Australian wonder batsman, putting a ball to the boundary during his magnificent innings yesterday of 309 not out in the Test match at Leeds. In a display of hurricane hitting he beat the Test record of 287 made by R. E. Foster in 1903 and joined the small company of Test batsmen who have scored a century before lunch. He is the only player to obtain a century in four successive Tests. Australia scored 458 for three. See also page 20.

DON BRADMAN

WHAT DOES
this Australian freak look like? This English crowd found out as Don went in to bat in the Test match at Leeds.

The Leeds crowd paves a path of honour for Bradman as he returns to the pavilion after his world record 334.

Bat used by Bradman in scoring his Test score of 334 against England at Headingley, Leeds July 1930. This total included 309 runs in one day.

BRADMAN V. ENGLAND:
309 AND STILL AT WICKET

TEST SCORE BOARD

AUSTRALIA—First Innings

W. M. Woodfull, b Hammond	50
A. Jackson, c Larwood, b Tate	1
D. Bradman, not out	309
A. F. Kippax, c Chapman, b Tate	77
S. McCabe, not out	12
Extras	9
Total (3 wkts)	458

Fall of Wickets.

1	2	3	4	5	6	7	8	9	10
2	194	423							

ONE MAN SHOW IN THIRD TEST

Unforgettable Innings of the Wonder Batsman

SMASHING RECORDS

EASTERN
DAILY PRESS
SATURDAY JULY 12
BRADMAN
VERSUS
ENGLAND

**Eclipses Record Test Score of 287
Made by R. E. Foster in 1903**

W. G. GRACE.

WEAK ENGLISH BOWLING FLOGGED

Sparkling 100 Scored Before Lunch—Chapman Loses Toss for First Time in Eight Tests

England's bowlers battered and exhausted; Don Bradman, aged twenty-one, the world's wonder batsman, triumphant and 309 not out after smashing still more records.

R. E. FOSTER

Such was the close of the first day of the Leeds Test match yesterday. "It was Bradman's day," says Mr. C. G. Macartney, the famous Australian cricketer, whose exclusive description of the match appears on page 6. Comments by Mr. P. J. Moss, the "Daily Mirror" Sports Editor, are on page 18.

By an amazing display of hurricane hitting Bradman beat the previous highest Test score of 287 made by R. E. Foster for England at Sydney in 1903, and his own personal record of 254 made in the match at Lord's. He nearly doubled the highest score (170) made by Dr. W. G. Grace, the "father" of cricket, against the Australians in 1886.

He is the only player to obtain a century in four successive Tests, and has equalled the feat of Trumper and Macartney in scoring a Test century before lunch. He has not yet made two separate centuries in a Test match. Bardsley did in 1909.

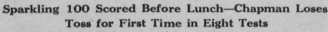

DON BRADMAN'S
AMAZING TREBLE CENTURY

Bradman late cutting a ball through the slips.

Applause for Bradman as he left the field.

Ashes won

THE ASHES
Urn containing the ashes of a bail with its embroidered velvet bag, presented to the Hon Ivo Bligh, captain of the English team in Australia 1882-3, to mark their victory by two matches to one against W. L. Murdoch's team

HE'S OUT

His phenomenal success was the beginning of Bradman's fame and adulation. In first-class matches on that tour he scored 2960 runs at 98.66 with 10 centuries.

AUSTRALIA WINS THE ASHES.

Don Bradman, the Australian cricketer, reading letters of congratulation on his test score, when en route to Bristol, after the match.

In 1882 the Australians defeated England at Kennington Oval by 7 runs. After the match the London "Sporting Times" created the ashes by publishing the following "In Memoriam" notice:—

In Affectionate Remembrance
of
ENGLISH CRICKET,
which died at The Oval on
29th August, 1882.
Deeply Lamented by a large
circle of
Sorrowing Friends and
Acquaintances.
R.I.P.

N.B.—The body will be cremated and the ashes taken to Australia.

He was a national hero, having lifted the Australian spirits in the tough times of depression and inspiring a national identity. More, his success against the might of the mother country forged a feeling that Australia was no longer an outpost, but a nation which could stand on its own.

And in England, Bradman was revered. The like of his scoring ability had never been seen before - and England knew he would be their most dangerous opponent for years to come.

"I DIPS ME LID!"

DON BRADMAN—

How He Captured the Imagination of Englishmen

From Lord's of Renown to Ragamuffins of the Street

AUSTRALIA'S CRICKET ROBOT.

What Bradman has Achieved in England.

THIRTY RECORDS.

Equalled or Broken in First Class Games: P. F. Warner's Eulogy.

Don's Test Record Stands Alone

PLAYING in nine Tests between England and Australia, Don Bradman has scored 1442 runs in 15 innings—average 103.

IN AUSTRALIA

Test.	First innings.	Second innings.
First	18	1
Third	79	112
Fourth	40	58
Fifth	123	37 n.o.

Australia—Total, 468.

IN ENGLAND

Test.	First innings.	Second innings.
First	8	131
Second	254	1
Third	334	
Fourth	14	—
Fifth	232	

English—Total, 974.

Don's Records

FROM BOWRAL TO THE OVAL.

The Evening News has tallied the performances of Don Bradman from his Bowral days to the Fifth Test. It is revealed that Bradman, although only 22 this month, has in all classes of cricket scored more than 12,000 runs. His full figures are:—

	Inn.	N.O.	H.S.	Runs	Aver.
1925-26					
Bowral	21	8	300	1318	101.38
1926-27					
Bowral	5	2	320*	560	186.66
St. George	7	1	110	289	48.16
All Games	27	5	320*	1576	71.63
1927-28					
St. George	10	3	130*	402	57.42
Sheffield Shield	10	1	134*	416	46.22
All Games	32	5	,134*	1123	41.59
1928-29					
St. George	4	0	107	261	65.25
Sheffield Shield	9	3	340*	893	148.83
Tests	8	1	123	468	66.85
All Games	42	8	340*	2616	76.94
1929-30					
St. George	6	2	187	484	121.00
Sheffield Shield	10	2	452*	894	111.75
All Games	39	10	452*	3368	116.13
1930					
In England	31	5	334	2662	102.46

HIS RECORDS.

Bigger and bigger grows the already amazing list of records standing to the credit of Don Bradman. Following are some of the more notable achievements of the batting champion:—

World's record individual score, 452 not out, N.S.W. v. Queensland, 1929-30.

Two highest scores on Sydney Cricket Ground—452 not out v. Queensland and 340 not out v. Victoria.

Highest score in a Test match—334 v. England.

Two highest scores for Australia in Tests—254 and 334.

Three double centuries in Tests—254, 334 and 232. Six centuries in nine Tests.

Six centuries in Tests (equals Trumper and Woodfull for Australia).

Four centuries in a series (equals Sutcliffe and Hammond).

Most runs for series of Tests—984.

Highest score in a Test at Lords (254), Leeds (334), and The Oval (232).

Century before lunch in a Test match (equals Trumper and Macartney).

Record aggregate for an Australian in an English season—2662 (unfinished).

Highest score for an Australian on first appearance in England—211 not out.

1000 runs in May—record for an Australian in England.

Record aggregate for an Australian season—1690 runs.

Seven centuries in an Australian season.

Century on first appearance for N.S.W.—118 v. South Australia.

Twice scored two centuries in first-class match—for N.S.W. v. Queensland and England.

Bradman's name is associated in several partnership records in Test matches, including that with Jackson for the fourth wicket in the Fifth Test.

BRADMAN,

ENGLAND.

Elstree Studios.
L to R: Mr. Arthur Whitelaw,
Geoff Whitelaw, Seymour Hicks,
Don Bradman, Margot Grahame and
one of the Western Brothers.

Kindly acknowledge receipt,
and oblige
J. Quail,
46 The Avenue,
GRANVILLE. N.S.W.

Bradman was so well known on
tour that he received letters from
Australia with only the postmark:
"Bradman, England."

Bradman holds a mirror for film
star Joyce Kennedy.

DON BRADMAN

*Australia's Most Popular
Young Man*

He was invited to the theatre, movie studios, tennis
tournaments and even had a game of billiards with
another Australian legend, Walter Lindrum.

Walter Lindrum shows
Bradman some tricks.

OUR DON BRADMAN

Snappy
Fox Trot
Song

by
JACK O'HAGAN

Written in appreciation of his match-winning and record-breaking efforts.

DON BRADMAN — AUSTRALIA'S BATTING PHENOMENON
Photo through Curtesy of the Melbourne "Herald."

Obtainable on
Regal Record No. G20744
and Player Rolls

ALLAN'S
MUSIC PUBLISHERS
MELBOURNE

COPYRIGHT
2/- NET

Columbia

HOW IT'S DONE — A FRIENDLY CHAT
By DON BRADMAN
(Australian Test Team, 1930)

REGAL
MADE IN AUSTRALIA

OUR DON BRADMAN
(Jack O'Hagan)
ART LEONARD—Baritone
With Novelty Accompaniment

G20744

Bradman was Australia's first and most enduring celebrity. He so captured the nation's imagination that Jack O'Hagan wrote a song about him, aptly entitled "Our Don Bradman."

The song was written "in appreciation of his match-winning and record-breaking efforts."

Bradman driving from the first tee at Sydenham in his plus-fours.

One of Bradman's great passions - and an outlet from the clamouring crowds and relentless cricket matches - was golf. He enjoyed it especially in England. Cartoonist Arthur Mailey equally loved drawing cricketers on the golf course, as he did with the Englishmen in Australia some years later.

SHY TEST HERO BAULKS AT SIGHT OF GREAT CROWD

Tumultuous Worshippers Smash Barriers and Mob Him

DON BRADMAN'S GREAT HOMECOMING

MELBOURNE, Sunday. — A wildly enthusiastic crowd of about 5000, which had waited for hours, broke the barriers at Essendon Aerodrome this evening and mobbed Don Bradman when he arrived by A.N.A. 'plane, over two hours late, from Adelaide.

The most surprised man was Bradman. He hesitated in the doorway of the 'plane amazed, and for a few seconds it seemed as though he would not face the hero-worshipping crowd.

Someone from behind pushed him forward. A smile flickered across his lips, and, waving his hand timidly, he stepped to the ground.

On his return to Australia Bradman was showered in publicity, much of which he found bewildering and overbearing.

At the request of his employers Bradman returned home ahead of his team. Once in Australia, he had to travel from Fremantle to Adelaide by train. Even though the train passed through deserted country such as the Nullarbor, crowds were there to greet Bradman at every stop the train made.

DON'S ARRIVAL MADE BOWRAL MAD WITH JOY

FROM CAR TO HIS MOTHER'S ARMS

SYDNEY TO-DAY

"GUARDIAN" SERVICE

BOWRAL, Tuesday.

Famous Don Bradman was cheered by perhaps a million people in the eight months he was away with the Australian Test team, but no welcome affected him more than the 500 who crowded round him when he reached his hometown this evening.

BOWRAL had never had such a day of excitement.

Earlier, Don Bradman had landed at Goulburn by plane from Melbourne and the first to greet him there were his father and brother, Vic.

As he alighted from the plane the gale which was blowing carried away his hat, but he raced across to greet his father and brother.

"Wizard" Smith drove the party to Bowral and when the car reached there the town was bright with bunting, a band was playing, and 500 excited people waited in Corbett Gardens, where the reception was held.

More tanned than when he went away, Don stepped out of the car into his mother's arms.

STILL SAME DON

The cheers of the crowd were deafening, and ten police had to keep his excited admirers sufficiently far away to enable the Bradman family to mount the specially erected dais.

Mayor Sheaffe said Bowral was there as an expression of its recognition of the wonderful cricket played by Don.

Ald. P. A. Westbrook, a former employer of Don, summed up the champion's efforts in the phrase, "He came, he played, and he conquered."

His success was largely due to his personal charm and ability, and he came back the same carefree clear eyed, clean limbed boy he was eight months ago.

Don's response was brief, as he was visibly affected.

It was more difficult, he said, to speak in his own town than anywhere else, because here they were all old friends while elsewhere they were strangers.

After the reception Don and his family were driven to a secret destination for a family re-union at the home of a relative.

Don wanted his first night home with just his people.

He will arrive in Sydney to-day. To-night he will attend a concert in aid of the United Charities Fund at the Town Hall.

Proud Mother, Emily, gratefully accepting a bunch of red roses.

He continues his spectacular displays against the West Indies and Sheffield Shield teams. In six Shield innings he scored 695 runs at 115, and after struggling in the opening two Tests against the West Indies, he unleashed innings of 223 in the third and 152 in the fourth. He also recorded his first duck in Tests when yorked by a slower ball from pace bowler Herman Griffith in the second innings of the fifth Test at Sydney.

When writing official letters and speeches, Bradman used a typewriter more often than not. He used a Royal typewriter for decades, never bothering to up-grade. Most of his correspondence as a cricket official after he retired was typed, and on this typewriter he collected in 1930 which he never replaced. He never ventured onto a computer.

Bradman's own Royal typewriter.

Orient Line
ENGLAND · AUSTRALIA

S. S. ORONSAY.

October 14

Dear Jack,

Your mother tells me you & Glenn are very keen cricket enthusiasts.

I sincerely hope you keep your love for cricket always for it is the greatest of games & even if one does not excel, a pleasure to play.

Best wishes for your future success.

Yours Sincerely

Don Bradman

Bradman was a prolific letter writer. Despite his phenomenal success in England, he spent time on the return cruise replying to his thousands of fan letters. One, to a young lad Jack Radford in Northampton, he wrote of "the greatest of games." Bradman did not worry about the origin of the country, the age group or denomination of those who wrote to him. He always replied, and by hand.

SIR RON BRIERLEY

(Investor and corporate raider who funded the establishment of the Bradman Museum, was a Trustee of the Sydney Cricket Ground 1988-96, and President of New Zealand Cricket in 1995)

We were an interesting mix, Don Bradman and me. We had two things in common - cricket and finance.

Bradman was the batsman without peer, the 'Boy From Bowral' who plundered bowlers around the world. I was the lad from Wellington in New Zealand who became an international corporate raider.

His fame was cricket and his profession was stock-broking. My fame is finance, but my passion is cricket.

So it was always interesting when we met. I always wanted to talk to Don about cricket but he was more interested in shares and interest rates.

I am just so pleased that we were able to meet, work together on such an important project as the Bradman Museum, and become friends.

Unfortunately I never saw Don play cricket. I was only 11 when he retired. But I knew he was a legendary figure, absolutely above everybody else in the game.

I recall the first time I met Don. Bob Vance, who ran New Zealand cricket, was manager of the 1973-74 touring team to Australia and he introduced me to Don during the January 1974 third Test in Adelaide. Don was a bit quizzical about why a corporate raider was at the Australia Day cricket. Even then he was more interested in the corporate side of things, certainly as far as I was concerned.

As with anyone with an interest in cricket, it was always a privilege to meet or talk with Don Bradman. I remember in the early days of my company International Equity that a colleague, who wasn't much interested in cricket but who was aware of Bradman's fame, told me he had phoned Don in Adelaide to pass on some information. I told my colleague that if there was any calling to be made to Don Bradman, it was chairman's material and I'd be doing it!

I had casual meetings with Don until 1988 and the start of the Bradman Museum, after which I would go to his home, chat and socialise and discuss the progress of the Museum. I was particular to have accurate facts and figures - Don didn't like generalisations.

The establishment of the Bradman Museum was a gesture by International Equity for the Bicentenary celebrations in 1988. Initially Don was neutral. He said we were welcome to do it but that he would not be promoting it. However as the years went by he became more involved and realised there was an important opportunity for him to be able to tell his true story. He saw too the chance to influence cricket in general about the way he saw the game, and how it should be played with sportsmanship and spirited passion.

I completely under-estimated what was involved with setting up and running a museum. We funded the project and it was a very big project, with the need to continually add to the collection. It has been very rewarding and today it is a marvellous tribute to Sir Donald Bradman.

When Don became involved, he wanted to influence things considerably. That meant he became more and more involved, and that gave me more opportunities to chat with him as I was on the board for a while. After that I did a lot of work on an unofficial basis - and still do - and left much to the late Bob Radford, the former secretary of the New South Wales Cricket Association and then boss at the Museum. He had a major influence on the success of the Museum.

I always tried to have a topic of interest when I spoke with Don - he was not the type for idle chat. At a dinner in the 1970s I was prepared, having unearthed the fact that Herbert Sutcliffe, one of the great English batsmen, had registered every score between 0 and 128 during his career. I mentioned this to Don and expected it would lead to an interesting conversation.

Don simply replied: "He had enough innings to make them in."

Maybe I should have suggested a share portfolio.

Bert Ironmonger and Bradman during the 1930-31 series.

THE VALUE OF DON BRADMAN

BEYOND all the denials, it appears to be established that the Australian cricket team is likely to lose Mr. Don Bradman, its most fertile run-getter.

Following a policy which began a few years ago, an English cricket club has made Mr. Bradman an offer which, with a view to establishing his future, he will possibly accept.

No doubt his acceptance would bring a certain criticism upon him by people who believe that he should stick to Australia and help to win Test Matches for her.

In a world in which talent is marketed like wheat or cotton or rubber, Mr. Bradman merely follows the usual procedure. He did not make the world, and it would be grossly unfair to blame him for following its usages. Australia's singers and artists and other professional folk go abroad, and, finding, as a rule, that they can do better abroad than in their own country, remain away. Few of us, if offered a sum which appeared as large to us as the very handsome wages offered must appear to Mr. Bradman, would refuse to go to London or anywhere else for it. In this case the admonition may well be quoted: "Let him that is without sin among ye cast the first stone."

At the same time it is most regrettable that the world is so constituted that talent should thus be marketed. So far, cricket has been a sport singularly free from the commercialism which bids for players. Far better for cricket should it remain so.

No doubt it is an excellent thing for a club to have a champion cricketer in its team, but the old system of breeding and training champions was a far more satisfactory way than buying them. It gave a genuine local pride which cannot be marketed nor valued— "the praise no man can buy."

That it will rebound to the general detriment of the game is certain. What pride can there be in England that a team of hired Australian professionals win a match against Australia?

At least the Australian artist abroad keeps his nationality. Melba was always the Australian prima donna, George Lambert signed his pictures frequently "G. W. Lambert, of Australia." The professional cricketer, after the statutory period of residence, becomes an English cricketer, and it becomes his painful duty to slog the bowling of his old team-mates or take the wickets which before it was his duty and pride to keep up. It is not a pleasant position for any man who has pride in the country of his birth.

Moreover, it tends to reduce Test cricket to a farce. If Great Britain is able to buy our most promising cricketers as they appear, and the habit grows, what Australian will be interested enough to go out to the Cricket Ground to see a team, largely composed of former Australian cricketers, wallop a team from which all the brightest talent has been bought by the enemy?

Bradman, playing for Australia on an Australian wicket, was a magnet to tens of thousands of enthusiastic spectators.

However, it is not much use to protest. If English clubs propose to strengthen their sides by purchase, there is no more to be said, and no young man can afford to reject a good offer from a mere reason of sentiment. It looks as if in future Australia may be the breeding ground of England's cricketers.

BUNGLING BOARD MAY BANISH BRADMAN

PUBLIC WILL NOT STAND
FOR DON'S
DEPORTATION BY DULLWITS

It's Time To Control the Controllers

IF BRADMAN boards a boat for Blighty to play as a professional for a Lancashire League Club, and is lost to Test cricket the Australian Board of Control will be blackguarded by every follower of the game. VIRTUALLY, the world's greatest batsman will have been deported by a band of buffers who, the majority of cricket enthusiasts declare, are not fit and proper persons to be controlling the national game. It seems to be a case of the Board getting rid of Bradman, or Australia first getting rid of the Board.

Don Bradman (right), who could have been a fallen idol had he succumbed to the Board's pinpricks, but "about" it the man who came through with flying colors.

WHAT HAS AUSTRALIA DONE FOR BRADMAN?

FINED HIM FOR EATING THE FRUIT
OF HIS OWN GENIUS

Emotional Outbursts About His Doing What Most Great Australians Have Done

DIDN'T GET HIS SKILL BY ACT OF PARLIAMENT

WHY all this outcry about Don Bradman? One would think the young cricketing genius had violated one of the commandments simply because he has enough business ability to consider his own future.

He has been offered a lucrative position in the English cricket world. Why shouldn't he accept it? There is no excuse for the pitiful wails which are resounding throughout Australia. Bradman is a free agent. A marvellous gift has been bestowed on him. It is sheer stupidity to imagine that it is his duty to remain in the land of his birth if his gift is more valuable elsewhere.

Bradman was keenly sought by Lancashire League clubs - the wealthiest in the world at that stage - immediately following the 1930 tour. Bradman considered an offer of 500 pounds a season for three seasons from Accrington but was castigated by the Cricket Board, which caused national uproar. The Board threatened that he would be ineligible to play for Australia if he played in England within two years of the 1930 tour. Bradman had the public's support to capitalise on a business opportunity - provided he could still play for Australia - but eventually he refused the offer when an Australian newspaper, radio station and sporting goods company joined forces to reward him handsomely to stay in Australia.

If Bradman Decided to Play For a Living He Could Start With an English Club at a Salary of About £1500 a Year. Not too Bad a Salary for a Young Man of 22.

WORLD WIDE WIRELESS **Radiogram**

AMALGAMATED WIRELESS (AUSTRALASIA) LIMITED

47 YORK ST. SYDNEY   67-9 QUEEN ST. MELBOURNE

Via Beam

K2102   NELSON LANCS   24   25TH   11 49AM

LCO CLAUDE SPENCER 278 GEORGE ST SYDNEY

LOCAL CLUB OFFERS FIVE HUNDRED POUNDS PER SEASON FOR 3

SEASONS PASSAGE BOTH WAYS CABLE REPLY

MARK YOUR REPLY "VIA BEAM"

CONSTANTINE.

Australian Board of Control for International Cricket.

TELEGRAMS AND CABLES :
"CRICKET" ADELAIDE
TELEPHONE
CENT. 1111 (5 LINES)
SECRETARY :
W. H. JEANES

MANUFACTURES BUILDING
14 PIRIE STREET
ADELAIDE
SOUTH AUSTRALIA

11th. September, 1931

Mr. Don Bradman,
C/- Mick Simmons Ltd.,
Haymarket,
S Y D N E Y

Dear Sir,

Your letter of the 9th. inst. was placed before the Board of Control at its meeting today.

Replying to your first question I was directed to say that the intention of the Board in framing Clause Twenty Seven of the Agreement in connection with the 1930 Australian Tour in England was to prevent any member of that Team returning to England for the purpose of playing cricket within a period of two years after the completion of the official tour.

Referring to the second question in your letter I am to say that the Board expects the Clause of the Agreement referred to to be observed by the members of the Team and if the Clause were broken by any member of such team the Board would not approve of his selection for Australia.

Yours faithfully,

SECRETARY

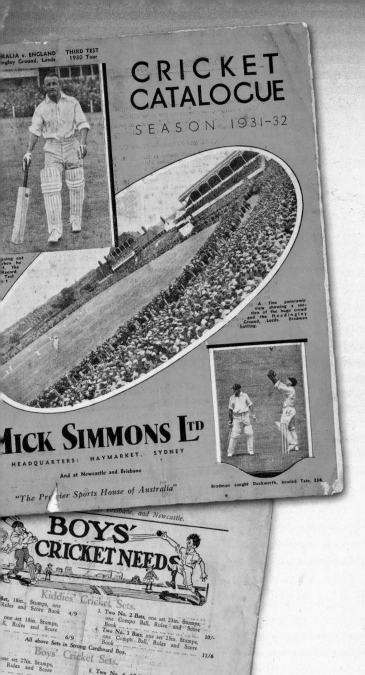

CRICKET CATALOGUE

SEASON 1931-32

AUSTRALIA v. ENGLAND — THIRD TEST
...ngley Ground, Leeds — 1930 Tour

A fine panoramic view showing a section of the huge crowd and the Headingley Ground, Leeds. Bradman batting.

MICK SIMMONS LTD

HEADQUARTERS: HAYMARKET, SYDNEY

And at Newcastle and Brisbane

"The Premier Sports House of Australia"

Bradman caught Duckworth, bowled Tate, 334.

...Brisbane, and Newcastle.

BOYS' CRICKET NEEDS

Kiddies' Cricket Sets.

...Bat, 18in., Stumps, one ...Rules and Score Book   4/9

3. Two No. 2 Bats, one set 23in. Stumps, one Compo Ball, Rules and Score Book   10/-

...one set 18in. Stumps, ...ll, Rules and Score   6/9

4. Two No. 3 Bats, one set 23in. Stumps, one Compo Ball, Rules and Score Book   11/6

All above Sets in Strong Cardboard Box.

Boys' Cricket Sets.

...one set 27in. Stumps, ...Rules and Score   12/9

8. Two No. 6 All-Cane Bats, Brass-top, ...

Don Bradman Has Been Saved for Australia!

Don Bradman signs the Australian contract.

LONDON June 11 1930

BRADMAN v. ENGLAND

EVENING NEWS 6.30

We've kept him here for you —

HOW IT WAS DONE

SEE HIM PALMER'S SYDNEY SPORTS ADVISER

Such was Bradman's scoring ability that on November 2, 1931, he scored 100 runs in three (eight ball) overs.

The occasion was the opening of the Blackheath Club's new malthoid wicket and Bradman and his NSW teammate Oscar Wendell-Bill were guest players.

Bradman scored 256, and having scored his century he decided to entertain the crowd. His scores during the next three overs were:

First over: 66424461 (33)
Second over: 64466464 (40)
Third over: 16611446 (27)

Wendell-Bill scored singles off the first and the fifth balls of the third over. Pictured left is the bat Bradman used in the innings and is on display at the Bradman Museum.

"It is important I think to emphasise that the thing was not planned. It happened purely by accident and everyone was surprised at the outcome, none more so than I." (Bradman on his innings at Blackheath in 1931 when he made a century in three overs)

The Don Bradman Special CRICKET BOOT

Material .... Size ....

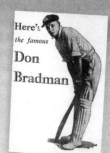

Here's the famous Don Bradman

QUALITY HATS

BY *Linney* LONDON

You may be sure the Wonder Batsman wears the best Cricket Boots obtainable anywhere. He's seen and tried many brands and from them all chooses McKeown's.

and here are his favorite

Boots

Leather Lined

Whole piece Backs

Finest Woven Canvas

Solid Welted Double Decker Soles

Double stitched Buck Back Strap

Now you can get exactly the same make and quality Boots as Don Bradman Wears—at DAVID JONES'

They've whole piece backs in selected fine woven canvas, solid leather double decker soles specially constructed to withstand spiking; white buck back-strap double stitched; and are leather lined throughout—each boot bearing a facsimile signature of Don Bradman himself. Special displays this week at both Stores.

Sizes and Half-sizes, **22/6** Youths' sizes, 1-4, **21/-**

Don Bradman AUTOGRAPH BATS

The first Australian shipment of Bradman Bats . . . especially for Mick Simmons, Ltd. Don Bradman, who is on the staff of this great Sports House, personally selected and autographed every one of these Bats at Sykes's famous Sporting Goods Factory, at Horbury, England.

Beautiful! That is the word that instantly escapes the lips of every cricketer who sees them. Every "Bradman" Bat, no matter what the grade, represents the highest standard of cricket bat craftsmanship ever introduced into Australia.

A Matchless Test Souvenir !

If you are a cricketer . . . you will appreciate the fact that one of these "Bradman" Bats with the glories that surround it . . . will one day become a priceless Test Souvenir. Any boy . . . in his hero-worship of the great Don Bradman . . . will treasure a "Junior" Bradman Bat beyond anything in the world that could be given him.

4 CROWN	65/-
3 CROWN	56/6
2 CROWN	47/6
CLUB	37/6
HARROW SIZE	37/6
JUNIOR SPECIAL	
No. 6	35/-
JUNIOR No. 6	20/-
JUNIOR No. 5	18/6
JUNIOR No. 4	16/6

Always Remember from January to December—

FOSTER'S

is the Bradman of Lagers

DON BRADMAN

Fosters "BLUE LABEL" LAGER meets all competition.

JOHN M. HEADRICK & CO., Local Agents

Bradman quickly developed a business acumen which propelled him to fortune as well as fame. He endorsed a variety of goods including beer (even though he never drank ale), ice-creams, hats, cricket bats, boots, hair cream and tea. He was one of the first sporting stars to capitalise commercially on his ability.

Featured in George Marlow's Gorgeous Xmas Pantomime, "Beauty and the Beast," at the Grand Opera House.
Produced by Nat Phillips.

EVERY DAY IS A RAINBOW DAY FOR ME

Australia's brightest star and the World's greatest batsman.. DON BRADMAN

Bradman even capitalised on his mucical talents. He wrote the music for Everyday Is A Rainbow Day For Me, recorded in Columbia Studios (pictured above) with words by Jack Lumsdaine. Everyone wanted Bradman to promote their wares. Marketing men cannot calculate how much money he would have been worth in the totally commercialised sports world of today - but all agree he could have commanded his own price and would have been by far the best paid cricketer in history.

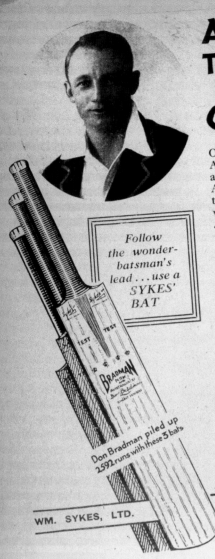

A GLOWING TESTIMONIAL
from the GREAT DON!

Follow the wonder-batsman's lead ... use a SYKES' BAT

On the eve of his departure for Australia Don Bradman, whose amazing performances during the Australian Tour of 1930 astounded the whole of the cricket world, wired us as follows:

"... Bats supplied have been excellent and played a big part in successful tour."

It is interesting to note that this great batsman has used no other bats than those manufactured by William Sykes Limited throughout the whole of his cricketing career, and that in compiling 2,592 runs during the 1930 English Season only three bats were used, all being in sound and first-class condition at the end of the season.

Sykes LTD
BRITAINS SPORTS SPECIALISTS
famous BATS

HORBURY, YORKS, ENGLAND

WM. SYKES, LTD.

Don Bradman piled up 2592 runs with these 3 bats

Autographing bats at Sykes' factory, Horbury (West Yorkshire).

Everyone wanted to know Don Bradman during and after the 1930 series - and every player wanted to use the bat recommended by The Don.

English bat company Sykes, realising the commercial value of having the prolific Bradman name branded on their bats, went on an advertising spree. They boasted he scored 2592 runs with three of their bats on tour, and then had him autograph for sale.

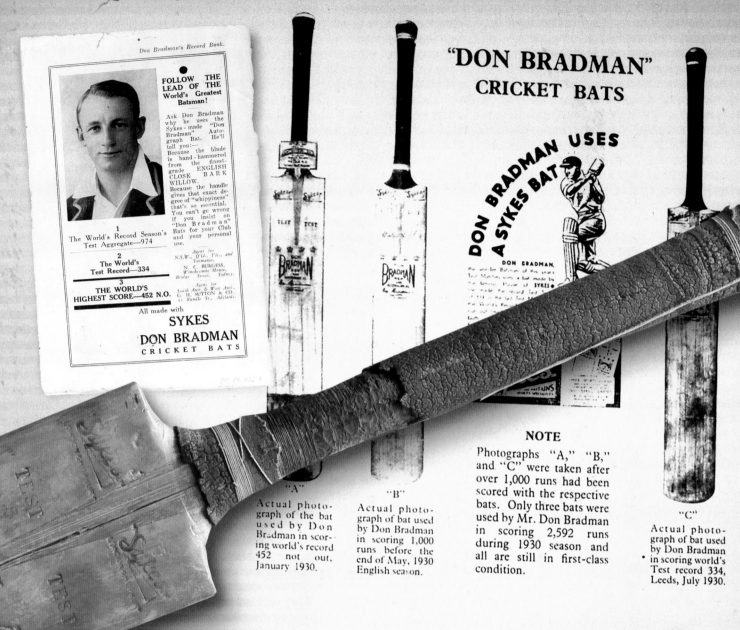

"DON BRADMAN" CRICKET BATS

DON BRADMAN USES A SYKES BAT

NOTE

Photographs "A," "B," and "C" were taken after over 1,000 runs had been scored with the respective bats. Only three bats were used by Mr. Don Bradman in scoring 2,592 runs during 1930 season and all are still in first-class condition.

"A"
Actual photograph of the bat used by Don Bradman in scoring world's record 452 not out, January 1930.

"B"
Actual photograph of bat used by Don Bradman in scoring 1,000 runs before the end of May, 1930 English season.

"C"
Actual photograph of bat used by Don Bradman in scoring world's Test record 334, Leeds, July 1930.

"D"
Actual photograph of Don Bradman bat autographed by Australian and English Teams, Final Test Match 1930.

Australia v. South Africa
Melb. Cricket Ground 1931

Back: L. to R.
S. McCabe, J. Fingleton, K. Rigg.
B. Ironmonger, L. Nash, L. Darling

Front:
C. Grimmett, A. Kippax, N. Woodfull.
D. Bradman, B. Oldfield

Amazing 299 N.O.

BIGGEST SCORE IN TESTS IN AUSTRALIA

Fifteenth Double Century: Record Aggregate

AUSTRALIA 513—205 AHEAD

(By ARTHUR MAILEY)

WITH the huge total of 299 not out in Australia's fourth Test score of 513, Don Bradman smashed several cricket records today.

His score is the highest individual total in Tests in Australia, R. E. Foster's 287 being the previous best; he is the only Australian batsman to make three double centuries against a visiting team; this is his fifteenth score of 200 or more in first-class cricket; and he has beaten the previous highest aggregate in Tests between the two countries—G. A. Faulkner's 732.

The South Africans were next to taste Bradman's blade, arriving in 1931/32, but only after Bradman was almost lost to Australia. Approached by an English Lancashire League club with a three year contract that was worth a fortune in that era, Bradman eventually remained in Australia after being provided a lucrative combined offer from Associated Newspapers, Radio 2UE and the department store chair, F. J. Palmer.

How Bradman Hit Up 219 Under Four Hours Against Springboks

BRADMAN'S FOURTEENTH DOUBLE CENTURY IN FIRST-CLASS CRICKET

Does Not Give a Chance Against High-class Bowling

(By "NOT OUT")

D. G. BRADMAN

That settled, Bradman rattled off innings of 226 in Brisbane, 112 in Sydney, 2 and 167 in Melbourne and 299 not out at Adelaide against the touring South Africans. In doing so he completed an unparalleled feat in Australian cricket by making seven centuries in consecutive matches. Although he was in the scorebook for the final Test, he injured his ankle in the dressing room matting before play. That ended his season.

BRADMAN BREAKS MORE TEST MATCH RECORDS

All of the seats in the main stand were occupied a good hour before play was resumed, and when Bell took up the attack against Bradman there appeared to be as many people present as there were on Friday afternoon. A single was scored off his first ball, and Bradman was off again towards another record. Six runs were scored from the over, four to Bradman and two to Oldfield. Morkel was the other bowler, and Oldfield took the honours for the first boundary of the day by snicking the first ball through slips for four. Bradman got the strike then, and put the ball in the same place, but his four was the result of a perfectly executed late cut. He followed with another boundary past mid-on, and took his total to 212, two runs short of the late Victor Trumper's record score of 214, made against the South Africans at Adelaide in 1911.

RECORD, THEN OUT.

There was a tumultuous roar in Morkel's next over when the champion smacked one to the leg boundary, and added just another record to his already formidable list.

His splendid knock was brought to an end in Vincent's next over, the left-hander adding to his laurels by getting the champion leg before wicket. Don had been treating him the same as Morkel, but the extra turn' imparted by Vincent got the ball past his bat when he stepped in front of the second delivery to pull it to leg. The innings of 226 had taken 277 minutes, and included 22 fours, four of which had been obtained to-day. After taking that wicket Vincent's figures were three for 74.

BRADMAN'S ABANDON.

The champion had made his extra 26 runs in a little over 20 minutes, an amazing rate of scoring for one who was opening to fresh bowling. He actually played as if there had been no break in his innings at all, and, while he could be pardoned for taking liberties with Morkel, who was sending them straight through, there was no excuse for his abandon when facing left-hander Vincent. The ball that got him was one which, ordinarily, he would have treated with respect, but in his merry mood he was prepared to hit at anything.

BRADMAN 226

Special to the "Ceylon Observer"—Copyright!

TO-DAY'S TEST AT BRISBANE

TWELVE thousand spectators witnessed the resumption of play and Don Bradman was lustily cheered on his way towards the breaking of the 20-year-old individual record held by the famous Victor Trumper. When he had succeeded in recording the required 15 runs—he started the day with 200 not out to his credit—the scene of enthusiasm was one of the most impressive ever witnessed on a Queensland ground. Bradman was cheered for some minutes and twice he was forced to acknowledge the prolonged and wonderful ovation.

HOW THE RUNS WERE SCORED

FIFTY in 44 minutes.
100 in 80 minutes.
150 in 127 minutes.
200 in 160 minutes.
250 in 186 minutes.
300 in 223 minutes.
350 in 251 minutes.
400 in 273 minutes.
446 in 299 minutes.

World's Champion Scores

226 vs. S. Africa

TEST AVERAGE 100

Australia 450 : South Africa 42 for 1 at Tea

Special to the "Ceylon Observer—Copyright

BRISBANE, Saturday

BRADMAN established a new record to-day in the first Test at Brisbane, for the highest individual score against South Africa, beating the previous record of 214 made by Victor Trumper at Adelaide in 1910.

Bradman's Test average is now 100.

At the lunch interval to-day Australia were 446 for 9.

Australia's innings terminated for 450, Oldfield being unbeaten at 56.

South Africa lost Curnow at 25 and at the tea interval had scored 42 for 1.

D. G. BRADMAN
NEW SOUTH WALES

DON BRADMAN'S

PICTORIAL TEST RECORD

S.AFRICA — AUSTRALIA CRICKET

Price 6D.   Copyright

BRADMAN

During the North American summer of 1932 Bradman joined a troupe led by Victor Richardson on a tour of Canada and the United States, where they played 51 matches. Bradman scored 3779 runs at an average of 99.45 - scoring 18 three figure scores on tour.
(These statistics are according to Alfred James in his book 'The Don vs The Rest', 2006)

Souvenir Programme

Australian Test Match XI
Touring Canada
1932

Australia
VS.
Western Ontario Cricket League

ONTARIO REFORMATORY GROUNDS
(By Courtesy Ontario Government)
GUELPH

July 4th, 1932

Play Commences at 11 A.M.

Bradman's 200, Not Out, Features Second Day Of Aussies' Visit

Bradman with the Women's World Championship basketball team, Edmonton Gardens, B.C.

"Brockton Point, Vancouver, BC Canada is without doubt the most beautiful cricket ground in the world...I cannot imagine a more delightful place for cricket. The ground is on the edge of a beautiful wooded park. Sitting in a deck chair on the veranda of the rustic pavilion, one can look across the field to the towering snow-capped mountains, while in the foreground an arm of the harbour runs behind the sightboard and lazy old ferries dawdle across the bowlers arm.

To the right are small clumps of ornamental trees. Then further on the right is the harbour where sea-planes come into graceful foamy landings and beyond is the city itself with its tall, stately buildings on the skyline."
(Bradman on his most picturesque ground)

Australian "Sports" In United States

AUSTRALIAN CRICKETERS.

Bradman's Double Century.

MONTREAL, July 8.
Don Bradman on Friday showed cricket enthusiasts why he is regarded as one of the best batsmen the game has produced, when, against the best local bowling, he scored 200 not out in the second of a series of three one-day matches between the Australians and an all-Montreal team. Montreal, batting 15, was dismissed for 77. The tourists scored 331 for three.

Above: AUSTRALIAN cricketers arrive back at Vancouver. Left to right, back row: A. Bremble, A. Vaughan, P. Carney, S. McCabe, W. F. Ives, L. Fleetwood-Smith, A. Mailey, H. Carter, E. Rofe. Front row: Don Bradman, Alan Kippax, V. Richardson (captain) Mrs. Bradman, R. Nutt, W. Carter

FOR CORRESPONDENCE ONLY

PLACE
STAMP
HERE

This group photo was taken in Montreal outside of Waterman's shop.

You can't see the features too clearly but guess you can recognise Some of us.

GOODWILL TOUR, AUSTRALIAN CRICKET TEAM, 1932

Dr. R. Pope (Physician); Hanson ("Sep") Carter; Don Bradman; E. K. Tolhurst; Mrs. Don Bradman;
L. O. Fleetwood-Smith; R. N. Nutt; Victor Y. Richardson (Captain); Arthur A. Mailey (Manager);
Alan F. Kippax; Stan J. McCabe; W. F. Ives; E. R. Rofe; P. H. Carney

BRADMAN—in a "Babe" Ruth outfit.

BABES OF THE WOOD

Bradman Meets Ruth

SURPRISING DON

A little tale of two Babes of the Wood—Ruth of the baseball willow and Bradman of the cricket willow.

Both Ruth and Babe Bradman sat together watching a big baseball match in New York a little over a month ago.

The two "giants" of their respective games found that they had a lot in common, and, judging by the newspaper stories, they were extremely polite towards each other.

"I'll try this cricket business," chuckled Ruth.

"Maybe it's my game. Now, why don't you put on a Yankee uniform and see what you can do against our kind of pitching?" he suggested to Bradman. "Maybe baseball is your game."

But Bradman "begged off."

The Babe—the original—was surprised by Bradman's lack of size and weight. "From what they were telling me I thought you were a husky guy," remarked Ruth to Don. "But us little fellows can hit 'em harder than the big ones," he roared.

KNOWLEDGE

Bradman also surprised Ruth by his knowledge of baseball.

"Now, watch this closely," suggested Guide Ruth, who was intent on teaching all the finer points to Bradman.

"Jove, a double play," ejaculated Don.

"Hey, what's this?" snorted the Babe. "I was told to point out the tricks of the game, and you holler 'double play.' You don't need any teaching."

Bradman confessed that he had seen a lot of baseball in Australia, and was keen on it.

During the tour he attended a baseball game and met champion American baseballer Babe Ruth.

Back row: Boris Karloff
2nd row from back: A. Mailey, (actor - unknown), V. Richardson, (director - unknown)
crouched in centre: H. Carter
3rd row from front: E. Rofe, R. Nutt, W. Ives, S. McCabe
2nd row from front: P. Carney, L. Fleetwood-Smith, Myrna Loy, K. Tolhurst, A. Kippax, D. Bradman
Front row: Desmond Roberts, (actor - unknown), Charles Aubrey-Smith

TONY GREIG

(Former England captain, Channel Nine commentator)

Having been dropped from the England team, I prepared myself for another winter of coaching schoolboys in South Africa. I had got as far as travelling there from England and beginning the term when a phone call from England altered all my plans.

It was Donald Carr, secretary of the Test and County Cricket Board, enquiring if I would be available to tour Australia with a Rest of the World team captained by Sobers.

The invitation was a surprise, even when I discovered that a number of earlier choices, South Africa's Mike Procter among them, had withdrawn. Sobers had put my name forward, conscious as ever of the all-rounder pursuing his own incomparable talent.

It was agreed that I would travel to Australia with Hylton Ackerman, the South African who had been my contemporary at school and was at that stage playing for Northampton.

My father saw the tour as my greatest opportunity, on hard Australian wickets that should suit my aggressive style. I needed no telling that, in his eyes at least, it was almost my last chance to prove that I could sustain a place in the top bracket of world cricket. I had already been selected and then dropped by England and, if I didn't make it this time, I would be under pressure to give up the game and find what Dad would have called 'a proper job'.

I can scarcely imagine a worse start to a tour than I experienced when Hylton and I arrived in Adelaide. My family had seen me off from South Africa and my father's final pep talk had included lengthy advice that I should listen to every word spoken by the man behind the tour, who just happened to be Sir Donald Bradman.

Bradman had been bred into my system from a very early age as I think he even topped Vera Lynn in my father's estimation. The only times that silence was ever demanded in our Queens-town home were when Vera Lynn was singing, the BBC World Service was crackling a Glasgow Rangers soccer commentary on the radio, or Dad was talking about Don Bradman.

I had never met Bradman and it was difficult to imagine his features from the faded photographs I had seen of him. It was a pleasure I was looking forward to as we flew towards Australia.

First stop was Perth, where Hylton and I were met by a group from the local Cricket Lovers' Society. It was midnight, but they took us into the airport buffet for a coffee and a chat, which made us feel flattered.

By the time we reached Adelaide we were both itching to catch a glimpse of the real Australia and the little man in dark glasses and cardigan who approached us as we entered the transit lounge looked just the sort we had been hoping to avoid.

Sure enough, he came out with the predictable lines, welcoming us to Australia and asking us to join him for a coffee. We were just not in the mood for another Cricket Lovers' ritual, so we gave the little man our bags and nipped into the toilet to think of a way out.

Fortunately, as it transpired, we decided not to be rude, and rejoined our new friend for the walk to the coffee bar. Two other guys were sitting at the table which he led us to, but their names meant nothing to us - and as the little chap had only mumbled his name by way of introduction I didn't have a clue who he might be.

Cricket chat developed in the expected fashion as we drank coffee, and the trio certainly seemed to know a thing of two. Turning to the cardigan-clad man on my right, I politely enquired if he had anything to do with cricket in the area.

With a surface smile that must have hidden a playful laugh, he replied that the three of them ran the local scene. Still, it all meant nothing to me - they might, after all, have been talking about the airport cricket club.

At about that point Sobers bounded through the swing doors and headed straight for the little chap. "How are you, Sir Donald?" he cried - and I don't think I've ever felt more foolish in my life.

Hylton had at least shown enough sense to remain reasonably silent during the chat. I had simply made an ass of myself, yet Bradman took it all with a laugh.

When we arrived in Melbourne, we gave the story to the press-men who met us. The next morning I easily conjured up a mental picture of my father, up early and collecting the papers to see how his boy had fared on arrival in Australia, only to be stunned by the "Greig snubs Bradman" headlines. It took a while but fortunately, he saw the funny side.

Since that day in Adelaide, every time I was lucky enough to meet Sir Don, a smile would appear on his face, and he would ask me 'if I had anything to do with cricket'.

Body-

W. M. Woodfull struck over the heart by a ball from H. Larwood.

Line!

"There are two teams
out there. One is
trying to play cricket,
the other is not..."
(Australian Captain, Bill Woodfull)

England paid Bradman the ultimate compliment when it devised tactics to curb his prolific scoring during the 1932/33 tour of Australia - bowling tactics known as Bodyline.

Bradman's phenomenal success in the 1930 Ashes series sewed the seeds for Bodyline. England was widely expected to easily beat Australia but Bradman's Test scores of 131, 254, 334 and 232 provided Australia with a 2-1 series victory.

Bradman's series Test average was 98.66. The 1932/33 England captain Douglas Jardine recorded that he saw Bradman flinch once or twice at short deliveries during the 1930 series. He instructed his two opening bowlers Harold Larwood and Bill Voce (both from Nottinghamshire) to bowl what he called 'leg-theory' (Bodyline).

Larwood, though small in stature, was a phenomenal athlete and had the ability to bowl very quickly and get the ball to lift. Voce was similarly quick and a left-hander which made him difficult to play off the body.

Essentially, Bodyline was a tactic used by fast bowlers to take wickets by intimidating batsmen with the ball. Quick bowlers would bowl short, rising deliveries aimed at the batsman's body. The batsman would be forced to fend the ball off defensively to a packed, close, leg-side field which would snap up the catches commonly offered.

During the 1932/33 series the Larwood-Voce partnership, under instruction from Jardine, bowled Bodyline at regular intervals. It was not a popular decision with Australian crowds who loudly heckled the Englishmen. Australian batsmen, especially the openers, Jack Fingleton, Bill Ponsford and Vic Richardson were struck many painful blows, much to the crowd's displeasure. Bradman was hit only once in the series, on the upper arm, but spent much of his time avoiding the ball at the expense of making runs. The tactic worked. He finished the series with an average of 56.57 - thanks largely to 103 not out in the second innings of the second Test at Melbourne. That was a dramatic drop from his 1930 average of 98.66, and England turned around a 1-2 loss to regain the Ashes 4-1.

Feelings came to crisis point during the third Test in Adelaide in January 1933. Australian Captain Bill Woodfull was struck a painful blow by Larwood over the heart. Larwood also hit wicket-keeper Bert Oldfield in the head and fractured his skull. The crowd threatened to invade the pitch and mounted police were ready to quell any violence.

At the end of the day's play the England manager Sir Pelham 'Plum' Warner visited the Australian dressing room to commiserate with the injured. The Australian captain Woodfull is reputed to have received him icily with the words; "I don't want to see you Mr Warner. There are two teams out there. One is trying to play cricket, the other is not."

Donald Bradman facing another hostile delivery from Harold Larwood during the "Bodyline" series against England.

M.C.C.
AUSTRALASIAN
TOUR
1932-3
ORIENT LINE s.s. "ORONTES" 20,000 TONS

AUSTRALIA
versus
ENGLAND
1932-33

TRIUMPH and CHAMPION
TEST MATCH
SOUVENIR
ALBUM

IS IT CRICKET?

If the fast bowler is permitted to bump balls at the batsman to unnerve him, why shouldn't the unnerved batsman be allowed to bash bats at the bowler?

By PERCY LEASON

A humorous look at Bodyline which may have helped alleviate the tensions caused by the tactic.

The depth of ill-feeling between the two teams led to the Australian Cricket Board of Control to write by cable to its England counterpart, the Marylebone Cricket Club on January 18, 1933.

"Bodyline bowling has assumed such proportions as to menace the best interests of the game, making protection of the body by batsmen the main consideration. Causing intensely bitter feeling between players as well as injury. In our opinion it is unsportsmanlike. Unless stopped at once likely to upset friendly relations existing between Australia and England."

The MCC took offence and a series of bitter exchanges ensued, at one point involving both countries' governments. There was never a formal acknowledgement from the England authorities that Bodyline bowling was unsportsmanlike but subsequent actions indicated a recognised culpability. Douglas Jardine would never again captain England against Australia while Harold Larwood never played Test cricket again, despite topping the England first class bowling averages in 1937. Another legacy of the tactic was a change in the cricket rules. Bodyline was banned and a law was introduced to limit only two fieldsmen gathering between square-leg, and the wicket-keeper.

Consequently, the 1934 Australian tour to England featured no Bodyline bowling and relations between the two teams quickly healed.

BRADMAN'S FUTURE IN CRICKET IS OBSCURE

JOB FIRST?

Don as Writer

Agreement Crops Up Again

By E. H. M. Baillie

WILL HE PLAY?

CONTROL BOARD RE-AFFIRMS WRITING BAN

CRICKET DRAMA WORTHY OF TEST FINALE

GAME, NOT MAN

BOARD WOULD CONSIDER HIS APPLICATION

A cricket drama worthy of the vital moments of a Test finale was staged in Sydney yesterday.

While the steamer Monowai was steaming into Sydney Harbor with Don Bradman aboard, returning from the tour of America and Canada, the Board of Control was re-affirming its embargo on player-writers.

The sensation caused by the board's announcement was followed by a still greater sensation with Bradman's declaration that if the board had said its last word he would not be available for Test cricket against the Englishmen.

"I have signed a contract to write articles," stated Bradman, "and I must keep it. I cannot let cricket interfere with my work."

It is, of course, unthinkable that Bradman will not play for Australia, and doubtless a satisfactory way out of the impasse will be found. Associated Newspapers Ltd. will not stand unreasonably in the way of Bradman playing Test cricket.

Bradman Has Decided— —It's Up To The Board!

NO TEST PLAY IF BARRED FROM PRESS CONTRACT

Refuses Financial Offer To Release Him

WORD ABOVE MONEY

Unless the Board of Control becomes reasonable, and ultimately reverses the decision of its chairman, there is little chance of Don Bradman appearing in the Test Matches this summer.

When the Chairman refused to consider Bradman's application for permission to write, by asking for information, which he knew perfectly well Bradman was unable to supply, Associated Newspapers offered to release Bradman from his contract, to enable him to play in the Tests.

Bradman stated in reply, "I have made a contract with Associated Newspapers, which I intend to honor. I am sorry, but I cannot accept your offer of release."

Bradman had another run-in with authorities prior to the 1932 tour by England when he insisted he write for his employer - which the Cricket Board demanded he could not do. Only when Associated Newspapers insisted that Bradman play for Australia and not write for the papers, did Bradman relent. He felt officialdom was attempting to force him to break a contract, which he maintained he would never do.

Bodyline was devised as a curb on Bradman

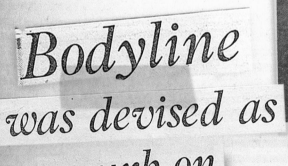

LARWOOD ... fastest in world.

HAROLD LARWOOD

The Australian captain, although not seriously hurt, was at this very moment lying on the massage table in his team's dressing-room receiving treatment for a great livid bruise on his chest.

"Plum," (later Sir Pelham) Warner, England's joint team manager, entered the Australian room to offer his sympathy. It was then that Woodfull, normally a man of quiet dignity and highly respected in Australia, made the remark that was to go down in cricket history.

"I don't want to see you, Mr. Warner," he began. "There are two teams out there on the Oval. One is playing cricket, the other is not. The game is too good to be spoilt. It's time some people got out of the game."

By this forthright avowal Woodfull brought bodyline into the open and summarily dismissed the views held by many people that it was nothing less than a newspaper invention.

Bradman bowled for 0.

Bradman had contrasting innings in the second Test at the MCG - out for a duck in the first innings and unbeaten on 103 in the second. He recalled both.

"Before an enormous crowd, I listened to a most inspiring ovation as I walked to the wicket. Herbert Sutcliffe, whom I passed on the way, commented on this wonderful reception and I replied, 'Yes, but will it be so good when I am coming back?' In a matter of seconds I was returning in deathly silence. Bowes' first ball pitched short and well outside the off stump, but aided and abetted by a faulty pull shot, hit my leg stump."

"Fortunately, I was able to make amends in the second innings by scoring 103 not out in a total of 191. It was amusing in the second innings when our last batsman, Bert Ironmonger, came in with my score in the nineties. The story is told of someone telephoning the ground to speak to him. On being told that Bert could not come to the phone as he had just gone in to bat, the enquirer said, 'Well, I'll wait'."

"I walked to meet Bert but he got in first with 'Don't worry, son, I won't let you down.' Hammond was bowling and never have I seen two balls go closer to any man's stumps. But Bert did not let me down."

MICK SIMMONS—"Leaders in Outdoor Sport and Home Entertainm   MICK SIMMONS—Men's High-Grade Mercery.

Australia v England at Melbourne Date 30th December 1932

Second Innings of Australia

	BATSMEN.	HOW OUT	BOWLER'S NAME	TOTAL
1	W. M. Woodfull	c. Allen	Larwood	26
2	J. H. Fingleton	c. Ames	Allen	1
3	L. P. O'Brien	bowled	Larwood	11
4	D. Bradman	Not Out		103
5	S. J. McCabe	bowled	Allen	0
6	V. Richardson	l.b.w.	Hammond	32
7	W. Oldfield	bowled	Voce	6
8	C. V. Grimmett	bowled	Voce	0
9	T. W. Wall	l.b.w.	Hammond	3
10	W. J. O'Reilly	c. Ames	Hammond	0
11	H. Ironmonger	Run Out		0
	SUNDRIES			9
	Byes 3 Leg-Byes 2 Wides X No Balls X			

| 1 for 1 | 2 for 27 | 3 for 78 | 4 for 81 | 5 for 135 | 6 for 150 | 7 for 156 | 8 for 184 | 9 for 186 | 10 for 191 | 11 for | TOTAL 191 |

BOWLING ANALYSES.

BOWLERS	1	2	3	4	5	6	7	8	9	10	11	12	13	14	15	OVERS	MAID-ENS	RUNS	WICK-ETS	WIDES	NO BALL	AVER-AGE
1 Larwood. H.																15	2	50	2	.	.	25.0
2 Allen. G.																12	1	44	2	4	.	22.0
3 Voce. W.																15	2	47	2	.	1	23.5
4 Bowes. W.																4	0	20	0	.	.	—
5 Hammond. W.																10.5	2	21	3	.	.	7.0
6																						
7																						
8																						

"Allen displayed strength of character in resisting Jardine's 'body-line' influence.

"I greatly regret Larwood's actions. As the finest fast bowler that England has seen for thirty years, he is too good to resort to any kind of leg theory.

"Unless the Marylebone Cricket Club does uphold the protest from the Australian Board of Control, the game will be ruined in the coming season. Even schoolboy fast bowlers, encountering difficult wickets and expert batsmen, will bowl bumpers deliberately at the man instead of the wicket.

"Body-line bowling must be abolished. The only solution is to give the umpire power to no-ball.

"AND IT MUST BE DONE BEFORE THE 1934 SEASON, AS JARDINE MAY STILL BE CAPTAIN WHEN THE AUSTRALIANS VISIT US."

Foster then concluded his statement to "Smith's Weekly" with a comment on Warner's presence in the visiting party, and a revelation regarding the body-line plan. Both were highly significant. Regarding Warner, he said:—

"In the whole history of cricket, there have never previously been two managers sent to Australia with an English Eleven. WARNER WAS SENT TO KEEP THE PEACE. THE CABLE SENT BY THE AUSTRALIAN BOARD OF CONTROL IS EVIDENCE THAT HE FAILED IN HIS OBJECT."

Bodyline was physical attack on batsmen devised by Jardine

Bradman c. Allen b. Larwood.

TENSE SCENES AT TEST.

Oldfield Struck by Ball.

CROWD HOOTS LARWOOD.

Australia 119 Behind on First Innings.

PONSFORD'S GREAT STAND FOR 85.

(FROM OUR SPECIAL REPRESENTATIVE)

ADELAIDE, Monday.

There was an ugly scene at Adelaide Oval this afternoon when the Australian wicketkeeper, W. A. Oldfield, who was batting in the third test match, was struck on the head by a ball from the English fast bowler, H. Larwood.

Oldfield staggered a few yards from the wicket and then fell to the ground. After assistance he was able to walk to the dressing-room, but later he was in a groggy state. He is now in the care of a doctor, who is a personal friend, and is reported to be "very comfortable."

The crowd demonstrated against the English players, especially Larwood, who was hooted continuously while he ran to the wicket during the next couple of overs. At one stage it appeared as if there might be serious developments, but the agitated crowd settled down to watch the Englishmen batting in their second innings.

Australia was dismissed for 222 runs. Ponsford continued a splendid stand, reaching 85, and Oldfield had batted pluckily for 41 before he was forced to retire.

England, with a first innings lead of 119 runs, lost Sutcliffe cheaply in the second innings, but Jardine and Wyatt had taken the score to 85 when stumps were drawn.

DON BRADMAN

Name BARR, F.
Berth No. 11
Car No. 2
NOT TRANSFERABLE.

DEPARTME
F. J. PALME

Sch
OF NORTH COA
Inclusive
TRANSPORT, MEALS,
and ACCOMMODATION,
£4/7/6
FOR CO

Schoolboys
"Goodwill"
Tour
1933

DON BRADMAN. STAN McCA

New South Wales Cricket Association

CABLE & TELEGRAPHIC ADDRESS: "STUMPS"
ADDRESS ALL COMMUNICATIONS TO THE SECRETARY
TELEPHONES: B3541, B5556
HH.HH

254A George Street, SYDNEY

Twentieth
February
1934

Mr. D.G. Bradman,
C/o Mr. J. Menzies,
MITTAGONG

Dear Sir,

    Your letter of the 14th inst.
notifying the Association of your intention
to live in Adelaide was read to the Association at its meeting last evening.

    I have been directed to inform
you that the decision was noted with regret.
The Association, however, decided to place on
record its appreciation of the wonderful services rendered by you to cricket in this State,
and instructed me to convey to you its best
wishes for your success in your new sphere of
life.

    I have very much pleasure in
conveying this resolution to you, and I would
like to add my own personal expressions of
appreciation and good wishes to the foregoing.

Yours sincerely,

SECRETARY

For the next seven years Don Bradman established himself as the greatest batsman the game had ever seen.

Following Bodyline, in the period between 1933 and 1940, he was an unstoppable batting machine.

In April 1932 he married Jessie Menzies and moved from St George to North Sydney, scoring a century in his second innings for the new club. He scored 200 against Queensland, 76 against South Australia, 187 not out and 77 not out against Victoria and 253 against Queensland before suffering a back injury.

His contract with Associated Newspapers, Radio 2UE and F. J. Palmer ended in February of 1934 and he announced he would join the stock-broking firm of H. W. Hodgetts & Co in Adelaide, and would move there to play for South Australia after the tour of England.

Bradman For S.A.
In Three Weeks

D.G. BRADMAN

IN BROKER'S FIRM

—

Champion Tells

BUSINESS FUTURE

(By A. G. Moyes)

Don Bradman will take up his residence in Adelaide in about three weeks and thus will make the move for qualification before he leaves for England with the Australian side.

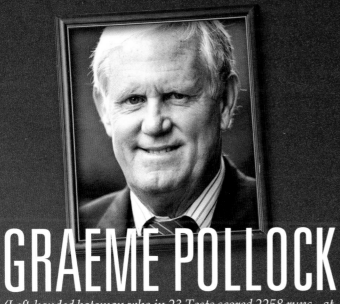

GRAEME POLLOCK

(Left-handed batsman who in 23 Tests scored 2258 runs - at an average of 60.97, second only to Sir Donald Bradman)

My memories of Sir Don Bradman go back to the early 1950's when as a young budding cricketer in South Africa, I was an enthusiastic follower of outstanding cricket. The name was synonymous with great batting achievements and I followed his career with great interest paying attention to the Ashes Tests.

I did however have another hero in Neil Harvey, in that he was a left hander like myself and also a prolific run-getter for Australian cricket.

I had the pleasure in 1963 of meeting Sir Don Bradman, as a member of the South African touring side when we arrived in Perth to begin our five month tour, Sir Don was the senior statesman for Australian cricket and was here to meet us on our arrival. He struck up a relationship in the 1930's with Ken Viljoen, our manager of the tour, and ensured everything was well organised. I was lucky enough to score 122 in Sydney and 175 in Adelaide in my third and fourth Tests and it was particularly gratifying to do so well in front of Sir Donald.

For a man of his stature and incredible feats, he was a very quiet, humble person and was never over critical of current cricketers in their endeavours to emulate his performances.

He was very helpful when asked, however he never ventured to give an opinion unless required to do so.

We had a successful series in 1963/64 and drew the series with Australia against all odds. I was a young side with players such as Eddie Barlow, Colin Bland, Denis Lindsay and many others who contributed to the amazing seven years of Test cricket before world isolation because of apartheid, put an end to SA cricket for 22 years.

In 1971, with the cancellation of the South African tour to Australia, I was fortunate enough to be chosen for a Rest of the World X1 which took the place of the SA Tour. In the side there were three South Africans; Hylton Ackerman, my brother Peter and myself. Tony Greig was also there. We knew him very well from South Africa, although he played his Test cricket in England.

The four of us were fortunate on one of the evenings of the Test in Adelaide to be invited for supper at 'Sir Don's' house. It was an incredible cricket evening listening to many stories and his views of his cricketing career and all those amazing achievements.

He was a magnificent, interesting and modest gentleman who did the game of cricket and his country proud.

I always remember a quote many years ago which was with me throughout my career "I can never remember playing a game of cricket without wanting to win". It is a motto for Australian cricket which has been customary in all the great Australian sides of the past.

It was the cricketing highlight of my career to meet this incredible cricketer and may this adulation and respect continue for ever.

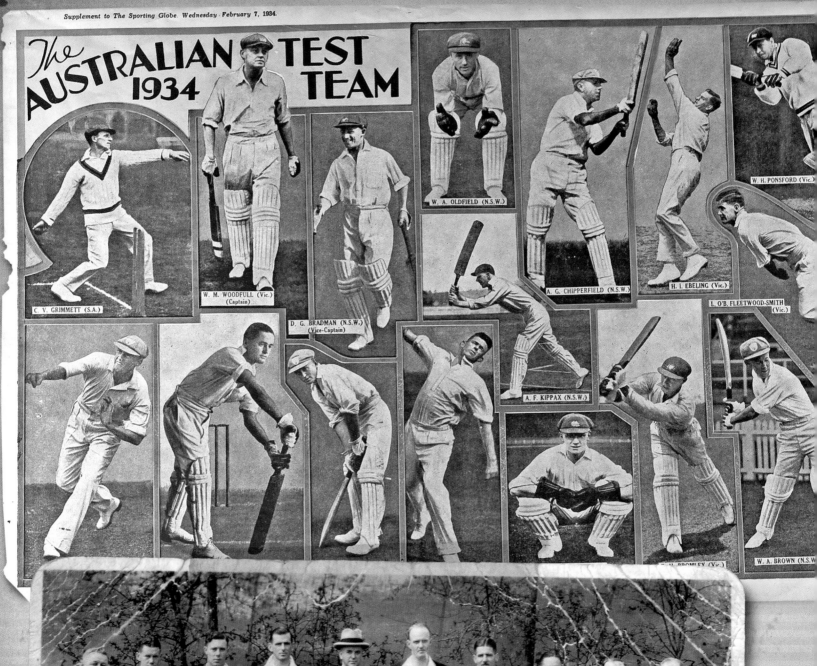

Supplement to The Sporting Globe, Wednesday, February 7, 1934.

The AUSTRALIAN TEST TEAM 1934

C. V. GRIMMETT (S.A.)

W. M. WOODFULL (Vic.) (Captain)

D. G. BRADMAN (N.S.W.) (Vice-Captain)

W. A. OLDFIELD (N.S.W.)

A. G. CHIPPERFIELD (N.S.W.)

H. I. EBELING (Vic.)

W. H. PONSFORD (Vic.)

I. O'B. FLEETWOOD-SMITH (Vic.)

A. F. KIPPAX (N.S.W.)

E. H. BROMLEY (Vic.)

W. A. BROWN (N.S.W.)

AUSTRALIAN CRICKET TEAM. ENGLAND, 1934

Standing: W. Ferguson, Brown, W. A. Bromley, E. H. Wall, T. W. H. Bushby, O'Reilly, W. J. Fleetwood-Smith, L. O'B. Darling, L. S. Grimmett, C. V. Wm. C. Bull
(SCORER)   (MNGR.)   (TREASURER)

Sitting: Ebeling, H. I. Chipperfield, A. G. Bradman, D. G. Woodfull, W. M. Kippax, A. F. McCabe, S. J. Oldfield, W. A.
(VICE CAPT.)   (CAPT.)

Front: Barnett, B. A. Ponsford, W. H.

COPYRIGHT

The Australian cricket team and the Davis Cup tennis team on board the 'Orford'.

IN QUEST OF THE ASHES 1934

THE DON BRADMAN SOUVENIR BOOKLET AND SCORING RECORDS

Like his team-mates, Bradman enjoyed sport on board to keep fit and focused.

VISIT OF THE AUSTRALIAN TEAM to ENGLAND 1934

Don Bradman

ORIENT LINE
ROYAL MAIL STEAMERS TO ENGLAND

ORIENT LINE. S.S. OTRANTO. 20,000 TONS.

AUSTRALIAN XI
ENGLISH TOUR
1934

The Ashes

ORIENT LINE R·M·S 'ORFORD'
20,000 TONS

King George shakes hands with Don Bradman and comments on his hand muscles.

JULY 21, 1934.

BRADMAN BATS AND BATS AND BATS

EVENING NEWS

CLOSE OF PLAY

BRADMAN ON LARWOOD

"Not Worrying About Him"

In 1934 he toured England for the second time, this trip as vice-captain, and opened with another double century against Worchester, scoring 206 despite being ill. He finished the tour with 2020 runs at an average of 84. The highlights were 304 at Leeds and 244 at The Oval. His five Tests netted him 758 runs at an average of 94. It said so much about expectations of his run-scoring ability that some people pointed out his average dropped from 139 in 1930 to 94 in 1934, as if he had been a moderate performer!

Bradman's autograph is still worth the bother of collecting it. Yesterday he carried his innings to 206 before being cleaned bowled by Howarth. Above: Leaving the field with one of his friends the autograph hunters,

WORCESTERSHIRE.

Mr. C. F. Walters lbw, b Grimmett	32	— c Ebeling b Wall	5
H. H. Gibbons b Ebeling	0	— c Bromley b O'Reilly	1
Nawab of Pataudi run out	14	— lbw, b Grimmett	27
M. Nichol lbw, b Grimmett	6	— c Ponsford b O'Reilly	1
S. H. Martin c and b O'Reilly	13	— c Bromley b O'Reilly	20
C. H. Bull st Oldfield b Grimmett	13	— b O'Reilly	1
Mr. B. W. Quaife c Oldfield b Wall	20	— not out	13
R. Howorth b Wall	16	— st Oldfield b Grimmett	14
G. W. Brook b Grimmett	3	— c Ebeling b Grimmett	2
P. F. Jackson lbw, b Grimmett	0	— b Grimmett	4
R. T. D. Perks not out	0	— c and b Grimmett	3
B 2, l-b 6	8	L-b	4
	112		95

AUSTRALIANS.

W. M. Woodfull c Perks b Martin	48	C. V. Grimmett c Brook b Howorth	7
W. H. Ponsford c Nichol b Jackson	13	H. I. Ebeling b Perks	13
D. G. Bradman b Howorth	206	T. W. Wall lbw, b Brook	24
A. F. Kippax b Jackson	0	W. J. O'Reilly not out	25
S. J. McCabe c Brook b Perks	20	B 26, l-b 5, n-b 5	36
E. H. Bromley c Brook b Howorth	45		
W. A. Oldfield c Martin b Howorth	67		504

AUSTRALIANS BOWLING.

	Overs	Mdns.	Runs	Wkts.	Overs	Mdns.	Runs	Wkts.
Wall	12.3	8	6	2	8	3	9	1
Ebeling	4	1	10	0	6	1	15	0
Grimmett	24	7	53	1	15.3	7	27	5
O'Reilly	16	6	35	1	13	6	25	4
Bromley					4		15	0

WORCESTERSHIRE BOWLING.

	Overs	Mdns.	Runs	Wkts.
Perks	26	2	83	2
Jackson	30	4	95	2
Martin	14	4	41	1
Brook	22	2	114	1
Howorth	23	0	135	4

Umpires: T. Oates and A. Dolphin.

Bradman compiled his second double-century against Worcester to open the 1934 tour and his reputation as a run-machine spiralled. So when he failed it was big news. A duck at Cambridge made headlines while English sailors in Melbourne were celebrating when The Don registered his first duck - well, in England anyway.

DON BRADMAN'S FIRST "DUCK"

BRADMAN 0

EVENING NEWS

LATE EXTRA

FIRST, AT LEAST, ON ENGLISH TOURS

"No one ever laughed about Bradman, he was no laughing matter."
(R.C. Robertson-Glasgow, England cricket writer)

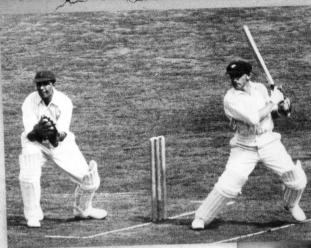

Bradman square-cutting
W.R. Hammond.

Cardus Says Bradman Is An Immortal

TRIBUTE TO BRADMAN

"Best Scoring Batsman I Have Seen"

ALL THE SHOTS

Headingley Wicket Still First-Rate

By WILFRED RHODES

HEADINGLEY, Saturday

THE scoring machine—that is Bradman—got to work again to-day and our bowlers had to pay tribute, as we all knew they would have to do, as soon as Bradman decided that the time had come for him to move seriously along the run-getting road.

He never hurried—never dashed, as cricketers say—yet at the end of a day on which he was at the wicket for five minutes less than six and a half hours he had 271 runs to his name. He scored over a hundred runs in the last hundred minutes, and just as there was no indication of quick-scoring in his general outlook, so, when he left the field, there was no suggestion that he was tired after the strain of standing at the wicket for so long.

Cricket legends, such as former England batting great Wilfred Rhodes and author Neville Cardus, were now hailing Bradman as a genius and the best scoring batsman they had seen. Bradman picked up where he left off in the 1930 tour - seemingly undaunted by the 1932 Bodyline series - and helped Australia regain the Ashes 2-1 after the 1-4 Bodyline disaster.

DON. BRADMAN
THE BREAKER OF CRICKET RECORDS

5TH AUSTRALIA.

MATCH BETWEEN Eng

at KENNINGTON OVAL. on and AUGUST

FIRST Innings of AUSTRAL

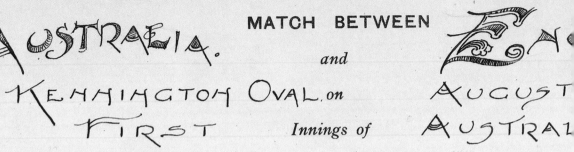

Date	Time In	Score	Adjm.	Score	Time Out	TOTAL		Name	Runs as Scored	
11.33	123	1.30	66	123	1/25	460	1	Ponsford W. H.	211 44 11 4 21 342 11 2 11 4112 442 2 114 12 2 112 1133 133 11 24 4 111111 41221141	
2.17	311	4.30	137	311		m			4111 44 1 41 4 11111 444 114112 4 1111111 441111 444 11 4111 4 111 2 131 42 1	
4.50	475	6.30	205	475						
11.35	475			475						
11.33	.				11/59	26 m	2	Brown W. A.	1 44 111 4.	
12.	71	1.30	43	123	6	316	3	Bradman Don.	4444 1111 42 44 1112 23 442 11 24 1111 2 4 14 112 14 14 442 12 14 1111 44 31 411 44	
2.17	123	4.30	150	311	2/3	m			1111111 412 312 112 412 112 442 14 11111 4412 14 2 14 61 2 4 1114	
4.50	311									
6.25	472	6/30	1	475	11/45	15 m	4	McCabe S. J.	1 4 412	
11.35	475									
11.47	488	4/30		574	7/57	143	5	Woodfull W. M.	1 1 13 11 1111 4 111 2 2 15 2 2 1 1 4	
2.17										
1.27	571	1/30		574	3/5	51 m	6	Kippax A. F.	41 1112 13 11 1 421	
2.17	574									
2/59	626				3/16	17 m	7	Chipperfield A.	111	
3/7	631				4/37	90 m	8	Oldfield W. A.	1 1114 4 11 4 1111 3 11 444	
3/18	638				4/5	47 m	9	Grimmett C. V.	1111 3	
4/7	676				4/20	13	10	Ebeling Hans	1	
4/23	687				4/57	14 m	11	O'Reilly W. J.	1411	

50	12. 24.	51 m	
100	1. 8	95 "	
143	1.30	117 "	lunch
151	2.35	135 "	
200	3. 9	169 "	
250	3.48	208 "	
300	4. 22	224 "	
311	4. 30	250 "	tea
350	5.10	276 "	
400	5. 48	305 "	
450	6. 5	325 "	
475	6. 30	350 "	
500	11.55	370 "	
550	12.52	431 "	
574	1.30	465 "	lunch

604	2.37	485 "
651	3.30	538 "
675	4. 2	570 "
700	4.34	602 "
701	4.37	605 "

Sat. Australia won toss and batted. day fine & warm.
good attendance   drinks 1/30. 3/20. 6/

monday. rain early & No 11 a.m. started play 11/35 a.m.
drinks 1/30. 3/30.

Umpires. F. Chester & Walden
Scorers W. Ferguson & H. Strudwick

Gregory fielded for Allen 1/40 for awhile

Time 605 minutes

	1	2	3	4	5	6	7
Fall of Wickets ...	21	472	488	574	626	631	638
Batsman Out ...	Brown	Bradman	McCabe	Ponsford	Woodfull	Kippax	Chipper
" Not Out ...	Ponsford 10	Ponsford 244	Ponsford 108	Woodfull 45	Kippax 45	Chipp 4	Oldfi

Partnership Ponsford & Bradman 100 at 1.27 pm 87 minutes
" " 200 3 30 168 "
" " 300 4.57 230 " "
" " 384 5.47 280 " "
" " 400 5 53 286 " "
" " 451 6. 23 316 " "

ƎAND.

18: 20. 1934.

— 18ᵗʰ (Saty.)

How Out	Bowled	Total	
//// Hit wkt.	Allen	266	Verity 244 1758
Bowled.	Clark	10	Woolley slips 118
			Wyatt midon
c Ames wkt.	Bowes	244	Wyatt, eg leg 57
Bowled	Allen	10	Wyatt. "
Bowled	Bowes	49	Woolley slips 71
			Woolley slips 18
LBW	Bowes	28	1747.
Bowled	Bowes	3	
Nos out.		42	
c Ames wkt	Allen	7	Verity slips
Bowled	Allen	2	
Bowled	Clark	7	
Byes 13		4	
Leg Byes ///// 2 2 3 / 2		14	
Wides 2		2	
No Balls ///////// ///////		13	

8	9	10		
676	682	701	TOTAL	701
Grimmett	Ebeling	O'Reilly		
Oldfield	Oldfield	Oldfield		
28	30	47		

THE TEST WRITING PAD

SECRET OF BRADMAN'S GREAT TEST INNINGS

CABLE FROM HIS WIFE

"Go to it, Don"

IN POCKET ALL DAY

While She Heard News on Radio

Australia won the opening Test at Nottingham by 238 runs and England responded to square the series with an innings and a 38 run win at Lord's. After draws at Manchester and Leeds, the Ashes were on the line at The Oval. Bradman (244) and Ponsford (266) shared a partnership of 451 as Australia went on to win by a staggering 562 runs

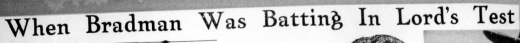

When Bradman Was Batting In Lord's Test

PERFECT STRANGERS SPOKE TO ONE ANOTHER

The Excitement Throbbed Visibly. The Tavern Emptied Temporarily

"Bradman Did Nothing Today That Victor Trumper Would Not Have Been Proud To Do."

AUSTRALIA'S HEROES

"I'VE SEEN ALL AND DON IS GREATEST"

Bobby Peel's Tribute to Bradman

Critics now concurred that lightning had struck twice and Don Bradman simply was the best - a batsman capable of winning Ashes battles off his own bat. All the columnists and critics, and former champions, sang his praises as he was the decisive factor in Australia regaining the Ashes twice on his two tours.

Don Bradman Considered
To Be Out Of Danger

At the end of the tour Bradman collapsed and almost died. He had acute appendicitis, which was almost gangrenous. Upon release from hospital, he holidayed in Switzerland and the Riviera and then spent three months recuperating at his father-in-law's Mittagong farm. He played no Sheffield Shield cricket during 1934/35 on medical advice.

OPERATION

DON BRADMAN

APPENDIX

"SOME ANXIETY"

("Sun" Special)

LONDON, Monday.

AN operation for acute appendicitis was performed upon Don Bradman to-day at the hospital of the noted Australian surgeon, Sir Douglas Shields, by his brother, Dr. Clive Shields.

MEN AND WOMEN OFFER BLOOD

| PROGRESS MUST BE SLOW | NATION IS WATCHING HIS FIGHT |

(SPECIAL BEAM SERVICE)

NEWS OF DON

Mrs. Bradman Speaks To London

IS REASSURED

MELBOURNE, Thursday.

MRS. BRADMAN spoke to London by radiophone this afternoon and received reassuring news regarding the condition of Don. After the talk she was much happier.

At the other end of the 'phone was a personal friend of Sir Douglas Shields, who had been asked by the eminent surgeon to ring her and tell her that, although they were still anxious, Don's temperature had gone down, and he was holding his own satisfactorily.

This message wsa cheering, pratically as Mrs. Bradman had heard in Melbourne the distressing rumors about Don's doeath, which were prevalent also in Sydney.

When Mrs. Bradman arrived in Melbourne from Sydney to-day, on her way to Perth to catch the Maloja for London, she was met at Spencer-street station by Canon Hughes and the secretary of the Vic-

everyone, from office boy to managing director.

In the city it was the one topic of conversation.

In offices, lifts, trams, shops, theatres—everywhere where there was a group of people—the question was "Is Bradman dead?"

Total strangers stopped each other in the street and asked the question. The very mention of the word "Bradman" in many cases brought passers-by into the conversation, and in every street small groups were to be seen discussing the rumor.

Hundreds of 'phone calls were received at "The Sun" office from 8 a.m. onwards, asking about the rumor.

It was the same in every place where possible confirmation could be found, such as broadcasting stations and cable offices.

How the rumor originated is unknown, but it will be comforting news to every Australian that their Don Bradman is not dead, even though his condition is still the cause of some anxiety.

DANCING DON

Don Bradman, after recovery from his severe illness, is seen here dancing with his wife at a "The Dansant" at the Battersea Town Hall. Their cheerful smile says that everything's all right again. 1934

Prayers For Don

A prayer that Don Bradman might be restored to complete health and strength was offered by Canon Begbie last evening at the weekly prayer meeting at St. Stephen's Church. Willoughby.

When in Sydney Bradman sometimes attended the service at St. Stephen's.

MELBOURNE, Thursday.

The Archbishop of Melbourne (Dr. Head) when asked this afternoon whether he would order general prayers for Bradman said: "I don't know that he is ill enough for that. There will be no chance for general prayers before Sunday. It is a most unusual thing to do, but I will think it over."

torian Cricket Association (Mr. H. Brereton).

They handed her a cable message which read:—

"I have arranged you telephone London, Thursday 3.30 p.m., Australian time. Important messages from Don and Sir Douglas Shields. Disregard wild rumors."

Mrs. Bradman was obviously greatly pleased at the prospect of the telephone call. She will leave for Perth in the transcontinental train this afternoon.

CITY RUMOR

Concern Is General

Fortunately untrue, a rumor that Don Bradman was dead spread like wildfire throughout the city and suburbs to-day.

Seldom has such general consternation and concern been manifest by

Cricket Heroism

Sportsmen everywhere will wish to extend their sympathy and good wishes to Don Bradman. He has been playing against a heavy handicap of ill-health for the last two years. His remarkable performances under the strain of Test Match conditions were more than exhibitions of genius. They were sporting heroism at its best. The world of sportsmen will join in the hope that this great cricketer soon will be completely restored to health. If good wishes could do it he would be well already.

He made his debut for South Australia in November of 1935. He began with 117, 233 and 357. In January 1936 he scored 369 against Tasmania, an innings which included 46 fours and four sixes, and which was his highest score for SA.

IMRAN KHAN

(Former Pakistan captain and all-rounder who in 88 Tests captured 362 wickets at 22.81 and scored 3807 runs at 37.69. He is now is a politician)

Cricket lovers will always know of Sir Don Bradman's batting statistics. He set the standard that has never been challenged in the 60 years since his retirement.

He is rightly considered the greatest batsman of all time. He was phenomenal, obviously. Anyone who could score that consistently and have that average of 99.94 must have been a genius. And I must admit his statistics fascinate me.

I think the best batsman I ever saw was Sir Vivian Richards. He didn't care about statistics and that is why I respected him so much. He performed on the big occasions. But when he lost interest he would give it away.

Bradman was a different breed. Clearly he never lost interest in scoring runs. He was just a run machine. Sir Don is beyond comparison so it is pointless comparing anyone with him.

The thing is that when I was growing up in Pakistan we all knew his statistics, but unless you were a reader of cricket books you didn't know much about him as a person or what he did after his playing days.

I am better read than most Pakistanis and I heard stories about him, and read about him, when I played around the world, and was studying at Oxford University and playing county cricket at Sussex and Worchester.

Unfortunately I never met the great Don. Although I toured Australia on several occasions with Pakistan, and played in Australia during World Series Cricket and when representing New South Wales, I never had the chance to meet him.

He has left a great legacy to cricket and to Australia's history. His statistics will last, and it is important that future generations should know more about him as a person.

The Don was alive for 40 years of my life but I had to read about him as a person in books and hear stories about him from those who knew him. The modern generation and future generations cannot meet him, yet his legend will live on because he was the greatest of them all.

DON. BRADMAN

D. G. BRADMAN

With best wishes from Don Bradman

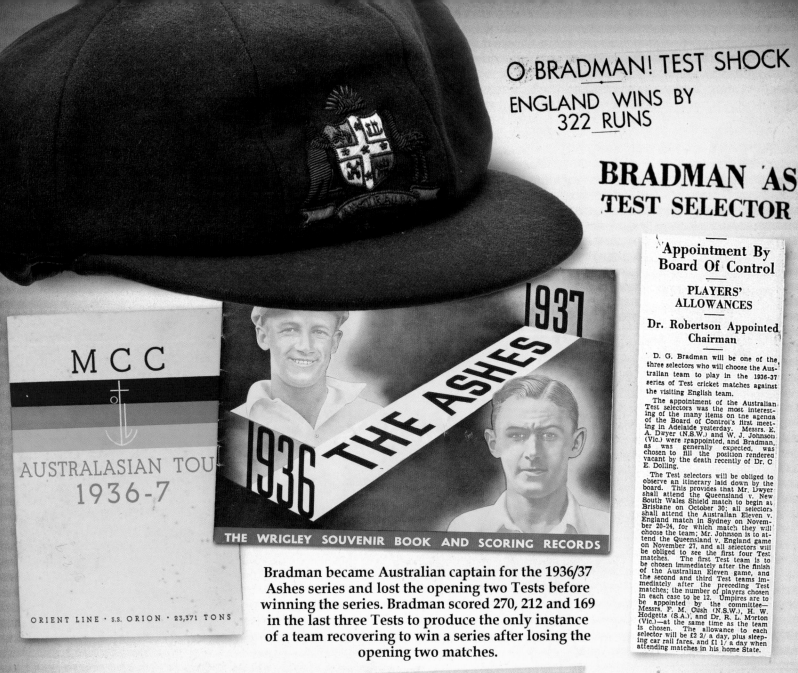

O BRADMAN! TEST SHOCK

ENGLAND WINS BY 322 RUNS

BRADMAN AS TEST SELECTOR

Appointment By Board Of Control

PLAYERS' ALLOWANCES

Dr. Robertson Appointed Chairman

D. G. Bradman will be one of the three selectors who will choose the Australian team to play in the 1936-37 series of Test cricket matches against the visiting English team.

The appointment of the Australian Test selectors was the most interesting of the many items on the agenda of the Board of Control's first meeting in Adelaide yesterday. Messrs. E. A. Dwyer (N.S.W.) and W. J. Johnson (Vic.) were reappointed, and Bradman, as was generally expected, was chosen to fill the position rendered vacant by the death recently of Dr. C E. Dolling.

The Test selectors will be obliged to observe an itinerary laid down by the board. This provides that Mr. Dwyer shall attend the Queensland v. New South Wales Shield match to begin at Brisbane on October 30; all selectors shall attend the Australian Eleven v. England match in Sydney on November 20-24, for which match they will choose the team; Mr. Johnson is to attend the Queensland v. England game on November 27, and all selectors will be obliged to see the first four Test matches. The first Test team is to be chosen immediately after the finish of the Australian Eleven game, and the second and third Test teams immediately after the preceding Test matches; the number of players chosen in each case to be 12. Umpires are to be appointed by the committee—Messrs. F. M. Cush (N.S.W.), H. W. Hodgetts (S.A.), and Dr. R. L. Morton (Vic.)—at the same time as the team is chosen. The allowance to each selector will be £2 2/ a day, plus sleeping car rail fares, and £1 1/ a day when attending matches in his home State.

M C C

AUSTRALASIAN TOUR 1936-7

ORIENT LINE · S.S. ORION · 23,371 TONS

1936 THE ASHES 1937

THE WRIGLEY SOUVENIR BOOK AND SCORING RECORDS

Bradman became Australian captain for the 1936/37 Ashes series and lost the opening two Tests before winning the series. Bradman scored 270, 212 and 169 in the last three Tests to produce the only instance of a team recovering to win a series after losing the opening two matches.

Fourth Test Match between England and Australia - Adelaide Oval, January 29th, 1937.

BRADMAN, 174, STILL THERE

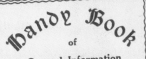

Handy Book
of
General Information
with
PROGRAMME
of
M.C.C. Cricket Tour
1936-1937

With the Compliments of
GEORGE ROBINSON
PTY. LTD.
28 GEORGE ST., SYDNEY
(OPP HUNTER ST.)
Makers of Personality Smart
Clothes for Men
TEL. B 4329
Also at 14 HUNTER ST.

Tossing the coin for the first
time with Sir George 'Gubby'
Allen, Brisbane 1936.

MELBOURNE CRICKET GROUND
THIRD TEST MATCH
Commencing JANUARY 1st, 1937
ADMIT
BLOCK RESERVED GRANDSTAND
FOR FULL MATCH
C Row B No. 11
1 2 3 4 5 6 7 8

Captaincy Has Not Affected Don

ANOTHER BRADMAN RECORD

His Fifty-sixth Century In First-class Cricket

By J. C. DAVIS ("Not Out")

WHEN Don Bradman completed the century and went on to his hilarious double-century in the Sydney testimonial match, he drew level with Warren Bardsley as the leading Australian century-maker in first-class cricket.

BRADMAN'S TENTH TEST CENTURY

BEST EFFORT YET IN AUSTRALIA

(By A. G. Moyes)

MELBOURNE, Tuesday.

WITH his century to-day, ten centuries have been scored by Don Bradman in his 21 Tests against England.

When he reached 124 to-day, too, he passed his previous highest tally in a Test in Australia against England, made in 1928.

His partnership with Fingleton, moreover, beat the record stand of 187 for the sixth Australian wicket, made by Armstrong and Kelleway in Sydney in 1921.

Bradman now has been associated with the Australian record Test partnerships for the second, third, fourth, fifth and sixth wickets.

A 248 NOT OUT REPLY TO HIS CRITICS

Record Stand; 624 Ahead With Four Wickets Left

By ARTHUR MAILEY

MELBOURNE, Tuesday.

IT was a great day's cricket today—for Australia. Terrible for England.

One wicket fell for a total of 306 runs, and Australia's score was raised from 5 for 194—it was 5 for 97 yesterday—to 6 for 500.

That magnificent record-breaking partnership between Bradman and Fingleton was responsible.

Both were superlative. Bradman, not the dare-devil we know he can be, but the grim fighter, the artistic destroyer of class bowlers; the captain who was determined to confound the critics who had said that the cares of leadership had seriously affected his batsmanship.

Fingleton, the persistent, tenacious bulldog that gets a grip and holds it.

A DAY OF TRIUMPH FOR BRADMAN.

INNINGS OF 174 NOT OUT.

One of Greatest of His Career.

English Test Team Fixtures
Season 1936-7
Oct. 16-19 — ENGLAND v. W. AUST.
Oct. 30 — ENGLAND v. S. AUST.
Nov. 3 — ENGLAND v. VICTORIA.
Nov. 5-10 — FIRST TEST at Brisbane.
Dec. 4-9 — SECOND TEST at Sydney.
Dec. 18-23 — THIRD TEST at Melb.
Jan. 1-6 — ENGLAND v. S. AUST.
Jan. 22-26 — FOURTH TEST at A'laide.
Jan. 29 — ENGLAND v. VICTORIA.
Feb. 3 — FIFTH TEST at Melb.
Feb. 19-23 —

TEST MATCH FIXTURES

1ST TEST MATCH
BRISBANE....DECEMBER 4TH 1936
AUSTRALIA v ENGLAND

1ST INNS.	234	1ST INNS.	358
2ND INNS.	58	2ND INNS.	256

RESULT. England by 322 Runs

2ND TEST MATCH
SYDNEY....DECEMBER 18TH 1936
AUSTRALIA v ENGLAND

1ST INNS.	80	1ST INNS.	6w 426
2ND INNS.	324	2ND INNS.	—

RESULT. England by Innings 432 Runs

3RD TEST MATCH
MELBOURNE....JANUARY 1ST 1937
AUSTRALIA v ENGLAND

1ST INNS.	9w 200	1ST INNS.	9w 76
2ND INNS.	564	2ND INNS.	323

RESULT. Australia by 366 Runs

4TH TEST MATCH
ADELAIDE....JANUARY 29TH 1937
AUSTRALIA v ENGLAND

1ST INNS.	288	1ST INNS.	330
2ND INNS.	433	2ND INNS.	243

RESULT. Australia by 148 Runs.

5TH TEST MATCH
MELBOURNE....FEBRUARY 26TH 1937
AUSTRALIA v ENGLAND

1ST INNS.	604	1ST INNS.	239
2ND INNS.	—	2ND INNS.	165

RESULT. Australia by Innings & Runs

My Favourite Cricketers are....
1. Bradman
2. O'Reilly
3. Hammond
4. McCabe

Bradman Won the Ashes

Charge to Governor-General's Account.

VIA IMPERIAL

PRIVATE SECRETARY TO THE KING

BUCKINGHAM PALACE

LONDON

PLEASE LAY BEFORE THE KING WITH MY HUMBLE DUTY THE FOLLOWING MESSAGE FROM MR. BRADMAN BEGINS PLEASE CONVEY TO HIS MAJESTY MY SINCERE THANKS FOR HIS MESSAGE OF CONGRATULATIONS ON THE SUCCESS OF AUSTRALIA IN TEST MATCHES FULLSTOP MEMBERS OF AUSTRALIAN TEAM FEEL VERY PROUD TO KNOW THAT HIS MAJESTY TAKES SUCH A GREAT INTEREST IN OUR NATIONAL GAME FULLSTOP I DEEPLY APPRECIATE THE COMPLIMENT WHICH HIS MAJESTY HAS PAID TO ME PERSONALLY SIGNED DON BRADMAN ENDS.

Admiralty House, North Sydney.   GOVERNOR-GENERAL.
        12th March, 1937.

No further evidence was needed of Bradman's status than a letter from the King at the end of Australia's remarkable 3-2 Ashes win in Australia under Bradman's captaincy.

URGENT.

Congratulatory Telegram

Office of Origin	Words	Time Lodged	
LAUNCESTON	37	12—3P	

MR BRADMAN
CARE BOARD OF CONTROL
MELBOURNE CRICKET CLUB MELBOURNE

HEARTY CONGRATULATIONS ON WINNING THE ASHES AND ON THE SPLENDID WAY IN WHICH YOU ALL DEMONSTRATED WHAT IS COMMONLY KNOWN AS PLAYING THE GAME

GOWRIE GOVERNOR GENERAL

THIS TELEGRAM HAS BEEN RECEIVED SUBJECT TO THE POST AND TELEGRAM ACT AND REGULATIONS

OFFICIAL SOUVENIR PROGRAMME

M.C.C. CRICKET TEAM AUSTRALIAN TOUR, 1936-37

ENGLAND v. AUSTRALIA

FIRST TEST — DECEMBER 4th

No. 29195

6d

ISSUED WITH THE AUTHORITY OF THE QUEENSLAND CRICKET ASSOCIATION

Brisbane's Leading Hotel

THE GRESHAM
100 Rooms

Hot and cold running water in every room
Telephone in Every Room
Rooms with Private Bath and Lav.
Automatic Lift to All Floors   Day and All Night Service
One minute from G.P.O.   One minute from Wharf
One minute from Railway

T. M. AHERN, Proprietor
Corner Creek and Adelaide Streets, Brisbane
Phone B 2351 (3 lines)

King's Test Message

CANBERRA, Thursday.

King George has sent a special cable of congratulation for the victorious Australian cricket team.

The Governor-General (Lord Gowrie) has received the following message from His Majesty:—

"Please convey to Mr. Bradman and the Australian cricketers my hearty congratulations on their victory in the Test match.

"I have followed with the closest interest the progress of the five well-contested matches, played in the friendliest spirit, in which Mr. Bradman has once more given evidence of his predominance as a batsman.

GEORGE R.I."

PRIME MINISTER,
CANBERRA.

CONFIDENTIAL.

6th March, 1937.

Dear Sir:

I desire to acknowledge the receipt of your letter of 10th February, in which you suggest that the bestowal of a Knighthood upon Mr. Don Bradman, whose pre-eminence in the world of cricket is so widely acknowledged, should be recommended to His Majesty the King

Your friendly interest in this matter is appreciated and the representations you have forwarded will be given careful consideration.

Yours faithfully,

Prime Minister.

Stephen St. John Martin, Esq.,
Grosvenor House,
Grosvenor Gardens,
St. Leonards-on-Sea,
ENGLAND.

KING'S MESSAGE TO DON BRADMAN

Although he was not knighted until after his retirement in 1948, clearly both the King and Australia's Prime Minister Sir Robert Menzies had it in mind a decade earlier!

DON BRADMAN
WONDER BATSMAN
CAPTAIN OF AUSTRALIA
1936-37

PREDOMINANT SKILL PRAISED

Congratulations On Test Victories

"FRIENDLIEST SPIRIT"

(From Our Special Representative)

CANBERRA, Thursday.

A SPECIAL message to Don Bradman from King George was contained in a cable received by the Governor-General (Lord Gowrie) to-day.

The cable reveals the personal interest taken by his Majesty in the Test series.

It is evident, too, that the King has followed closely the wonderful batting performances of Bradman, for there is reference in the message to his "predominant skill."

The King's cable is as follows:—

"Please convey to Mr. Bradman and the Australian cricketers my hearty congratulations on their victory in the Test Matches. I have followed with the closest interest the progress of the five well-contested matches played in the friendliest spirit, in which Mr. Bradman has once more given evidence of his predominant skill as a batsman.

(Signed) George R.I."

The Australian Test Team—Back Row: C. L. Badcock, W. A. Brown, J. H. Fingleton, E. L. McCormick, W. J. O'Reilly, Mr. W. H. Jeanes (Manager), E. White, L. Fleetwood-Smith, F. A. Ward, C. L. Walker. Front Row: A. L. Hassett, A. G. Chipperfield, S. J. McCabe (Vice-Captain), D. G. Bradman (Captain), B. A. Barnett, S. Barnes, M. G. Waite.

LAUREL *The all-purpose kerosene* **WINS EVERY TEST**
For Lighting, Cooking, Heating, Cleaning, Freezing and Incubation

In 1938 he made his third trip to England, his first as captain. It was the start of a leadership that netted him 21 wins from his last 22 Tests as Australian captain. For the third time he began with a double century against Worcester, scoring 258. For the tour he averaged a remarkable 115.66 with 2429 runs and 13 centuries.

Bradman, now a celebrity who was more relaxed with his public stature, enjoyed the company of tennis stars en route to England, as well as a joke in a dress-up party with a cheeky passenger, and, above all, some quality time reading and writing in his cabin.

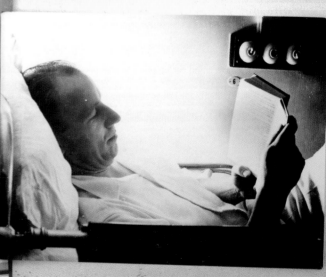

In bed with a sore throat and temperature.

ORIENT LINE

AUSTRALIAN XI
ENGLISH TOUR 1938

ORIENT LINE R.M.S 'ORONTES' 20,000 TONS

In his first six innings of the 1938/39 season in Australia, Bradman rattled off scores of 118, 143, 225, 107, 186 and 135 not out to equal C.B. Fry's record for the most centuries in succession in first-class cricket.

..... e, R.D., R.N.R.
..... F. J. L. Butler, R.D., R.N.R.
..... Comdr. H. Petit-Dann, R.D., R.N.R.
PURSER: H. N. M. Herapath.
SURGEON: B. Muir, M.R.C.S., L.R.C.P.
CHIEF ENGINEER: G. D. S. White, M.I.Mar.E.

ITINERARY

BRISBANE	dep.	Wed.	Mar. 2	PORT SAID	Sat.	Apr. 9
SYDNEY	,,	Wed.	Mar. 9	NAPLES	Wed.	Apr. 13
HOBART	,,	Sat.	Mar. 12	VILLEFRANCHE	Thur.	Apr. 14
MELBOURNE	,,	Tues.	Mar. 15	TOULON	Fri.	Apr. 15
ADELAIDE	,,	Thur.	Mar. 17	GIBRALTAR	Sun.	Apr. 17
FREMANTLE	,,	Mon.	Mar. 21	SOUTHAMPTON	Wed.	Apr. 20
COLOMBO		Wed.	Mar. 30	LONDON	Thur.	Apr. 21
ADEN		Tues.	Apr. 5			

AUSTRALIAN CRICKET TOUR

1938

19th VISIT TO ENGLAND

Foreword by A. E. R. GILLIGAN
Edited by - - - A. W. SIMPSON
Compiled by - - W. FERGUSON

6^D

FIXTURES, PHOTOGRAPHS,
AUTOGRAPHS AND RECORDS
of Past & Present, Players & Teams

'ENGLAND! WE'RE HERE'

"I've brought you a very happy team." Don Bradman's own world-famous smile is here to leave no doubt about that first remark of his on landing at Southampton yesterday. The mighty hitter and his merry men, youngest Australian Test team ever to fight for the Ashes in England, had a rousing welcome.

"Chuck" Fleetwood-Smith and
Bradman were in good spirits on
their arrival.

Bradman looks ashore on arrival at Southampton.

WHO'S WHO

D. G. BRADMAN (Captain South Australia) : Captain of Australia. Born 27th August, 1908. Brilliant and enterprising right-handed batsman. Holds most batting records, including world record individual score (452 not out), highest Test score in England-Australia series (334) and record first-class aggregate for an Australian (this season he passed Hill's record of 17,221). Toured England in 1930 and 1934 and headed Australia's batting averages each time. Is a remarkably fine fieldsman, with lightning throw. In 1930, scored 3170 runs at an average of 99.06, and in 1934, scored 2106 at 81.00. In Tests against England has made 3406 at 89.63 (twelve centuries).

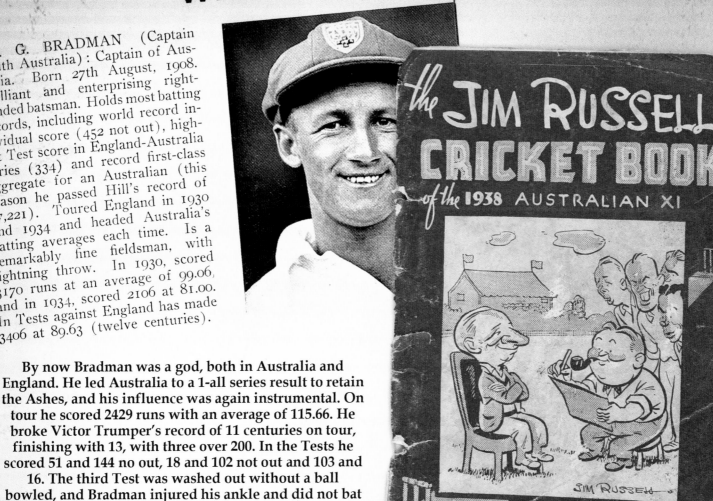

By now Bradman was a god, both in Australia and England. He led Australia to a 1-all series result to retain the Ashes, and his influence was again instrumental. On tour he scored 2429 runs with an average of 115.66. He broke Victor Trumper's record of 11 centuries on tour, finishing with 13, with three over 200. In the Tests he scored 51 and 144 no out, 18 and 102 not out and 103 and 16. The third Test was washed out without a ball bowled, and Bradman injured his ankle and did not bat in either innings of the final Test. So he finished with 434 runs at an average of 108.5.

"ABOVE ALL"
AEROPLANE JELLIES

AUSTRALIAN TOURING TEAM - 1938

TOP ROW :- A.G.CHIPPERFIELD. L.OB.FLEETWOOD-SMITH. D.G.BRADMAN. W.A.BROWN. S.G.BARNES.
CENTRE ROW :- E.C.S.WHITE. W.J.O'REILLY. CL.BADCOCK. B.A.BARNETT.
BOTTOM ROW:- A.L.HASSETT. M.G.WAITE. C.W.WALKER. E.L.McCORMICK. J.H.FINGLETON. F.A.WARD. S.J.McCABE.

Bradman's more relaxed outlook could be underlined by his acceptance of a new nickname, Braddles, when he toured England in 1938. He was to carry it for the rest of his life.

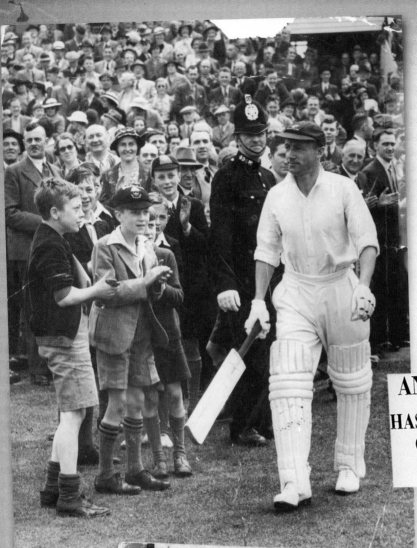

The Don Is "Braddles"

AUSSIES HAVE NEW NICKNAMES

BRADMAN, PUBLIC ENTERTAINER No. 1

ANOTHER RECORD TO BRADMAN

HAS NOW MADE SHIELD CENTURY IN EACH INNINGS TWICE

THE FASTEST HUNDRED

Bradman's Brilliant Display

OLD TRAFFORD SPELL BROKEN

From Our Own Correspondent

Don Bradman has hit a century at Old Trafford at last and must therefore not only be a happy man, but must have gained confidence for his next visit there, which will be on the occasion of this season's third Test.

The result of the match with Lancashire, a draw, was a foregone conclusion before the day's play began and, therefore, did not matter. What did matter was the fact that it was Bradman's eighth century of the tour and the fastest of the season, being made in 73 minutes, two minutes shorter time than that compiled by C. W. Packe for Cambridge University against the Army on May 31. It was a wonderful effort after a morning of deadly dullness and sent 5,000 people home delighted.

If there was an error in Bradman's innings at all it came when a ball from Wilkinson went off the bottom of his bat and just missed the stumps. For the rest his driving, pulling, hooking, leg hitting, and cutting bore the hall mark of a master batsman, and he hit fifteen 4's. Eight came in his first 50 in 33 minutes, and the rest in his second 50, made in 35 minutes. Having reached his century he declared with his side leading by 293 runs with 8 wickets standing, and in the last hour or so Lancashire obtained 60 for 3 wickets.

BRADMAN LOOKS SET FOR THE DAY

PITY SOMEONE DIDN'T INVITE HIM TO ASCOT.

1938——
Australian XI
Tour in . . .
Great Britain

BRADMAN BATS ALL DAY, SEES AUSTRALIA SAFE

England reveres W.G. Grace, so it was a bold statement from former captain Plum Warner to suggest that Bradman had proven himself a greater player.

"In the many pictures that I have stored in my mind from the burnt-out Junes' of more than a century, there is none more dramatic or compelling than of this small serenely-moving figure in its big peaked green cap coming out of the pavilion shadows into the sunshine, with the concentration, ardour and apprehension of surrounding thousands centred upon him and the destiny of a Test match in his hands." (Doyen English cricket writer, E.W.Swanton, 1962)

MICHAEL CLARKE

(Current Australian Test cricketer with 2212 runs at 47.06 in 35 Tests, and one-day international vice-captain)

Every Australian cricketing kid grows up knowing of Don Bradman. In my case, the history lesson came from my grandfather who talked about him all the time - and he still tells me of his deeds and how he was the best.

I unfortunately have seen Bradman only on movie footage. But his statistics are unbelievable and you can only imagine how good he was.

I can't comprehend just how much pressure he must have been under throughout his career. Probably the closest example to him in the modern era is India's Sachin Tendulkar. The expectations on him by the Indian fans to score a century every time he bats must be enormous. Imagine what it must have been like for Bradman, with an entire nation looking to him to succeed during the Great Depression and after the Second World War.

The amazing thing about him - and I think it is the greatest accolade - is that he rarely let anyone down because he scored so many hundreds and was so dominant almost every time he walked out to bat. He set all sorts of standards and records. And he conducted himself so well off the field, during his playing days and then throughout the rest of his life. People are always looking for the next Don Bradman to come along. I don't know if we will ever see another like him.

I scored a century on my Test debut, against India in Bangalore in 2004. My mother and father and grandparents flew over for the match and it was fantastic to get that century. I was very nervous, especially after receiving my Baggy Green cap in the pre-match ceremony.

Every cricketer dreams of a century on Test debut and that was a real thrill. To score consistently and maintain a high standard after that is difficult enough, but more so if people somehow think you may be another batsman of Bradman's run-scoring ability.

Nobody has ever done it better than Bradman, and I doubt anyone every will.

Bradman Gets His 1,000—Second Time

Don Bradman— wins race for 1,000 runs

DON BRADMAN won the 1,000-runs-before-the-end-of-May-race yesterday by taking a century off the Hampshire bowling at Southampton.

This is the second time he has accomplished the feat, the last time being in 1930 on the same ground. Incidentally, he is the first player to make 1,000 runs so early in the season.

In 1927 Walter Hammond made his 1,000 by May 28, so that the Don beats him for speed by a day, but Hammond still has a chance of emulating Bradman.

He requires 106 more runs for his 1,000, and Edrich needs only 19 more. W. G. Grace was the first batsman to score 1,000 runs before the end of May. This was in 1895, and a national testimonial fund brought him £7,356 from an admiring public.

WORLD'S RECORD

BRADMAN earns another distinction. He is the only player who has twice scored 1,000 before the end of May.

Rain nearly foiled him yesterday. The Hampshire players sportingly continued to field in heavy rain, and eventually a boundary off Baring, who dismissed him for a duck four years ago, took his score to 125 and made his aggregate 1,000 and 1.

This was Bradman's fifth century of the present tour. He was warmly congratulated by his team-mates and the Hampshire team.

TWO new cricket records were set up when Don Bradman, the Australian captain, became the first cricketer to reach 1,000 runs for the season at Southampton yesterday.

No other batsman has ever scored 1,000 runs before the end of May more than once.

No other batsman has succeeded in reaching his 1,000 so early in the season. In 1927 Hammond got his on May 28, a day later than Bradman.

Bradman has scored his runs in 24 playing days—258 of them on the last day of April. Hammond's performance in 1927 was achieved in 22 playing days—May 7 to 28. Incidentally, Bradman's previous feat was completed on the same ground in 1930.

There is still time for two Englishmen to get to the 1,000 mark before the end of May. Hammond, who scored 113 yesterday, needs 106, and Edrich only 19. Both are playing in matches starting to-day.

EDRICH'S CHANCE

Yet another record will be set up should either or both of them succeed, for never before has more than one batsman scored 1,000 runs before the end of May in the same season.

One more record remains—that of being the first batsman to score 1,000 runs in the month of May alone. Here Edrich stands the best chance, for he needs only 40 more, whereas Bradman needs 237.

W. G. Grace, when nearly 47, was the first player to attain a four-figure aggregate during May. That was in 1895, and the performance was recognised by a National Testimonial fund that resulted in some £7,356 being presented to "W. G."

Bradman was heartily congratulated by all his team mates when he returned to the dressing room at Southampton yesterday.

"We are all very pleased that he has achieved the feat," said Mr. W. H. Jeanes, the Australian manager. "It is a fine performance to get 1,000 runs before the end of May twice. Bradman does not talk about himself, and he has not said very much about it, but he is very pleased about getting the runs."

£50-A-WEEK OFFER TO DON BRADMAN TO STAY IN ENGLAND

By JOHN THOMPSON

ON the eve of the second Test match at Lord's, Don Bradman, Australia's captain, was last night made a sensational offer by a London firm of bookmakers.

Details of the proposal were given to me at Dorland House in the West End of London by a director of the firm concerned, the Sports Investors Society, Ltd., which has been for some time conducting the business of bookmaking along co-operative lines.

OFFERS TO BRADMAN POUR IN

News that the Australian Cricket Board of Control had refused permission for Jessie Bradman to travel to England to accompany her husband home caused a flurry of offers from English businesses who wanted him to settle permanently in England.

Bradman, with support from the players, pushed the issue and eventually won the day, with his wife joining him at the end of the tour.

Unhappily Bradman chipped a bone in his ankle in the final Test at The Oval. He recovered and enjoyed Jessie's comfort as he did not play again on tour. He also knocked back the lucrative offers to return to Australia.

BIG MONEY IN ENGLAND

Don's New Request To Board

From A. G. MOYES—Copyright—All Rights Reserved.

MANCHESTER, Thursday.

On the eve of the third Test, Don Bradman is being inundated with attractive financial offers from people who are unable to credit the Australian Board of Control's refusal to allow Mrs. Bradman to go to England and travel home with her husband.

The Australian captain, however, remains silent. He has no intention of dishonoring his contract with the board, will do nothing stupid, and will return to Australia with the team.

The special representative of the London "Star" says that Bradman is likely to refuse to visit England again unless the board's form of contract with the players is altered to permit wives to meet their husbands in England at the conclusion of a tour. Bradman is reported to have cabled the board, asking for reconsideration of his request.

The players feel the board has no moral and legal right to raise the question of wives, and have sent a strong cable to the board.

Don Bradman May Force Wives Crisis

WIFE BAN CAN'T BE ENFORCED

CHANGE IN CONTRACT NEXT TOUR

Bachelors Support The Marrieds

REFUSAL BY THE AUSTRALIAN CRICKET CONTROL BOARD TO ALLOW MRS. BRADMAN TO JOIN HER HUSBAND IN ENGLAND AT THE END OF THE SEASON MAY LEAD TO THE AUSTRALIAN CAPTAIN MAKING A STISFCTORY CLEAN-UP OF THE WIVES QUESTION A CONDITION FOR HIS NEXT TOUR HERE.

From A Special Correspondent

DON BRADMAN is to issue a statement to-night, the eve of the third Test, at Manchester, on the Australian Board's decision.

I understand that all the members of the team are very upset and disappointed.

There is no question of the ban on Mrs. Bradman being defied, but it is likely that Bradman will refuse to make another visit to England unless an alteration is made in his contract.

CALLED A MEETING

Before Bradman made his request for his wife to be allowed to come over in September, he called a meeting of the players and told them of his intention.

They raised no objection; in fact, they were enthusiastically in favour.

Don was not asking for special dispensation in his case.

It is open for any member of the team to make a similar application.

He had precedent in his favour, for in 1934 Mrs. Woodfull, wife of the then Australian captain, was allowed to join the team at the end of their tour.

36 POINTS IN CONTRACTS

Before the men left Australia they had to sign contracts of 36 articles, bristling with legal terms, and governing eating, drinking, smoking, wives, mothers-in-law, modes of travel, broadcasting, talking to newspaper men, entrances to dressing rooms, blazers, sweaters, caps, ties, etc.

Any infringement of one of the 36 clauses renders a player open to a fine of up to £150.

There are no moral or legal right to make them sign on the question of wives.

But there is so little time between the selection of the team and the departure from Australia that they have no opportunity to fight the conditions.

SIGN NOW OR NEVER

It is a case of signing the contract immediately or being left out of the team.

The present party includes eight married men, and eight bachelors. And the bachelors are supporting Bradman in his claim.

Here are the married men: Bradman, McCabe O'Reilly, Chipperfield, Fleetwood-Smith, Walker, Waite and Ward.

The bachelors are: Brown, Fingleton, Badcock, Barnes, White, Barnett, Hassett and McCormick.

The Australian Press accuse the Board of being dictatorial. A leading article says:

"We have rocked with laughter at some of the things Fascism has imposed on totalitarian countries. Can we hear their shrieks of laughter now?"

Public opinion is divided, says British United Press.

One section is angry, in view of Bradman's great value to Australian cricket; the other says there should be no discrimination in favour of one player.

The issue of wives joining their husbands at the end of tours was highly embarrassing for Australia's cricket administrators. Bradman, as a legend, held the high moral ground because he had done so much for the game. Also, he had the support of other married members of the touring team, as well as vocal support from the bachelors who had no complaints. Critics suggested that as Bradman had nothing in his touring contract to prevent his wife from joining him, they could face a legal battle. Eventually commonsense prevailed.

Has Signed No Contract With Board

Cable From Don Causes Board To Reconsider Veto; Telegraphic Vote Being Taken

NEITHER THE CRICKET BOARD OF CONTROL NOR THE AUSTRALIAN LAWN TENNIS ASSOCIATION WOULD HAVE A LEG TO STAND ON IF BRADMAN AND HOPMAN DEFIED THEM ON THE "WIVES BAN," SYDNEY LAWYERS DECLARE.

Even worse, they say, would be the position of the Board of Control if it tried to take action in the event of Mrs Bradman going to England despite the Board's refusal to give her permission.

In both cases the question of public policy is involved, and assert the lawyers, no contract that is against public policy can be enforced.

Bradman's contract provides that he shall not be accompanied "on the tour or any part thereof by his wife or any member of his family or any relative."

But the law says that an agreement which provides for a separation to take place between a husband and wife at some future time is void, as contrary to public policy.

WIFE IS FREE AGENT

Mrs. Bradman has signed no contract and is free, at law, to leave for England at any moment she likes. Even assuming the event of the cricketer's contract being held as legal, Bradman could not be held responsible for a breach brought about by his wife.

There is a law which provides that an agreement for a gift to a married woman on a condition that brings about a separation will be treated as unconditional. The condition is void as encouraging her in a breach of her duty.

"I would not mind arguing the converse of that in support of the right of Bradman to have his wife with him if he desires," a barrister said yesterday.

In the case of the Hopmans, both have signed contracts—but, if the lawyers are right, the separation clause is voidable on the ground of public policy.

To the extent that both the Board of Control and the A.L.T.A. could refuse to select Bradman or the Hopmans for future tours, they hold the whip hand.

But imagine the public uproar should Mrs. Bradman go to England despite the Board and Bradman be omitted from the team at any time he is available.

BRADMAN OUT OF TEST

CHIPPED BONE IN ANKLE

May Not Play Again On Tour

ONLY 12 FIT

From A. G. Moyes—Copyright—All Rights Reserved.

LONDON, Tuesday.

Don Bradman, who is out of the fifth and final Test at Kennington Oval, will probably be unable to play again on the tour.

While bowling to-day, during England's innings of 7 for 903, Bradman stumbled in a pot-hole made by Fleetwood-Smith's scuffling feet. To-night, X-rays showed that there is a "chip fracture" of the tibia, at the right ankle.

Three attempts were made by a doctor to patch up Fingleton, who is suffering from a pulled muscle, but it was found impossible to get him to the wicket. It is hoped that Fingleton may be able to play again towards the end of the tour.

As McCormick is suffering from neuritis and Chipperfield is convalescing from an appendicitis operation, the Australian team is reduced to 12 reasonably sound men.

In Australia's first innings, three wickets are down for 117.

Bradman is lying in his hotel room, with a crutch alongside the couch. His ankle is badly swollen and discoloured.

To avoid sending Bradman to a hospital for examination, Dr. Isaac Jones, who is an Australian, had a cable run from an X-ray van in the street through a sitting-room window on the second floor of the hotel, and thence to Bradman's room.

The injury was X-rayed, and the plates were developed in the van in three minutes. They were inspected by the doctor and by a radiologist. Two further photographs confirmed the diagnosis that a piece of bone has been chipped from the tibia.

Late to-night, Bradman dined with the manager, Mr. Jeanes, and with members of the team. He is not suffering much pain.

Will Never Bowl Again

It is ironical that Bradman was injured during his first spell of bowling of the tour. To-night he announced his retirement from bowling. "That's definite," he said smilingly as he lay on a couch undergoing treatment. I reminded him of his statement earlier in the day that he would never bowl again. "Yes, I was talked into it to-day, but that's the finish," replied Don.

It is now impossible for Bradman to reach 3000 runs for the tour, and be the first Australian to achieve this feat.

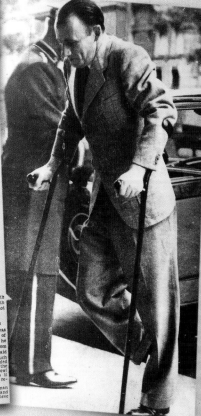

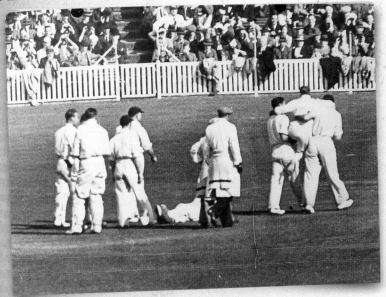

The final Test of 1938 was a dark one for Bradman. He watched as 22-year-old Len Hutton eclipsed his Test record score of 334 by 30 runs, and then he broke an ankle bone while bowling. To add insult to injury, Australia lost the Test and the series was drawn 1-1.

BRADMAN BREAKS A LEG BONE
BRADMAN'S SHIN BROKEN

BRADMAN WILL CHASE C. B. FRY'S RECORD TO-DAY

By GEORGE THATCHER.

SOUTH AUSTRALIA, with eight wickets in hand, requires a mere 130 to equal the N.S.W. total in the Shield game being played at the S.C.G.

Bradman wants 78 for his century. Main interest to-day will be centred in Don's attempt to equal C. B. Fry's record of six consecutive first-class centuries.

New South Wales fared quite as well as expected on Saturday. Generally the batsmen displayed a pathetic lack of judgment.

Five wickets fell before lunch. Solomon alone looked like staying. He was caught off a full-toss. Earlier he had swept Ward on to the top of the new stand, the ball rebounding into the Show Ground.

Pepper and McCaffrey were out to poor shots off Grimmett, and it was left to R. James and Hynes to show that the bowling could be hit.

James is a breezy youth, who plays brilliant shots and then introduces an execrable cross-bat stroke. Hynes, who has been out of touch, chanced his arm. He was a shade fortunate, but played the correct game.

The partnership of 77 provided the brightest batting of the day.

Syd Barnes played over a yorker from P. Riding, while Chipperfield hung out his bat to Waite.

In Walker's absence Bradman kept wickets. He accepted one chance and missed a stumping on the leg side.

To keep faith with the hillites, who had sat throughout the heat wave, Don came to the wickets after K. Ridings had gone l.b.w. to Cheetham.

Don batted with his eye on the clock. He may be more venturesome to-day.

Whitington batted in a style that suggests he may develop into a Test opener. He has a shot through the covers that recall's Rock's famous push past point.

Weak Attack

The N.S.W. bowling was never of a high standard. Chipperfield will have to don his thinking cap early to-day, particularly if Bradman and Badcock get a good sight of the ball.

The wicket played well, although Grimmett spun more than is his wont on the first day of a match.

Umpire Borwick once no-balled Cotton for throwing.

To-day's pre-lunch crowd will probably be much bigger than usual. If Bradman gets over the first three overs Fry's record will probably go.

THE SCORES

N.S.W.—First Innings

A. G. CHEETHAM, c Bradman, b Grimmett		10
B. V. McCAULEY, l.b.w., b Grimmett		25
S. G. BARNES, b P. Ridings		12
A. G. CHIPPERFIELD, c Cotton, b Waite		15
C. SOLOMON, c P Ridings, b Ward		34
C. PEPPER, c Waite, b Grimmett		17
V. McCAFFREY, c P. Ridings, b Grimmett		6
R. JAMES, b Cotton		45
L. C. HYNES, not out		63
S. SISMEY, c P. Ridings, b Cotton		6
L. O'BRIEN, b Cotton		0
Sundries		13
Total		**246**

Fall of wickets: 32, 46, 50, 90, 102, 118, 143, 220, 246.

BOWLING

	O.	M.	R.	W.
Cotton	10.6	1	44	3
Waite	11	1	49	1
Grimmett	15	3	53	4
P. Ridings	7	1	37	1
Ward	7	0	41	1
K. Ridings	2	0	9	0

Byes 8, no-balls 4 (Cotton 2, P. Ridings 2), Waite bowled a wide.

SOUTH AUSTRALIA—First Innings

K. RIDINGS, l.b.w., b Cheetham		28
R. S. WHITINGTON, l.b.w., b Barnes		59
D. G. BRADMAN, not out		22
F. A. WARD, not out		4
Sundries		3
Two for		**116**

BOWLING

	O.	M.	R.	W.
O'Brien	4	0	25	0
Hynes	6	0	27	0
Cheetham	7	0	32	1
Barnes	3	1	4	1
Pepper	5	0	25	0

O'Brien bowled 3 no-balls.

DON AGAIN

Six Hundreds In Row

MELBOURNE, Sunday.—Don Bradman scored his 85th Sheffield Shield century and his sixth in succession when he reached 107 yesterday.

Thanks to a magnificent fighting knock by Lindsay Hassett, who was unconquered at 211, Victoria totalled 499 in the first innings.

Hassett played shots to all parts of the ground, and revealed his artistry with scintillating drives that gave the fieldsmen no chance.

Fast scoring was the feature of the Victorian innings, the 499 occupying 215 minutes.

Form Reversal

Fleetwood-Smith, often described as the world's worst batsman, knocked up 43 in smart time.

The slow bowler scored 16 off one over from P. Ridings, and took 13 off three balls from Test team-mate Merv Waite.

South Australia began well and had lost 4-240 at stumps. K. Ridings and Whitington opened vigorously, and Whitington played a great knock for his century.

Bradman was always in control of the situation and is batting in his usual form.

Jack Badcock was caught and bowled by McCormick for one. Charlie Walker and Ward will resume to-morrow.

Walker allowed no byes in the big Victorian score.

PLAYER'S CIGARETTES

S.A.C.A.

D. G. BRADMAN

War began in September 1939 but the government asked for the 1939/40 Sheffield Shield season to continue. Bradman scored 1475 runs at 122.91, with a highest score of 267. However he rated his two innings against NSW at Adelaide, of 251 not out and 90 not out, as his best in Shield matches. He scored the runs against Bill O'Reilly at his peak.

EASY TO DON: Records come easily to Don Bradman's flashing blade. Yesterday he scored his sixth consecutive century in first-class cricket, equalling the record of Englishman, C. B. Fry, which has stood since 1901. Bradman's sequence is 118, 143, 225, 107, 186 and 135 not out.

Bradman's South Australian Cap.

World War II deprived Bradman of six years of his cricketing life, and almost sent him into retirement.

He enlisted in the Australian Royal Air Force but after a delay in his formal enlistment he transferred to become a physical training instructor at the Army School of Physical and Recreational Training. He had a rank of lieutenant.

BRADMAN JOINS R.A.A.F.

In a regulation test at Frankston in Victoria for the Army, his eyesight was found to be below average, a fact that didn't surprise him but stunned the cricket fraternity.

The Bradmans . . .

AUSTRALIA taking its hat off to Don Bradman and son. Don just enlisted with the Air Force, and son John Russell celebrates his first birthday this Wednesday. "No party, he is too little," says his mother.

Animals are John's first love, but lately he's been intrigued with a miniature bat. He doesn't hesitate to swing it, and loves to tap it on the crazy pavement in the garden.

Mrs. Bradman is not yet making any special plans for herself and John when Don is called up, but she will probably keep their Adelaide home going.

She's an expert knitter, and is a member of the Kensington Park Red Cross circle.

DON BRADMAN ENLISTS IN AIR FORCE

DON Bradman today joined the Royal Australian Air Force.

With flying colors the Australian Test captain passed his medical examination at the North terrace recruiting depot and subsequently was sworn in for service in an R.A.A.F. air crew. He was placed on reserve and will be called up later for training.

In the meantime, Bradman with other members of the air crew reserve, will attend special study classes organised for reservists.

The Lord Mayor (Mr. Barrett), who is chairman of the Air Force Recruiting Committee, said: "It should be an inspiration to every sportsman in Australia to see a cricketer of such international fame in the R.A.A.F. Let us hope now that Bradman will get centuries as readily in the air as he has on the ground."

Don Bradman

ADELAIDE, Friday. — Don Bradman joined the Royal Autsralian Air Force today. He passed the medical examination, and subsequently was sworn in as a member of the air crew reserve.

It is likely to be some time before he is called up for service, but in the meantime he will attend night study classes.

The Lord Mayor (Mr Barrett), who is chairman of the R.A.A.F. Recruiting Committee, said that Bradman's action was an inspiration to all sportsmen of Australia.

Don Bradman

A BATSMAN WHO CARRIES A CANE

Exchanging white flannels for khaki, Don Bradman, famous Australian test cricket captain, is now a lieutenant in the Australian Army.

1941/42 Army School of Physical & Recreational Training, Frankston Victoria

His new physical work produced a succession of muscle problems, diagnosed as fibrositis.

He had three spells in hospital before he was invalidated out of the Army in June, 1941. He returned to Bowral to recuperate, unable to lift his arm to comb his hair. His wife had to shave him.

P. T. Squad at Frankston, December 1940.

Bradman played only two matches in 1940-41. He was bowled first ball on Christmas Day in Adelaide in 1940 (and managed only six in the first innings) in a match for charity between South Australia and Victoria.

Then he was dismissed for another duck and scored only 12 in his only first-class appearance for his XI versus Stan McCabe's XI in Melbourne in January of 1941.

After the birth of his daughter Shirley in 1941, Bradman returned to work in stockbroking and in 1943 was elected a member of the Adelaide Stock Exchange. In July, 1945, his employer's firm, H.W.Hodgetts, collapsed and Bradman went into business on his own. He also replaced Hodgetts as South Australia's representative to the Australian Cricket Board of Control.

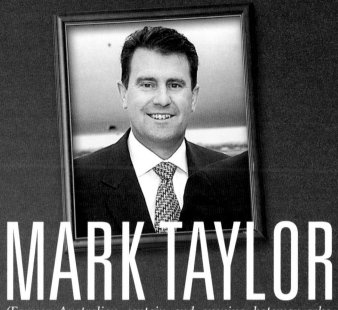

MARK TAYLOR

(Former Australian captain and opening batsman who scored 7525 runs at 43.49 and a record 157 catches in 104 Tests. Now Cricket Australia board member)

It was a nice thought that two blokes, born 56 years apart but growing up in the same neck of the woods in rural NSW, could share an Australian Test batting record.

Yet that was the case and a memorable link I enjoyed with the greatest batsman the game has known, Sir Donald Bradman.

And it was simply a quirk of fate. I never intended to finish the second day of the 1998 Peshawar Test against Pakistan on 334 not out. I actually received a couple of deliveries to end the day, but hit them to fieldsmen and didn't score

Then, when stumps were drawn, I realised I was on that famous number 334 - Don Bradman's Australian Test record score against England at Leeds in 1930.

I had all night to think about what I was going to do: declare or bat on for 10 minutes to keep Pakistan in the field for just that bit longer.

If I had taken Bradman's score out of the equation I might have batted on. But I really gave Bradman's score a lot of thought. I figured that if I batted on and then declared after a couple of overs and broke his record, there could have been a school of thought that I batted on only to make sure I passed his score. That was the last thing I wanted to do.

In the end it was an easy decision. To equal Don Bradman's record was a great honour - to pass i in such circumstances could have bordered on treason! One of the ironies was that when I reached 210 in that very innings I passed Bradman's Tes aggregate of 6996 runs - it had taken me only ar extra 87 innings to do it!

Bradman sent me a letter after the Pakistan tour He congratulated me on the score and was delighted that we held the record together (Matthew Hayder took it away with 380 against Zimbabwe in Pert in 2003).

He also congratulated me and the team on the way we were playing. It was a letter to cherish.

Bradman also offered me an invitation to catch up Naturally, I made contact and in the December of that year of 1998 I went to his house in Kensington and spent two hours engaging in memorable conversation with the great man.

My lasting memory was that, even at the age of 90 he still had his finger on the pulse of world cricket He asked me as many questions as I asked him about his illustrious career.

It was the time of betting and bribery scandals and he was keen to learn all about such issues. He was contemporary in this thinking then and clearly didn't live in the past.

I was always connected with Bradman, who was dubbed the 'Boy From Bowral' even though he was born in Cootamundra. I was born in Leeton, which is not far away, even though I have been more associated with Wagga Wagga where I wen to live in 1972 when I was eight.

Bradman's legacy is his statistics, and the entertaining way he played the game. I have looked at the black and white films of The Don playing cricket, and even though there was a depression and war, people flocked to see him play. They may have had only a few coins in thei pockets in those days, but they were prepared to pay to see Bradman bat.

It just goes to show what a drawcard he was, what a national hero he was. No doubt watching him play was worth every penny.

Bradman, after six years away from the game, gave serious thought to a comeback at the cessation of war. He was an Australian selector and member of the Board of Control, and equally was heavily committed to his stock broking business and family. Despite misgivings about his health, he decided to play for South Australia against a Services XI because it was for charity.

His 112 in that match gave him the incentive to return to international cricket. Although clearly not his old self, he scored 76 and 3 for SA against the MCC and then 106 for an Australian XI against the MCC, before 116 for SA against Victoria in the lead-up to the first Test.

This cap is the first to depart from the metallic bullion emblem and adopt cotton thread embroidery. Cotton thread is still used today to fashion the Australian emblem.

The resumption of Test cricket after the Second World War was warmly received by the Australian public who flocked to the matches to watch Australia eventually defeat a weakened England team. During this series Bradman and Sid Barnes famously made a record 5th wicket partnership of 405 runs in the Sydney Test. Both batsmen coincidentally made 234 runs each.

PLAYER'S CIGARETTES

D. G. BRADMAN (N. S. WALES)

Bradman scored his maiden Brisbane Test century with 187, and followed up with 234 in the Sydney Test. Scores of 79 and 49 followed at Melbourne, 0 and 56 not out at Adelaide and 12 and 63 at Sydney to conclude a fairytale comeback. The series yielded 680 runs at an average of 97.14 - an exceptional return for a man of 37 who had not played for six years!

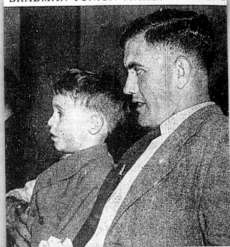

BRADMAN JUNIOR MAKES A FRIEND

John Bradman, seven-year-old son of Don Bradman, met Alec Bedser, of the English cricket team, on his first day in Adelaide, and since then John has constantly sought out his new friend. He went to the English dressing room on Saturday and asked for "Mr. Bedser, please." Bedser came out and was soon engaged in a rapid fire cricket conversation led by young Bradman, in which some of the youngster's mates joined. In this picture Bradman junior is seen watching the game with Bedser.

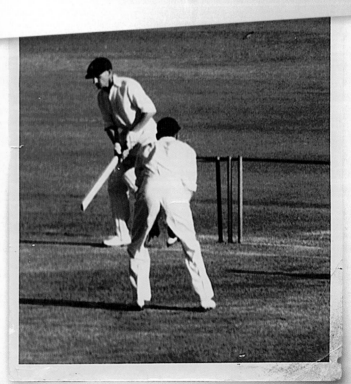

Bradman bowled for nought by Alec Bedser, Adelaide Oval, February 1947

FINE TEST CENTURY BY ARTHUR MORRIS
Death Blow To England's Hopes

The Wizardry Of Don Bradman
AMAZING 234 IN WORLD RECORD STAND

(From JIM MATHERS)

MELBOURNE, Saturday.—Eighty thousand people gave Arthur Morris an ovation this afternoon when he scored a century in the Third Test.

Morris failed to get going in the previous Tests, but today he was seldom in trouble and kept his end up while other star batsmen came and went.

He effectively dispelled England's hopes of forcing a win, which were high at one stage, when Barnes, Bradman and Hassett were back in the pavilion.

52-YEARS-OLD RECORD TO BRADMAN, BARNES

MICHAEL HUSSEY

(Australian batsman who in 25 Tests has scored 2325 runs at an average of 66.36, currently second only to Bradman)

Records are made to be broken but Don Bradman has one that I don't think anyone can, or will, ever beat.

That is boasting a Test average of 99.94. I just cannot comprehend how he kept making such prolific scores. Every batsman goes through tough times, but the only time Bradman wasn't up around the century mark was during the Bodyline series, and he still averaged 56.

It is unbelievable that anyone could maintain that average. He must have been a freak of nature to have the talent, temperament, drive and passion to do that.

Bradman obviously is the best batsman to play the game - it is just amazing that anyone could average almost twice what anyone else can achieve.

I have looked at old film of him in action. It is very difficult to judge eras and you wonder how he would get on today. But I am absolutely convinced he still would be twice as good as anyone else. He would have access to the latest technical aids and equipment.

It is not my goal to be regarded as the man with the second highest Test average to Bradman. I am resigned to the fact that my average will come back, as everyone else's has through the generations - except for Bradman.

One of the difficulties for anyone with a high average is that people expect big scores all the time. Of course, that is a big ask. How Bradman did it year after year, series after series is just staggering. He had huge expectations from the public and he just kept delivering. He is the biggest legend the game has ever had, and probably ever will have.

SIR CLIVE LLOYD

(Former captain and champion West Indian batsman who in 110 Tests scored 7515 runs at an average of 46.67. Recently appointed chairman of the International Cricket Council's cricket committee)

When I injured my back in a fielding accident in Adelaide during the Rest Of The World series in 1971-72, I didn't know if I would walk again. It was a very worrying time but as I lay in hospital Sir Donald visited me and we spent the best two hours I've ever had chin wagging about cricket. He told me that if I wanted to stay in Australia - become a resident - he would personally sponsor me.

That chat was so relaxed and informative. It lifted my spirits no end, and, I'm sure, helped me recover and to go on to enjoy a wonderful career. He told me that he thought (Sir) Everton Weekes was the best of the three W's - Weekes, (Sir) Clyde Walcott and (Sir) Frank Worrell - and we discussed the no-ball rule and the future of cricket and all sorts of cricket-related matters.

That he went out of his way to visit me, and to spend so much time with me and also to offer to sponsor me if I wanted to migrate to Australia, was just a wonderful experience. When we arrived in Adelaide with the Rest Of The World team, big South African Hylton Ackerman had us in fits of laughter. He looked at this little bloke scurrying around sorting out luggage and he asked 'who is that busy little fella?'

Obviously Hilton had no idea who he was, and it was Sir Donald just doing his best to help us out. He was that sort of person. Bradman is an icon to all of us who have played the game, or who are in administration. In fact, he is a life model.

He was not only Australia's icon. He was the cricket icon everyone aspired to be like. He was known and loved throughout the cricket world: he was the sport's flag bearer. He epitomised everything that is great in the sport: skill, sportsmanship, devotion and passion.

He was so modest. On all the occasions I met him, he was modest and easy going. He never talked about himself. He was more interested in the players of the day, the good of the game, the planning for the future and how to improve the spectacle so that the public would be as enthralled with the game as he was. It was a privilege to meet him and to get to know him as a person, not just the man with the unbelievable statistics.

I once heard a couple of prominent sports people suggesting that the three greatest athletes in the history of sport were soccer champ Pele, boxer Muhammad Ali and golfer Tiger Woods. Then someone mentioned Sir Donald, his average, his contribution to the sport, to the Australian national ethos, and a lot more accolades. The order quickly changed and Bradman was on top of the list - where he deserved to be.

I have tried to follow Sir Donald's lead in cricket administration. People too easily forget about his days as a selector and administrator, and the massive influence he had on the game for decades after he retired as the world's undisputed best batsman. I am now chairman of the West Indies, on the committee at Lancashire, a recently retired match referee and now chairman of the International Cricket Council cricket committee. I take these duties extremely seriously because I know how much Sir Donald put into the game after his playing days, and I intend to do the same.

Bradman was a god in the cricket world during his life, and he will remain so.

**This ball was used during the
3rd Test, Australia-England,
Melbourne, Janurary 1947.**

Australia won the series 3-nil, with Bradman scoring heavily, and once again moulding a young team that was to become immortal within a year in England. During his career Bradman averaged 130.08 when Australia won, 111.90 when Australia drew and 43.27 when Australia lost. He scored 26% of the team's score in his career and this series was typical of his influence.

THE PARLIAMENT OF THE COMMONWEALTH.

LEADER OF THE OPPOSITION,
CANBERRA, A.C.T.

20th March, 1947.

My dear Don,

I would not like the 1946/47 Test Season to pass into Limbo without dropping you a line to say how much I admired your unique contribution to victory.

As a highly interested onlooker I was constantly fascinated by the skill with which you controlled the game at all stages. There are very many of us who think that we have never seen a better or more subtle exhibition of Captaincy.

You no doubt have your critics and I suppose, like all the rest of us, you occasionally deserve them! But you can certainly look back over these Test victories with unadulterated pride.

With very kind regards,

I am,

Yours truly,

(R.G. MENZIES.)

D.G. Bradman, Esq.
- - - - - - - - - - -

Sir Robert Menzies, then leader of the Opposition, was an unabashed cricket devotee. He wrote to Bradman in March of 1947 to congratulate him on the Ashes success, especially his supreme captaincy.

BRADMAN'S 100 CENTURIES

Made at Average of One In Every 3 Hands

The bat used by Don Bradman when he scored his 100th century in first-class cricket at the Sydney Cricket Ground, November 1947 against India.

Bradman's hundredth century

By GINTY LUSH

DON BRADMAN may score his 100th century in first class cricket in the present match at the Sydney Cricket Ground between an Australian XI and India.

Bradman's 99 first-class centuries to date put him 46 centuries ahead of Warren Bardsley, who is next on the Australian list of century-makers.

This season in big cricket Bradman has had only three innings, and two of them yielded centuries.

Each time, Bradman hit out to score quickly after the century, instead of settling down for 200.

If he sticks to these tactics, he will lessen the strain on his physical condition and probably last a few more seasons before retiring altogether from big cricket.

Despite his 99 centuries, Bradman is a long way down the list of century-makers at large.

Ten English batsmen have scored more than 100 centuries:

J. B. Hobbs	197
E. Hendren	170
W. R. Hammond	156
C. P. Mead	153
H. Sutcliffe	149
F. E. Woolley	145
W. G. Grace	126
A. Sandham	107
T. Hayward	104
E. Tyldesley	102

Bradman comes next after those 10. He is likely to pass only the last three of them—Tyldesley, Hayward, Sandham.

But compare the number of Bradman's innings with the Englishmen's, and you find him far superior to them as a run-getter.

A top-line player in England can have as many as 60 first-class innings in a season.

The most Bradman has ever had in an Australian season is 24.

Jack Hobbs, who has scored more centuries and more runs than any other cricketer, batted 1315 times. He scored 61,221 runs, for an average of 50.63.

In contrast, Bradman has had only 294 innings, and scored 24,395 runs.

Since he entered first-class cricket in the 1927-28 season he has averaged more than 94 for every one of his 294 innings (37 not outs).

Bearded W. G. Grace made more centuries than Bradman has made to date. Grace scored more than twice as many runs as Bradman.

But Grace played 43 years for his 54,896 runs, whereas Bradman is entering his 18th season.

Some of Bradman's Test innings will live forever in cricket history. He is the only batsman to have exceeded 300 in an innings twice in Tests.

Both of these innings, 334 in 1930 and 304 in 1934, were at Leeds.

Bradman's score of 334 was his contribution to a total of 566; Kippax was the only other Australian to exceed 50 in that match.

In that Test series, Bradman's top scores were 334, 254, 234, and 131.

Bradman virtually failed in the first three Tests on his second (1934) visit to England.

His highest score for the series was 36 when he went in to bat at Leeds in the Fourth Test.

Australia had lost 3-39 when Bradman joined Ponsford. The fourth wicket fell at 427 when Ponsford hit his wicket playing defensively to Verity.

Bradman continued, and scored 304 out of 583.

Bradman and Ponsford repeated the dose in the Fifth Test, adding 451 for the second wicket, Ponsford making 266 and Bradman 244.

Bradman's most memorable innings was in January, 1930, when he scored 452 not out in a Sheffield Shield match against Queensland at the Sydney Cricket Ground.

This was a chanceless innings, lasting six hours 46 minutes and including 49 fours.

At one stage Bradman was the youngest batsman ever to score a century in a Test match.

After playing in the First Test in Australia in 1929, he was 12th man in the Second Test, but played in the Third Test, scoring 79 and 113.

He was 20 years and four months old at the time.

Archie Jackson came out in the next Test at 19 years of age and made 164.

So the honor of being the youngest to score a Test century passed from Bradman to Jackson.

"I think of all my experiences in cricket that was the most exhilarating moment on the field. The huge crowd gave me a reception which was moving in its spontaneous warmth." (Bradman after scoring his 100th first-class century).

DON BRADMAN SCORING HIS 100th CENTURY

On 15th November, 1947, playing for an Australian XI against India on the Sydney Cricket Ground, Don Bradman played a superb innings of 172 in compiling 100 centuries in first-class cricket. He received a hearty and breath-taking ovation from a thrilled crowd of 32,000. His score of 172, made just three minutes short of three hours, included 18 boundaries and one six. Scoring was made at a very fast rate after the century in 132 minutes —150 in 161 minutes, and 172 in 177 minutes. Keith Miller, his partner, also played a great knock, and the partnership of 252 lasted 154 minutes—the last 50 in 16 minutes.

Bradman celebrated his 100th first-class century during the 1947/48 season, enjoying yet another golden Summer in which he gave the touring team from India a display of batsmanship that enhanced his reputation.

He started with 156 and 12 for SA against the tourists, then scored 100 for South Australia against Victoria in his only Sheffield Shield match of the summer.

He went to Sydney in mid-November 1947 to represent an Australian XI, and produced 172 in the first innings to notch his 100th century milestone.

SYDNEY CRICKET GROUND 15th NOVEMBER, 1947.

Sydney Smith making a presentation to Don Bradman from the NSW Cricket Association to mark the occasion of his making his 100th century in 1st class cricket at the Sydney Cricket Ground - December 13th, 1947.

AUSTRALIA 1947-48

at SYDN[EY]

Date	Time in	Score	Adjn.	Score	Time Out	Total
15	12·52				1⁻	8
15	12·52	·	1·32		1·17	25
15	1·2	11	1·32 2·7 4·58	11 101	5·4	177
15	1·19	31	1·32 2·17 4·58	8 64	4·56	154
15 17	4·58	283	6ᵖᵐ 12·3	6f 25	12·21	75
15 17	5·4	237	6f 12·3	80	12·27	75
17	12·23	346			12·25	2
17	12·26	346			12·55	9
17	12·29	346			12·55	26
17	12·37	348			1·10	33
17	12·57				1·10	13

50 IN 45 MIN.
100 IN 83 MIN.
150 IN 113 MIN.
200 IN 149 MIN.
250 IN 167 MIN.
300 IN 202 MIN.
350 IN 274 MIN.
400 IN   MIN.

LUNCH.
BRADMAN
MILLER
2·04

TEA
BRADMAN
MILLER
2·140

STUMP[S]
HAMENC[E]
HARVEY 4·34

J. PETTIFORD (12 MAN) 4·34

TIME of INN. 304 MIN

In scoring his 100th first-class century, he was the first and only to reach the milestone without having played county cricket in England. He took approximately half as many innings to achieve this result as the next fastest, Denis Compton (295 innings to 552).

MATCH BETWEEN

AN AUSTRALIAN XI   *and*   INDIA

CRICKET GROUND   *on*   14 - 15 - 17 - 18 NOV. 1947

FIRST   *innings of*   AN AUSTRALIAN XI

Name		Runs as Scored	How Out	Bowled	Total
...WN	W. A.	4121 /	CGT HAZARE *1st SLIP*	SOHONI	8
...ERS	R	1112224421 /	RUN OUT		16
...DMAN	D. G.	2111111112312111111111112411421111112111142422121411111411111122111112411114411 44412442444146114 /	CGT AMARNATH *DEEP MID OFF*	HAZARE	172
...LLER	.K. R.	1211122441121111111111122111122141212141141214411111 /	BOWLED	MANKAD	86
...MENCE	R	11114111211111141111 /	CGT HAZARE	SOHONI.	27
...RVEY	.N.	2111112141441111211112 /	CGT MANKAD	HAZARE	32
...XTON	.S.	0 /	CGT IRANI	SOHONI	0
...GGERS	R. A.	1 /	CGT IRANI	SOHONI	1
...OLAND	.B.	11111 /	L. B. W	MANKAD	5
...RBERT	M	432412211411	NOT OUT		26
...HNSTON	W	11 /	CGT IRANI	AMARNATH	2

BRADMAN - MILLER 50 P·SHIP 43 MIN   BRADMAN - MILLER 100 P·SHIP 73 MIN
BRADMAN 50 IN 78 MIN   "   " 150 " 110 MIN
   " 100 " 132 MIN   "   " 200 IN 136 MIN.
   " 150 " 181 "   "   " 250 IN 152 MIN
MILLER 50 IN 98 MIN

How Out		
Byes 12		2
Leg Byes 11		
Wides		
No Balls		

	1	2	3	4	5	6	7	8	9	10		
Fall of Wickets -	11	31	283	287	346	346	346	348	366	380	TOTAL	380
Batsman Out - -	BROWN	ROGERS	MILLER	BRADMAN	HAMENCE	LOXTON	HARVEY	SAGGERS	DOOLAND	JOHNSTON		
" Not Out	ROGERS 3	BRADMAN 7	BRADMAN 168	HAMENCE 0	HARVEY 32	HARVEY 32	SAGGERS 0	DOOLAND 1	HERBERT 14	HERBERT 26		

BRADMAN SCORE 172 GIVES HIM HIS 100 CENTURY IN FIRST CLASS MATCHES.

"Bradman was a player who appears not once in a lifetime but once in the lifetime of a game."
(England cricket legend Denis Compton)

"TRUNK LINE CALL —" To Jolly Good Fellows — INDIA XI

THE TOAST IS OUR VISITORS!

MENU DONALD DUCK

Dinner
in honour of the visit of the
Indian Cricket Team

Menzies Hotel   3rd January, 1948

His form continued in the opening Test in Brisbane, with 185, and in the third Test at Melbourne in January.

No. 7.—D. G. Bradman

OFFICIAL MAGAZINE

AUSTRALIA
V.
ALL-INDIA

TESTS
1947-48

★

PRICE :
ONE SHILLING

BRADMAN, DOUBLE CENTURY

By H. A. de LACY

Not only did Don Bradman thrill the big crowd at the MCG today by completing a dual century, but he took his total for the season past 900.

LATE in the afternoon Bradman, that amazing run-making machine, developed a frictionless drive and, hitting fours at will, amassed another century. Following his 132 in the first innings, the Test can be rightly called Bradman's match.

This was his 103rd century in first-class cricket and his sixth for the season.

Bradman's scores this season have been 156, 12, 100, 172, 26, 185, 13, 132, and today's score—a total of 796 runs before to-day's innings began.

It is the fourth time that Bradman has made a century in each innings in first-class cricket, but the first time in a Test.

SCORE BOARD AT MCG

At MCG. Third Test. Third Day. India, 6/262 (Phadkar 52 not out, Rai Singh 2 not out) resumed first innings.

Official attendance, 48,674. Takings, £4994. Giving a grand total for the three days of 137,870, with takings £14,073—a bonanza for the Indians, who played for rain-soaked peppercorns at Brisbane and Sydney.

AUSTRALIA
First Innings 394

INDIA
First Innings
Mankad, c Tallon, b W. Johnston 116
Sarwate, c Tallon, b W. Johnston 36
Gul Mohamed, c and b Dooland 12
Hazare, c Tallon, b Barnes 17
Amarnath, lbw, b Barnes 0
Adhikari, st Tallon, b I. Johnston 26
Phadkar, not out 55
Singh, c Barnes, b I. Johnston 2
Rangnekar, c and b I. Johnston 6
Sen, b I. Johnston 4
Nayudu, not out 4
Extras 13
　　Nine wickets (dec.) for 291
Fall: 124, 145, 188, 188, 198, 260, 264, 280, 284.

BOWLING

	O.	M.	R.	W.
Lindwall	12	0	47	0
Miller	13	2	46	0
W. Johnston	12	0	33	2
I. Johnston	14	0	59	4
Dooland	12	1	68	1
Barnes	16	1	25	2

AUSTRALIA—Second Innings
I. Johnson, c Hazare, b Amarnath 0
Dooland, lbw, b Phadkar 6
W. Johnston, lbw, b Amarnath 3
Barnes, c Sen, b Amarnath 15
Bradman, not out 124
Morris, not out 90
Extras 4
　　Four wickets for 242
Fall: 1, 11, 13, 32.

Bowling (at 5.0).—Phadkar, 1/28; Armanath, 3/34; Mankad, 0/42; Hazare, 0/45; Sarwate, 0/7; Gul Mohamed, 0/1.

Bradman scored 132 and 127 not out, the first time he had completed the feat of a century in each innings in a Test.

MATCH *AUSTRALIA* V. *INDIA* – *3RD TEST*. 1st Jany. 1948.

Australian 1st INNINGS.   PLAYED AT *MELBOURNE*

BATSMAN	RUNS	HOW OUT	BOWLER	TOTAL
1 S. BARNES		Bowled	MANKAD	12
2 A. MORRIS		Bowled	AMARNATH	45
3 D. BRADMAN		L.B.W	PHADKAR	132
4 L. HASSETT		L.B.W	MANKAD	80
5 K. MILLER		L.B.W	MANKAD	29
6 R. HAMMENCE		Stp. SEN	AMARNATH	25
7 R. LINDWALL		Bowled	AMARNATH	26
8 D. TALLON		C. MANKAD	AMARNATH	2
9 B. DOOLAND		NOT OUT		21
10 I. JOHNSON		L.B.W	MANKAD	16
11 W. JOHNSTON		RUN OUT		3
			SUNDRY	1
BYES				
LEG BYES				
WIDE BALLS		TOTAL FOR INNINGS		394

MATCH *AUSTRALIA* V: *INDIA* (*3RD TEST*)

AUSTRALIA 2ND INNINGS.   PLAYED AT *MELBOURNE* 1st JAN. 1948

BATSMAN	RUNS	HOW OUT	BOWLER	TOTAL
1 I. JOHNSON		C. HAZARE	AMARNATH	0
2 B. DOOLAND		L.B.W	PHADKAR	6
3 W. JOHNSTON		L.B.W	AMARNATH	3
4 S.G. BARNES		C. SEN	AMARNATH	15
5 A. MORRIS		Not Out		100
6 D.G. BRADMAN		Not Out		127
7				
8				
9				
10				
11				
BYES				
LEG BYES				4
WIDE BALLS				
NO BALLS				
	4 Wickets (DECLARED)	TOTAL FOR INNINGS		255

Runs at the Fall of each Wicket	1 for	2 for	3 for	4 for	5 for	6 for	7 for	8 for	9 for	10 for	Total
	1	11	13	32							

SCORE	1	2	3	4	5	6	7	8	9	10	11	12	13	14	15	16	17	18	19	20	21	22	23
	31	32	33	34	35	36	37	38	39	40	41	42	43	44	45	46							
	61	62	63	64	65	66	67	68	69	70	71												
	91	92	93	94																			

DON BRADMAN NOT RETIRING

Will Play Indian XI

Don Bradman will continue to play first-class cricket next season.

Many enthusiasts expected Bradman, who is 38, to announce his retirement from Shield and Test cricket after the Fifth Test ended yesterday.

Bradman said last night that he hoped to play in some matches against the Indians in Australia next season.

Praise For English Team

He could not say yet whether he would go with the Australian team to England next year.

Bradman said: "Now that the final ball has been bowled this season, I feel there is much for which we should be most grateful.

"The English team endeared itself by its gallant efforts and modest bearing.

"It was fitting that the final game should have provided such thrilling cricket.

"It would like to see more matches played under conditions which give the bowler a real chance."

The English captain, Walter Hammond, congratulated Australia on winning the Ashes.

He said: "The clear-cut margin of three wins and two draws indicates Australia's superiority in all branches of the game.

"Australia will be strong for some years, but England will make a powerful challenge for the Ashes in 1948."

Stump Souvenir

Australia won the Fifth Test on the Sydney Cricket Ground yesterday by five wickets, five minutes before the day's play would have ended.

Another day was left for play, but Australia forced the scoring to avoid the risk of rain robbing her of victory.

Bradman, who was missed in slips when he was two, was largely responsible for Australia's win.

He went on to make 63.

Keith Miller made Test history when he souvenired a stump while running the final three runs.

Before the last over began he had promised Compton, English batsman, a stump.

He handed the stump over after the match ended.

Miller grabbed a ball in the first run; and when he pulled out a stump as he turned for the second run the English team looked amazed.

Police Protect Turf

When the third run had been completed, the players rushed for the remaining stumps, and 5000 spectators jumped the fence to inspect the wicket.

A dozen policemen protected the turf.

Early in the day, Australian wicket-keeper Don Tallon threw the ball to George Tribe at the end of the English innings.

Tribe leaves next week to play cricket in the Lancashire League.

Australia had to score 214 runs in 238 minutes to avoid play today.

Eighteen minutes before stumps Australia still needed 24.

Miller then hit Bedser with tremendous force twice—over mid-off's head and straight for the sightboard.

An on-drive off Wright flashed inches past Bedser's head at forward short leg.

Miller's hitting in the final ten minutes was the most powerful seen at the Sydney Cricket Ground since Warwick Armstrong's famous 158 in 1920.

Australia has won 60 of the 148 Tests in the series, which began in 1877. England has won 55, and 33 have been drawn.

LUCK FAVORS BRADMAN

EXCLUSIVE electric eye pictures of the crucial point in the last day's play of the Fifth Test yesterday—Bradman missed when he was two. 1. Bradman snicks the ball to Edrich in slips.

2. Edrich ready for an easy catch.

3. The ball goes through his hands, and falls to the ground. Bradman went on to score 63—and Australia won.

This cartoon appeared on the menu card when the Institute of Journalists gave a luncheon in London to the Australian cricketers. It carried the following caption: "News item, 1998.—It is expected that Don Bradman will retire from international cricket this year, as usual."

BRADMAN WILL RETIRE THIS YEAR

English Tour As Finale

DON BRADMAN, world's greatest cricketer, will retire from the game after the Test tour of England this year.

He will be playing his last first-class game in Australia in the fifth Test against India, which starts at the M.C.G. today.

He will then make himself available for the English tour, which starts next April, and leave the game completely at the end of the tour.

Nothing could stop his avalanche of runs. He followed with 201 in the first innings in the fourth Test in Adelaide, ending the series with 715 runs at an average of 178.75.

Bradman then prepared for his farewell to cricket - the 1948 tour of England.

Don Bradman has announced that he will not play cricket after the end of the English tour this year.

"Well, things are beginning to look brighter, all right. It says here Bradman's only coming over once more."

SIR ALEC BEDSER

(Champion England bowler, chairman of selectors, president of Surrey and one of the greatest English cricketers of the 20th century, in 21 years taking 1924 first-class wickets in 485 matches)

It is a privilege to help honour Don in his centenary year because he was not only a superb cricketer, selector and administrator, a true legend throughout the cricket world and a wonderful ambassador for Australia and sport, he also was one of my closest friends.

I was fortunate to strike up a friendship with Don the first time we met, which was during the 1946-47 series in Australia 61 years ago. We stayed pals for the next half century, and we were in regular contact either on the phone or by letter until his death. I miss him greatly.

Don was kind to me from the start. I didn't have much first-class experience when I arrived in Australia in 1946. Although I had taken 11 wickets in each of my first two Tests against India earlier that year, I'd played only 12 first-class games before that. I didn't bowl a ball for two years when I was in the RAF and serving in Dunkirk, Italy, North Africa and Austria, and I was 28 on my Test debut.

However playing Australia, particularly Don Bradman, was a different ball game altogether. I was in awe of Don, but he immediately made himself known to me and made me feel most welcome. When both teams caught the train from Brisbane after the First Test, Don walked down the carriage and gave us some beers.

I think he was a good human being, but he was selective about who he liked and trusted and he was a most private man. When you knew him - and, importantly, when he knew you - he was a most generous and friendly man.

When we were in Australia for the 1950-51 tour, I had the flu in Perth and was struggling considerably. Don was at Adelaide airport to meet me when the team arrived. The hotel rooms were not available until midday, so Don took me home to his place and put me to bed to rest and recuperate.

Like Don, I tried to put as much back into cricket as I gained from it. After my retirement in 1960, I served as an England selector for a record 23 years, and was chairman between 1969 and 1981. As well, I was deputy manager to the Duke of Norfolk to Australia in 1962-63, and manager in 1974-75 and 1979-80. I fell in love with Australia on my first visit in 1946-47 and that was the only place I wanted to go as manager, because I had such wonderful memories.

When I was manager, Don and I would play golf in the morning and then go to Adelaide Oval for the cricket. He was a far better golfer than me, but it gave us a chance to have private chats. Don seemed to me the sort of bloke who did not make friends easily, but if you were one, he was a true friend to you. I would never have done anything to compromise that friendship.

We actually had a lot in common after our playing days. He was a marvellous administrator and selector and he was knighted for his services to the game. I too was a long time selector and I was knighted in 1996, which gave us both a bit of fun - a boy from Bowral and a lad from Yorkshire.

My playing days against Don provided me with mixed success. We played in 10 Tests against each other, five in 1946-47 and another five in 1948.

It was a tough start when he made 187 at the Gabba and 234 in Sydney, and I captured 1-159 off 41 eight-ball overs in the first match and 1-153 off 46 eight-ball overs in the next. He followed with 79 and 49 in Melbourne, while I captured six wickets for the match.

I first captured his wicket when I bowled him for a duck in Adelaide. As I matured I learned how to swing the ball, and although my stock ball was a late in-swinger, I perfected what people today call a leg-cutter. I pitched one on leg and took his off stump. I'm not sure who was more surprised that day, him or me!

Don scored 12 and 63 in the second innings in Sydney, when I again claimed his scalp, when Len Hutton caught him in the covers. That was the start of a surprising sequence.

When Don made his farewell tour of 1948, I had him caught by Hutton again - but only after he made 138 in the first innings at Nottingham - and then I got him for his second duck in three Tests.

Then I dismissed him for 38 in the first innings at Lord's, and amazingly for a fifth straight time for 89 in the second innings. On the last four occasions Hutton was at a short leg gully.

Although Don was near 40 on his final tour he was an exceptional batsman. I'm glad I ran into him at the end, not at his peak. He didn't slash the bowling. He kept the ball on the ground and just kept scoring runs.

During 1946-47 I captured 16 wickets at 54.75 from 1971 balls, and in England it was 18 wickets at 38.22 from 1647 balls. I loved bowling and it is fair to say I was improving - and I improved a fair bit when Don retired!

I captured 69 wickets at an average of less than 17 during the next 10 Tests I played against Australia, and I was honoured to read that Don put me in his Best Ever XI, the only Englishman in his elite group.

The last time I spoke to Don was when he was close to the end. I rang him on his 90th birthday and we spoke regularly on the phone, and also corresponded by letter. I remember he wrote that it was no fun getting old and that I should make the most of my health and play golf for as long as I could. I had to give it up when I was 86 because of a really bad left knee. Turning 90 on July 4 this year reminded me of Don's warning about getting old.

One of my great regrets is that I didn't know Don needed only four more runs to finish with an average of 100, and that I wasn't bowling at the time. I would have bowled him a full toss to give him the boundary, because he was the closest thing to perfect and deserved a 100 average. It was a real pity that he missed by those four runs, although nobody knew it at the time.

Now we are celebrating his 100th year. It just shows that his influence on the game has not diminished. And it never will while the game is played, because he will always be the benchmark.

In March 1948, captained by the world's greatest batsman Don Bradman, the Australian Test team sailed for England. Their tour was to end some eight months later where the Australian team, not having lost a single match, were dubbed 'The Invincibles' - the greatest Australian side in history to leave our shores.

AUSTRALIAN TEST TEAM—1948

SELEC
AND
DO

1—231
crick

2—104
with
runs

3—High
cricl

4—Two
mat

5—Thr
day
193

6—Yo
300
cric

7—Ho
any
in

8—Mc
cri
tra

Back Row: R. N. Harvey, S. G. Barnes, R. R. Lindwall, R. Saggers, D. Ring, W. A. Johnston, E. R. H. Toshack, K. R. Miller, D. Tallon, S. Loxton.

Front Row: Mr. K. O. E. Johnson (Manager), R. Hamence, I. W. Johnson, A. L. Hassett (Vice-Capt.), D. G. Bradman (Captain), W. A. Brown, A. R. Morris, C. L. McCool, Mr. W. Ferguson (Scorer).

The 1948 team surpassed all records by winning four out of the five Tests and remaining undefeated throughout the tour. They remain the only side not to lose a match on tour.

D HIGHLIGHTS
CCORDS FROM
BRADMAN'S
CAREER

tches in first-class
for 27,851 runs.

ings in test cricket
h average of 99.94
r innings.

score in first-class
—452 not out.

ple centuries in test
s.

hundred runs in one
09 not out at Leeds,

st player to score
d 400 in first-class

highest aggregate
e series of tests. 9
0.

runs in first-cla
than any other Aus
.

In winning they were extremely convincing. In half their matches they won with an innings to spare, two by 10 wickets, one by 9 wickets, two by 8 wickets and one by 409 runs. Seven of the seventeen players completed 1000 runs. Eleven batsmen between them hit 50 centuries while the English batsmen could only manage 7. The Australian bowlers took 89 Test wickets while the English took 50.

1948
TESTS

AUSTRALIAN XI'S
ENGLISH TOUR

Proceed

P

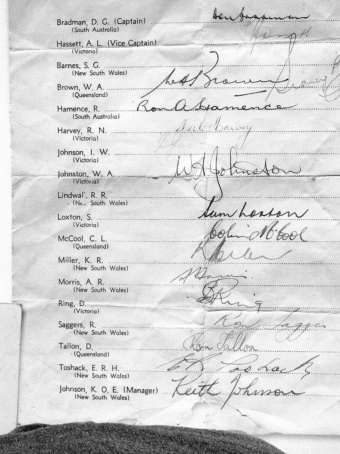

With the Compliments of
20th Australian Team to Great Britain 1948

Bradman, D. G. (Captain)
(South Australia)

Hassett, A. L. (Vice Captain)
(Victoria)

Barnes, S. G.
(New South Wales)

Brown, W. A.
(Queensland)

Hamence, R.
(South Australia)

Harvey, R. N.
(Victoria)

Johnson, I. W.
(Victoria)

Johnston, W. A.
(Victoria)

Lindwall, R. R.
(New South Wales)

Loxton, S.
(Victoria)

McCool, C. L.
(Queensland)

Miller, K. R.
(New South Wales)

Morris, A. R.
(New South Wales)

Ring, D.
(Victoria)

Saggers, R.
(New South Wales)

Tallon, D.
(Queensland)

Toshack, E. R. H.
(New South Wales)

Johnson, K. O. E. (Manager)
(New South Wales)

Don's family see him off on final tour

EGGS BEFORE RUNS is slogan of young John Bradman, who is a keen poultry farmer.

Wife has followed his cricket career since earliest matches

By FREDA YOUNG, staff reporter

When Don Bradman goes to England this month for his fourth series of English Test matches, bringing to a close the most spectacular career of cricket history, he will leave behind him three of his keenest fans . . . his attractive wife, 8-year-old son John, and daughter Shirley, aged 6.

MRS. DON BRADMAN and her children, Shirley and John, with the family pet, Sally, at the side gate of their home.

Bradman Says Good-Bye

This was a tour of a lifetime, a team of outstanding cricketers. Bradman was given the honour of a Knighthood bestowed upon him, a distinction never before awarded to a cricketer while still active in the game.

Bradman and Ian Johnson look down at lumpers who knocked off work to see them and other friends just before the Australian test team sailed on the "Strathaird" to England from Fremantle.

Australian Cricket Team, Bradman third from left.

"It may be that Bradman had not the sheer grace of Victor Trumper, the versatility on all wickets of Jack Hobbs, the annihilating unorthodoxy of Gilbert Jessop but for sheer ruthless efficiency no cricketer in the post-Grace era could compare with him." (E.W.Swanton, 1962).

Don Bradman's day case on the successful tour of England in 1948.

P&O. R.M.S. "Strathaird"
22,500 Tons.

QUIS NOS SEPARABIT

PENINSULAR AND ORIENTAL STEAM NAVIGATION COMPANY

AUSTRALIANS ARRIVE—
AND START THEIR PRACTICE TO-DAY

Clearly the Australians had a very strong side that dominated the entire English summer. Behind Bradman was a phenomenal batting combination, which amassed 15,120 runs for an average at just under 50 per wicket. In addition they scored the runs quickly in their desire to play entertaining cricket.

When one batsman failed there was always another to score the runs. Indeed for players down the order, it was common to hear good-humoured complaints that they were not getting a chance to bat!

The bowling was outstanding, with eight Australians bowling over 350 overs on the tour. England had no answer to the speed and accuracy of the pace men. Nor were they able to adjust to the spin. In addition to this the Australians rarely dropped a catch and under Bradman and Hassett's leadership kept a very tight, competitive and well thought out field.

THE BRADMAN BOOK

THE STORY AND REC[ORD] OF THE WORLD'S GR[EATEST] CRICKETER.

Compiled by "OUTFIELD"
Drawn by WILL MAHON[Y]

Dedicated to Don Bradman——Our Australian Cricketer

MIGHTY DON

Words and Music by
PEGGIE THORNE

Price
2s.

Australia so dominated the series that Lindsay Hassett, Bill Johnston,
Ray Lindwall, Arthur Morris and Don Tallon were named Wisden's five cricketers
of the year. Bradman, arriving in England, proudly introduced his team,
including the 'boy wonder' Neil Harvey (3rd from right).

THE SAME BRADMAN HERE AGAIN

His 107 had all the shots on parade

From CRAWFORD WHITE

WORCESTER, Thursday.

BRADMAN failed ! At least, Worcester folks think so. On each of the three previous occasions he played here he scored a double century.

His aggregate on this ground was 700, and his average 233.3. Today he had to content himself with a paltry 107.

But don't be misled by this early sign of "weakness." This was the same Bradman of yesteryear—of 1930, '34 and '38—the ruthless, competent, run-making machine, who is going to trouble us again throughout his last season of first-class cricket.

In the two and a half hours he was at the wicket he hit 15 fours and I saw no sign of age—he will be 40 this year—or injury. He was still down the pitch like a dancer to the slows and sometimes to the pacey Perks as well. His timing was perfect and his running between the wickets just as fast and fine as ten years ago.

Still on his pedestal

As ever, it was his amazing footwork that made it all seem so sure and easy and his incredible placing, which made the field always look full of holes. His cover-drive, the straight-drive, the pull, the leg-glance and the late cut were all on parade in full glory.

Yes, this was the Don of cricket, the greatest of them all still on his pedestal.

Bradman had only one team meeting on the ship en route to England and demanded the team play entertaining cricket. He showed the way with 107 in the opening match against Worcester - giving him four tour successes of 236, 206, 258 and 107. The team obliged too, scoring 721 runs in six hours at Essex.

THOSE AMAZING AUSTRALIAN CRICKETERS ARE AT IT AGAIN

721 RUNS: 6 HOURS

Bradman's men break world records

Most runs ever scored in one day

By JOHN WADHAM

IT'S those Australians again. This time Don and Co. treated our bowlers with such high disdain that ere the close they had scored 721 runs, and that, believe me, breaks all records for the highest number of runs scored in a first-class match in one day.

Back in 1909 Surrey set up a world record for one team when they cracked 645 for four against Hants at the Oval. And in 1920 the same Surrey (607 for four dec.) and Northants (59 for two) set up the all-time record of 666 for the highest number of runs in a match in any one day.

Look at the scores, you England bowlers, and weep. Four centuries, shoals of boundaries.

Once more Don the Magnifico stole the show. It wasn't cricket. It was an exhibition of strokes whose variety beggars description.

In all 187 streamed from his bat in 125 minutes. Boundaries? Why he had 32 of them, plus a 5.

"THE DON" DOUBLES UP—winded by a ball from R. Smith (Essex) at Southend. Australia's captain hit a dashing 187 in 125 minutes.

DON BRADMAN and his team of swashbuckling super-batsmen caught one of the scoreboards on the hop at Southend yesterday. When the score reached 700, the overworked staff couldn't find a " 7 " to fill the gap! The mammoth innings finished at 721, which is the highest number of runs ever made in one day, and easily beat the 666 scored by Surrey and Northants in 1920.

Long ago I used up all my superlatives to describe Don's batting, but now I suppose I shall have to dig up a few more. Ray and Peter Smith, Frank Vigar, Trevor Bailey and Eric Price all had a go at him, but he scored 42 in 20 minutes before going in for his lunch. Spin-bowler Vigar, in particular, was put off his feed, for Don smacked him for 20 off his first over.

It was Don's fourth innings this tour, his third century, the 105th of his career, and his first ever against Essex. When he came in Bill Brown already had 62 on the board, but Don closed the gap at a gallop. And later he also hit Price for 20 runs in one over!

It has always come easy to Don ever since he used to practise with a stump and a golf ball at Bowral and played his first match at Sydney in braces. He reached his hundred yesterday in 70 minutes, and with Brown put on 219 in 90 minutes.

The 1948 tour was a fine finale for Bradman. He enjoyed captaining an undefeated team that many would consider the strongest side to ever take the field. He felt he was leaving the Test arena with Australia in a strong position.

Bradman's favourite trophy, 'The Worcester Vase' presented to him for his extraordinary batting performances on each of his four tours.

Pre-view At Lord's

AT Lord's the Australians won the toss and the great crowd basking in the sunshine knew at once that the happiest team of batsmen that can ever have left the Dominion would revel in their strength.

Today's daybreak queues told of London's teeming enthusiasm for cricket. The sport holds its own. Indeed, with present-day holiday difficulties, top-level cricket in London has a special appeal.

If the Australians caught an impression of a lynx-eyed crowd today, they must have known why.

For the first time they were meeting most of the potential English team for the first Test at Nottingham on June 10. The spectators were having something like a pre-view.

The absence of any acrimony and untoward incidents in the matches the Australians have played so far has naturally made for their popularity.

Bradman is not only the world's greatest batsman. As the years have added to his skill, he has become the perfect cricket ambassador.

Their feats attracted unprecedented crowds to the Tests. Fans queued all night to be guaranteed entrance to Lord's for the 2nd Test. Bradman and the players were presented to the King and Queen and, of course, won the match.

All Night Queue To See Bradman

QUEUES FOR THE MCC v AUSTRALIANS' MATCH STRETCHED FOR HUNDREDS OF YARDS OUTSIDE LORD'S CRICKET GROUND HOURS BEFORE PLAY WAS DUE TO START TODAY.

With two hours still to wait special police, summoned to marshal the crowds, estimated at 30,000, were lined up.

THOUSANDS TURNED AWAY

THIRTY THOUSAND people who packed into Lord's today for a Test "preview" saw Australia's first wicket fall to the M.C.C. for 11 runs after 15 minutes. Then they saw Don Bradman bat.

Mounted police, called in to control the six-deep, half-mile queues of cricket enthusiasts waiting to see the match described the crowds as "the biggest since the war."

TURNED AWAY.—A microphone announcement that the ground was full dashed the hopes of many people who helped to form a queue 12 deep and hundreds of yards long outside Lord's today. Extra police were called out to control the huge crowds, the earliest of whom had waited all night. To relieve the congestion in the surrounding streets, the gates were opened early. Many of those in the picture were unable to hide their disappointment and shouted protests.

The King and Queen—and crowd of 30,000—at Lord's

BRADMAN'S MEN ARE PRESENTED

The Australians scored at a furious rate throughout and attracted big crowds wherever they played. They scored 350-plus in 24 innings. Bradman scored 11 centuries on tour - equalling Victor Trumpher's tally of 1902 - and only two shy of his own record 13 in 1938.

The grand old man of cricket celebrated his 40th birthday on August 27 and the Australians were only too keen to enjoy the moment, gathering in front of the pavilion at Lord's during a match against the Gentleman of England. Bradman celebrated too, scoring 150 in the match. He received so much mail as he toured England, fans could be guaranteed to find him - even with unconventional letters (above).

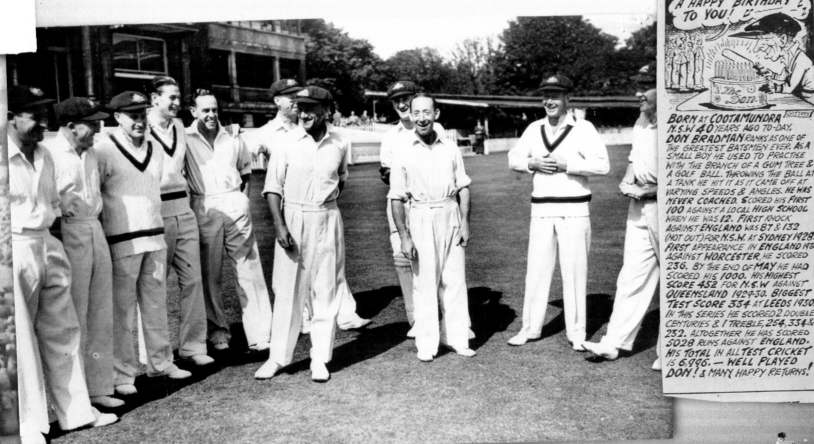

The tour was not all cricket. Bradman loved his golf and the theatre - and he was happy to pose for pictures, even with the constabulary (with Sam Loxton). Everywhere he ventured, even on a golf course, he was surrounded by fans, especially the young. And he was so relaxed that he smiled and laughed, by now totally in control of his destiny.

At the Coloseum Theatre, London, 1948 to see a performance of 'Annie Get Your Gun'.

At official functions mixing with royalty (seen below with Prince Philip) or showing youngsters the art of bowling, Bradman took time to savour the final adventure of his playing days.

Bradman with Prince Phillip.

Here is Don's dismissal in Australia's second innings at Trent Bridge - for 0!

England paceman Alec Bedser, a great friend of Bradman, was also an excellent foe. He dismissed Bradman for his first duck in a Test in England. Bedser dismissed Bradman five consecutive times in Tests - the first in the final Test of 1946/47 and ending with the second innings of the second innings of the 2nd Test at Lord's - which earned him a place in cricket history.

Australians Set 98 to Win

Lose 2 Wickets

SHOCKS IN TEST: DON—0

Bedser - Hutton Do It Again

Although out for his first "duck" in Test play in England, Don Bradman was not at all unhappy. Even at the time of his dismissal victory for his side was in sight, and shortly after four o'clock Australia had won the First Test by eight wickets.

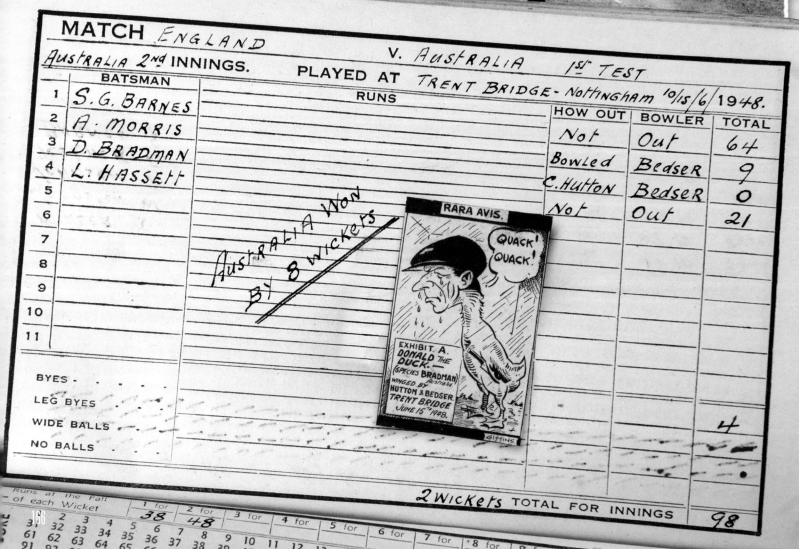

MATCH ENGLAND V. AUSTRALIA 1ST TEST				
Australia 2ND INNINGS. PLAYED AT TRENT BRIDGE - Nottingham 10/15/6/1948.				
	BATSMAN	RUNS	HOW OUT	BOWLER	TOTAL

	BATSMAN	RUNS	HOW OUT	BOWLER	TOTAL
1	S. G. BARNES		Not	Out	64
2	A. MORRIS		Bowled	Bedser	9
3	D. BRADMAN		C. Hutton	Bedser	0
4	L. HASSETT		Not	Out	21
5					
6					
7					
8					
9					
10					
11					

Australia Won By 8 Wickets

RARA AVIS.

QUACK! QUACK!

EXHIBIT. A. DONALD THE DUCK.— (SPECIES BRADMAN Australis) WINGED BY HUTTON & BEDSER TRENT BRIDGE JUNE 15th 1948.

BYES -
LEG BYES -
WIDE BALLS -
NO BALLS -

4

2 WICKETS TOTAL FOR INNINGS   98

Runs at the Fall of each Wicket	1 for	2 for	3 for	4 for	5 for	6 for	7 for	8 for	9 for
	38	48							

Bradman in off drive position at Lord's on the 1948 UK Tour.

SPORTING LIFE Cricket Guide

AUSTRALIAN TEAM'S 1948 TOUR OF ENGLAND

Programme of matches

107 April 28. Worcester at Worcester.
81 May 1. Leicester at Leicester.
May 5. Yorkshire at Bradford. 33·173* July 22-27. FOURTH TEST at Leeds.
146 May 8. Surrey at the Oval. 62 July 28. Derbyshire at Derby.
May 12. Cambridge Uni. at Cambridge. July 31. Glamorgan at Swansea.
187 May 15. Essex at Southend. 31·13* August 4. Warwickshire at Birming-
May 19. Oxford Univ. at Oxford. ham.
98 May 22. MCC at Lord's. 28·133* August 7. Lancashire at Old Trafford.
11·43 May 26. Lancashire at Old Trafford. August 11. Durham at Sunderland.*
86 May 29. Notts at Trent Bridge. 0 August 14-19. FIFTH TEST at the
June 2. Hants at Southampton. Oval.
109 June 5. Sussex at Hove. 65 August 21. Kent at Canterbury.
138+0 June 10-15. FIRST TEST at Trent 150 August 25. Gentlemen at Lord's.
Bridge. August 28. Somerset at Taunton.
June 16. Northants at Northampton. 143 Sept. 1. South of England at Hastings.
54·36 June 19. Yorkshire at Sheffield. Sept. 8. Leveson-Gower's XI at Scar-
38·89 June 24-29. SECOND TEST at Lord's. borough.
128 June 30. Surrey at the Oval. 153 Sept. 13. Scotland at Edinburgh.*
July 3. Gloucester at Bristol. 27 Sept. 17. Scotland at Aberdeen.*
7·30 July 8-13. THIRD TEST at Old 123 *Two-day matches, not reckoned in
Trafford. No. first-class averages of tour.

6 July 17. Middlesex at Lord's.

SPORTING LIFE, May, 1948   Page Twenty-one

Bradman scored 138 in the first innings at Nottingham when Australia won by eight wickets. He was out for a duck in the second innings, having fallen both times to Alec Bedser. He contributed 38 and 89 in the 409 run win at Lord's, again falling both innings to Bedser.

Bradman managed seven and 30 not out in the rain interrupted drawn third Test at Manchester.

He led from the front in the classic victory at Leeds, when Australia required 404 on the final day and achieved the mammoth task in 114.1 overs, with 15 minutes to spare.

After scoring 33 in the first innings, Bradman remained unconquered on 173 after sharing a second wicket partnership of 301 with Arthur Morris (182).

Bradman and Morris resuming during their historic run chase at Leeds.

AUSTRALIA WINS FOURTH TEST

Morris, Bradman Make Fast-Scoring Centuries

Daily Telegraph Service and A.A.P.

HEADINGLEY, Tuesday.—Australia won the Fourth Test today by seven wickets and with 15 minutes to spare.

England had set Australia 404 in 345 minutes for victory. Morris (182) and Bradman (173 n.o.) made the win possible with fast scoring.

DON HITS OUT IN VICTORY BID

BRADMAN PLAYS HIS LAST TEST MATCH AT HEADINGLEY : The Australian skipper, now nearing the moment of retiring, playing this chanceful but forceful innings in the Fourth Test where, with Morris as his partner, he flogged the English bowling, almost in the old grand manner. He has never seemed so purposeful, although a little of his former magic has gone with the year.

Harvey, 19, Scores Century In Great Test Debut

THE DON GETS A GREAT OVATION

Bradman was next man in and he was escorted through the crowd of people who lined his way to the wicket from the pavilion, by a police sergeant.

This was his farewell innings on the Headingley ground, and he was given a wonderful ovation, the crowd standing and clapping him all the way to the wicket. It was a grand tribute to a great player, and one that Bradman is likely to remember the rest of his life.

Neil Harvey began his Test career in England in astonishing fashion. The 19-year-old left hander went to the crease with Australia 3-68 (Bradman out for 33) and produced a quality innings of 112. He then had the satisfaction of hitting the final boundary of the Test to register an historic win.

Morris And Bradman With Great Stand Of 301 Force Thrilling Test Win

LEEDS, July 27.—Australia won the fourth Test at Headingley to-day by seven wickets but with only 13 minutes to spare. The tourists had been set to get 404 runs in 345 minutes.

Brilliant batting by Morris (182) and Bradman (173 not out), who added 301 for the second wicket, put an end to England's hopes. Neil Harvey, who came in when only eight runs were needed, made the winning stroke with a boundary.

It was Bradman's 19th century in Tests against England.

Norman Yardley, after using the heavy roller, allowed England's innings to continue for only a few minutes before declaring at 8-365.

YARDLEY'S RIGHT TO USE HEAVY ROLLER

BRADMAN ACCEPTS ENGLAND'S CHALLENGE

GREAT STAND WITH MORRIS

Two Centuries in Sparkling Play

Morris-Bradman Revel in

Big Aussie Victory Bid

150 RUNS SCORED IN 85 MINUTES

By "THE SPECIALIST"

TEST EXCITEMENT REACHED FEVER PITCH AT HEADINGLEY THIS AFTERNOON AS MORRIS AND BRADMAN LASHED THE ENGLAND BOWLING IN A BOLD AUSTRALIAN BID FOR VICTORY.

So completely were the batsmen masters that the first 85 minutes of their partnership produced 150 runs.

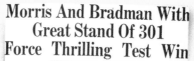

Bradman and Arthur Morris shared many outstanding partnerships, but none more memorable than in the second innings of the 4th Test at Headingley. Set 404 runs to win after England batted for 15 minutes on the final day, they shared a union of 301 to ensure a most unlikely victory.

England				
L. Hutton b Lindwall	81	c Bradman b Johnson	57
C. Washbrook c Lindwall b Johnston	143	c Harvey b Johnston	65
W. J. Edrich c Morris b Johnson	111	lbw b Lindwall	54
A. V. Bedser c and b Johnson	79	c Hassett b Miller	17
D. C. S. Compton c Saggers b Lindwall	23	c Miller b Johnston	66
J. F. Crapp b Toshack	5	b Lindwall	18
N. W. D. Yardley b Miller	25	c Harvey b Johnston	7
K. Cranston b Loxton	10	c Saggers b Johnston	0
T. G. Evans c Hassett b Loxton	3	not out	47
J. C. Laker c Saggers b Loxton	4	not out	15
R. Pollard not out	0		
B 2, l-b 8, w 1, n-b 1	12	B 4, l-b 12, n-b 3	19
	496	Eight wkts., dec.	365

Australia				
A. R. Morris c Cranston b Bedser	6	c Pollard b Yardley	182
A. L. Hassett c Crapp b Pollard	13	c and b Compton	17
D. G. Bradman b Pollard	33	not out	173
K. R. Miller c Edrich b Yardley	58	lbw b Cranston	12
R. N. Harvey b Laker	112	not out	4
S. J. Loxton b Yardley	93		
I. W. Johnson c Cranston b Laker	10		
R. R. Lindwall c Crapp b Bedser	77		
R. A. Saggers st Evans b Laker	5		
W. A. Johnston c Edrich b Bedser	13		
E. R. H. Toshack not out	12		
B 9, l-b 14, n-b 3	26	B 6, l-b 9, n-b 1	16
	458	Three wkts.	404

Australia Bowling

	O.	M.	R.	W.	O.	M.	R.	W.
Lindwall	38	10	79	2	26	6	84	2
Miller	17.1	2	43	3	21	5	53	1
Johnston	38	13	86	1	29	5	95	4
Toshack	35	6	112	1				
Loxton	26	4	55	3	10	2	29	0
Johnson	33	9	89	2	21	2	85	1
Morris	5		20					

England Bowling

	O.	M.	R.	W.	O.	M.	R.	W.
Bedser	31.2	4	92	3	21	2	56	0
Pollard	38	6	100	3	22	6	55	0
Cranston	14	1	51	0	7.1	0	28	1
Edrich	3	0	19	0				
Laker	30	8	113	3	32	11	93	0
Yardley	17	6	38	2	13	1	44	1
Compton	3	0	15	0	15	3	82	0
Hutton					4	1	30	0

FALL OF WICKETS

ENGLAND—First Innings:

1	2	3	4	5	6	7	8	9
168	268	423	426	447	473	486	490	496

ENGLAND—Second Innings:

1	2	3	4	5	6	7	8
129	129	232	260	277	278	293	330

AUSTRALIA—First Innings:

1	2	3	4	5	6	7	8	9
13	65	68	189	294	329	344	355	403

AUSTRALIA—Second Innings:

1	2	3
57	358	396

Umpires: F. Chester and H. G. Baldwin.

Bradman Goes For Those 404 Runs

England

Batsman	1st Innings		2nd Innings	
L. Hutton	c Tallon b Lindwall	30	c Tallon b Miller	64
J. G. Dewes	b Miller	1	b Lindwall	10
W. J. Edrich	c Hassett b Johnston	3	b Lindwall	28
D. C. S. Compton	c Morris b Lindwall	4	c Lindwall b Johnston	39
J. F. Crapp	c Tallon b Miller	0	b Miller	9
N. W. D. Yardley	b Lindwall	7	c Miller b Johnston	9
A. Watkins	lbw b Johnston	0	c Hassett b Ring	2
T. G. Evans	b Lindwall	1	b Lindwall	8
A. V. Bedser	b Lindwall	0	b Johnston	0
J. A. Young	b Lindwall	0	not out	3
W. E. Hollies	not out	0	c Morris b Johnston	0
	B 6	6	B 9, l-b 4, n-b 3	16
		52		**188**

Australia

S. G. Barnes c Evans b Hollies	61	R. R. Lindwall c Edrich b Young ... 9
A. R. Morris run out	196	D. Tallon c Crapp b Hollies 31
D. G. Bradman b Hollies	0	D. Ring c Crapp b Bedser 9
A. L. Hassett lbw b Young	37	W. A. Johnston not out 0
K. R. Miller st Evans b Hollies	5	B 4, l-b 2, n-b 3 9
R. N. Harvey c Young b Hollies	17	
S. J. Loxton c Evans b Edrich	15	**389**

Australia Bowling

	O.	M.	R.	W.		O.	M.	R.	W.
Lindwall	16.1	5	20	6		25	3	50	3
Miller	8	5	5	2		15	6	22	2
Johnston	16	4	20	2		27.3	12	40	4
Loxton	2	1	1	0		10	2	16	0
Ring						28	13	44	1

England Bowling

	O.	M.	R.	W.
Bedser	31.2	9	61	1
Watkins	4	1	19	0
Young	51	16	118	2
Hollies	56	14	131	5
Compton	2	0	6	0
Edrich	9	0	38	1
Yardley	5	1	7	0

FALL OF WICKETS

ENGLAND—First Innings:

1	2	3	4	5	6	7	8	9
2	10	17	23	35	42	45	45	47

ENGLAND—Second Innings:

1	2	3	4	5	6	7	8	9
20	64	125	153	164	167	178	181	188

AUSTRALIA—First Innings:

1	2	3	4	5	6	7	8	9
117	117	226	243	265	304	332	359	389

Umpires: D. Davies and H. G. Baldwin.

Bradman b. Hollies 0.

The historic win at Leeds paved the way for Bradman's farewell and expectations were sky-high from the adorning English crowd. On a green and moist pitch at The Oval, Australia dismissed England for only 52 and late in the day Bradman strode to the wicket to a rousing ovation, with the English players giving him three cheers and a chorus of "For he's a jolly good fellow". He was bowled second ball by Eric Hollies for a duck.

Bradman's last Test match appearance has probably become one of the most talked about moments in cricket history.

Hollies was to write later, "I don't think Don saw it properly. He seemed to have tears in his eyes."

Bradman's great mate Alec Bedser commented: "One of my great regrets is that I didn't know Don needed only four more runs to finish with an average of 100 and that I wasn't bowling at the time. I would have bowled him a full toss to give him the boundary, because he was the closest thing to perfect and deserved a 100 average."

Bradman missed a Test total of 7000 runs by just 4 runs, (finishing with 6996 total Test runs), which would have given him a Test career average of 100, instead of 99.94.

Bradman wrote in Farewell to Cricket, 1950, "I dearly wanted to do so well. It was not to be. That reception had stirred my emotions very deeply and made me anxious - a dangerous state of mind for any batsman to be in. I played the first ball from Hollies, though not sure I really saw it. The second was a perfect length googly which deceived me."

Batting with Bradman at the time was Arthur Morris, who went on make 196 runs. Keith Miller was in the dressing room when Bradman returned from the crease, and according to Miller, when Bradman was unbuckling his pads, he simply said "Gee whiz, fancy doing that!"

England All Out 52—Don A "Duck"

(TRUTH'S SPECIAL SERVICE.)

THE OVAL, Saturday.—After Yardley had won the toss, England collapsed dramatically in the Fifth Test today and were all out after two and a half hours for 52—the lowest Test score ever recorded by them in England.

The first wicket fell five minutes after play began and from then on there was a continuous procession of batsmen making their way dejectedly back to the pavilion.

Hutton played a valiant lone-hand innings. scoring 30 of England's total. He was the last man dismissed, and was unfortunate not to join R. Abel, who remains the only Englishman to carry his bat through a Test innings.

The innings was a personal triumph for Australian fast bowler Ray Lindwall who took 6 wickets (four bowled) for 20 runs. Miller took 2 for 5.

Today's collapse was a particularly bitter pill for the English as in the corresponding game on the last tour of England in 1938 England compiled the record Test score of 903 for 7 wickets and beat Australia by the record margin of an innings and 579 runs.

Of the three players who represented England in that game who played for England today, two recognised batsmen failed utterly on both occasions—Edrich 12 in '38 and 3 today, Compton 1 in 1938 and 4 today—while the third, Hutton, scored the world's individual record Test score of 364 in 1938 and today proved the only prop in the English side.

England's lowest score in all Anglo-Australian Tests is 45, recorded at Sydney in 1886.

Their previous lowest in England stood at 53, made at Leeds in 1888.

Lowest Test score ever recorded was Australia's 36 at Birmingham in 1902.

The Australian openers, Morris and Barnes, passed the English total before tea in 57 minutes.

Morris and Barnes doubled the English total before Barnes was caught behind off Hollies, the Warwickshire spinner, who had taken eight for 107 against the tourists early this month—including Bradman and Harvey.

Bradman, playing in his final Test, received a magnificent ovation as he walked out to bat, the entire oval standing as a man and cheering him all the way. Yardley met him near the crease, and, after shaking his hand, called for three cheers from the English team.

The day of sensations, however, had not ended. After blocking the first ball he received from Hollies, Don went forward to the next and was completely beaten and bowled. Bradman returned to the pavilion as big a grin as he had when he left it.

Stumps score was two for 152—Morris 77, Hassett 10.

Arthur Morris scored a magnificent 196 in the difficult conditions to guide Australia to victory and a crushing 4-nil series result.

MORRIS

THANKS FOR THE MEMORY MR. BRADMAN!

But *YOU* Will Remember This Test Match, Too

By VIVIAN JENKINS

ENGLAND'S fifth Test match of 1948 will be remembered not for Don Bradman's farewell alone. As though determined to give him the send-off he deserved, the Australian team went berserk with the most astonishing bowling and fielding performance for 60 years.

In two and a half hazy, crazy hours they shot out the cream of England's batting for a paltry 52 runs, our second lowest score since Tests between the two countries started and the lowest-ever score in a Home Test match. "The Don" was like an excited schoolboy in the field, startled by the success which even he could hardly have expected, but when he came in to bat the unbelievable happened : he was out for a "duck."

To watching eyes, accustomed as they are to seeing England's cricketers in the doldrums, the whole thing took on the appearance of some fantastic ballet.

Magnified Australian cricketers, with huge yellow eyes in the middle of their green caps, cavorted and whirled in a frenzy of destruction.

Wickets hurtled through the air like flailing boomerangs, gargantuan arms stretched out to take unimagined catches. Round and round the mad vortex went, while in the centre the England batsmen did a pitiful halting little dance of death.

Only when a batsman left, spat out from the maw of destruction, did the wild fandango subside.

Then came another to take his place, and all lapsed into unreality again.

Here they were, the cream of England's cricketers, gods in their own sphere and county boundaries.

Edrich, Compton, Crapp, Yardley, and the pride of Glamorgan, 26-year-old Alan Watkins, the one-time baker's boy, playing in his first match for England.

So much for unsubstantial earthly fame. Along came a fiend incarnate. Ray Lindwall, Australia's fast bowler, belching unseen flame to cast them into limbo and destruction.

Six wickets fell to him, four clean bowled, by batsmen who felt a wind pass by, and that was all.

Only Len Hutton stuck it out—"our Len" of the far-flung Yorkshire acres, with a broad, solid puddeny bat which seemed to say: "Somebody must be mad round here, but not I."

Last out, while unbelievable things happened at the other end. Hutton batted 2¼ hours for 30 runs.

Young Watkins carried a piece of white heather from his wife for luck. But it was like trying to stop a runaway train with a walking-stick.

Some said Yardley should have put Australia in to bat when he won the toss. "What have we been waiting for all this rain for ? " they said.

But Yardley was quite right. There was nothing wrong with the wicket. "Slow and easy" was the general verdict, but the trouble was the bowling "fast and far too difficult."

Bradman would give no verbal farewell message to the Press for the British public. "My contract with the Australian Board of Control prevents it," he said.

While all this was going on Bradman himself chuckled and chortled, clapped his players on the back and rubbed his hands in huge delight. What a play, and what a producer !

Stayed to Wonder

Thus the one-time unknown boy from the bush, son of a carpenter, "Bowral's Boy Beauty," the "Cootamundra Kid," saw the dream-end of his career beginning to arrive.

"It is a trait in my make-up which it is quite impossible to explain, that I am almost a total stranger to that species of nervousness common to most people wherever involved in an unusual happening." (Bradman on his lack of anxiety in new or stressful situations - an emotion that unfortunately deserted him in his final Test innings).

ENGLAND		First Innings		Second Innings	
1 Hutton, L.	Yorkshire	c Tallon, b Lindwall	30	c Tallon, b Miller	64
2 J. G. Dewes	Middlesex	b Miller	1	b Lindwall	10
3 W. J. Edrich	Middlesex	c Hassett, b Johnston	3	b Lindwall	28
4 Compton, D.	Middlesex	c Morris, b Lindwall	4	c Lindwall, b Johnston	39
5 Crapp, J. F.	Gloucestershire	c Tallon, b Miller	0	b Miller	0
6 N. W. D. Yardley	Yorkshire	b Lindwall	7	c Miller, b Johnston	9
7 Watkins, A.	Glamorgan	lbw b Johnston	0	c Hassett, b Ring	2
8 Evans, T. G.	Surrey	b Lindwall	1	b Lindwall	8
9 Bedser, A. V.	Middlesex	b Lindwall	0	b Johnston	0
10 Young, J. A.		not out	0	not out	3
11 Hollies, W. E.	Warwickshire	b Lindwall	0	c Morris, b Johnston	0
		B6, l-b, w, n-b	6	B9, l-b4, w, n-b 3	16
		Total	52	Total	188

FALL OF THE WICKETS

| 1-2 | 2-10 | 3-17 | 4-23 | 5-35 | 6-42 | 7-45 | 8-45 | 9-47 | 10-52 |
| 1-20 | 2-64 | 3-125 | 4-153 | 5-164 | 6-167 | 7-178 | 8-181 | 9-188 | 10-188 |

Bowling Analysis	First Innings						Second Innings					
	O.	M.	R.	W.	Wd.	N.b.	O.	M.	R.	W.	Wd.	N.b.
Lindwall	16.1	5	20	6			25	3	50	3		
Miller	8	5	5	2			15	6	22	2		1
Johnston	16	4	20	2			27.3	12	40	4		
Loxton							10	2	16	0		
Ring							28	13	44	1		2

AUSTRALIA		First Innings		Second Innings	
1 S. G. Barnes	N.S.W.	c Evans, b Hollies	61		
2 A. R. Morris	N.S.W.	run out	196		
*3 D. G. Bradman	S.A.	b Hollies	0		
4 A. L. Hassett	Victoria	lbw b Young	37		
5 K. R. Miller	N.S.W.	st Evans, b Hollies	5		
6 R. N. Harvey	Victoria	c Young, b Hollies	17		
7 S. R. E. Loxton	Victoria	c Edrich, b Young	15		
8 R. R. Lindwall	N.S.W.	c Crapp, b Hollies	9		
‡8 D. Tallon	Queensland	not out	31		
10 W. A. Johnston	Victoria	c Crapp, b Bedser	0		
11 D. Ring	Victoria	c Crapp, b Bedser	9		
		B4, l-b2, w, n-b 3	9	B, l-b, w, n-b	
		Total	389	Total	

FALL OF THE WICKETS

| 1-117 | 2-117 | 3-226 | 4-243 | 5-265 | 6-304 | 7-332 | 8-359 | 9-389 | 10-389 |
| 1- | 2- | 3- | 4- | 5- | 6- | 7- | 8- | 9- | 10- |

Bowling Analysis	First Innings						Second Innings					
	O.	M.	R.	W.	Wd.	N.b.	O.	M.	R.	W.	Wd.	N.b.
Bedser (A.V.)	31.2	9	61	2								
Watkins	4	1	19	0								
Young	51	16	118	2								
Hollies	56	14	131	5								
Compton D.	2	0	6	0								
Edrich	9	1	38	1								
Yardley	5	1	7	0								

*Captain   ‡Wkt.-keeper

Umpires—H. G. Baldwin & D. Davies

Toss won by ENGLAND

Result—Australia won by an innings and 149 runs.

HOURS OF PLAY for 5 days 11.30—6.30   Lunch 1.30

CUSHIONS MAY BE HIRED 6d. EACH PER DAY

LIST OF FIXTURES ON BACK OF CARD.

Printed on the Ground by the Surrey County Cricket Club Printing Department.

England 52; Bradman bowled for duck

From Arthur Mailey

London, Saturday.—After England had been sensationally dismissed for 52 in the fifth Test match against Australia at Kennington Oval today—Lindwall taking 6/20—Australia passed the English score without loss.

Barnes went for 61. Then Bradman, after receiving a tremendous greeting from the crowd and the English players in his last Test match. was bowled second ball.

ENGLAND'S total was the lowest made by England in a Test at home. Previous lowest was 53, made at Lord's in 1888. Australia's smallest score in England was 36—at Birmingham in 1902.

Ring was included in the Australian team with Ian Johnson twelfth man, but the spinner did not bowl. It was an all-pace attack led by Lindwall which caused the damage.

Half-hour delay

Play began at noon—half an hour late—and Yardley, winning the toss, decided to bat.

Disaster came early to England when Dewes, 21-year-old Cambridge lefthander, was bowled in Miller's first over.

Twenty minutes later Edrich was caught at square leg. Soon after a similar shot brought the dismissal of Compton, and at lunch the score was 4 for 29.

The early rebuff to England's hopes was not completely caused by the state of the pitch. Bumping deliveries could have been left alone, and it is possible the reappearance of Barnes at "suicide point" affected the batsmen.

He stood as close as he was when Pollard struck him at Manchester, keeping his provided to be back at "the old address."

At lunch critics were condemning Yardley for electing to bat, but I believe Bradman would have done the same. When the sun shone soon after the start there was no discernible difference in the pitch, although it was expected to play a few tricks.

The plain fact is the early batsmen expected the pitch to be difficult and batted nervously. Hutton did not seem perturbed, and the early debacle was due to bad batting against efficient bowling.

After lunch Lindwall took five of the six wickets which fell in rapid succession. His success was due to sheer speed.

The end of the tour was a highlight for all, with Bradman and the team
visiting Balmoral Castle as guests of the King and Queen.

**Gathering at Balmoral
Castle, Scotland**

**Bradman with King George VI and other
cricketers and Royals at Balmoral.**

ARTHUR MORRIS

(Champion opening batsman and 1948 Invincible who scored 3533 runs at 46.48 in 46 Tests)

I was lucky enough to share one of the Test cricket's most memorable partnerships with Don when we steered Australia to an historic victory against England at Leeds in 1948. We scored 404 runs in less than a day to win the Ashes.

Unfortunately, I also hold a unique place in Don's cricketing life - I was at the other end when he made that famous last innings duck at The Oval that series which deprived him of an average of more than 100.

Naturally I prefer to recall our successes. Our partnership at Leeds re-wrote history and it was totally unexpected, especially by the English press who had predicted an England triumph that day.

This was only my 13th Test, and Don's second last of 52. I had already scored four centuries against England (three at home the previous summer and another at Lord's in the second Test) and I have never batted as well as I did this day to score 182, although the only press clippings I recall stated that I was lucky!

England made it really tough. They batted for five minutes on the final day (it was a sixth day pitch because we didn't play on Sundays) and Lindsay Hassett was out early for 17. We had six hours less 15 minutes to make 404. Don and I made it through to lunch, and then accelerated in the middle session and suddenly we started to think about a win. We made the runs with 15 minutes to spare. It was a great feeling because such a chase had never been achieved before.

Don had contributed an unbeaten 173, which, when you think about it, was a tremendous achievement for a batsman only a month shy of his 40th birthday. He rose to the challenge, and we shared a second wicket partnership of 301. It was a result that guaranteed the Ashes, and was the final of his 29 centuries.

It was, however, a build-up to his grand finale and English cricket lovers packed The Oval to pay homage. Our partnership that day lasted two balls - and the Don's career was over.

The thing I remember most about the moment was the silence that immediately followed his dismissal. It was like being at a funeral.

The crowd had cheered him all the way to the wicket, and the English players raised their caps and gave him three cheers and a round of He's A Jolly Good Fellow. The noise was unbelievable in this build-up. And then, when Eric Hollies bowled him second ball, there was deadly silence. As usual, Don simply tucked the bat under his arm and walked off. I think everyone was stunned: me, the English players, the crowd, and our boys in the dressing rooms.

The thing was that we had bowled England out for 52 and Sid Barnes and I had put on 117 for the opening wicket, so you knew Don wouldn't get a second innings, and his Test career was all over.

I must admit I was surprised he came in so late in the day. Probably it was because he didn't want to disappoint the capacity crowd who had come to see him. I thought he would have sent in a night watchman, but Don never wanted to let down the audience when he was playing.

I just stood there and took it all in. I figured I had better get plenty of runs now that Don was out. I finished with 196. There was plenty of juice in the pitch, as you can gather from England's first innings of 52, Barnes' contribution of 61 and the next highest score was 37 by Lindsay Hassett.

The papers the next day were all about Bradman. I think someone mentioned somewhere that I batted well, but nobody was interested in my 196 that followed my 182 at Leeds - everyone wanted to talk and read about Don.

That's the way it was. Don Bradman was a cricketing god. And on this his farewell tour he was a celebrity like I've never seen before or since.

It is amazing to think that in 14 Tests I played with Don Bradman, I was at the other end when he was out for a duck - twice! The other occasion was at the Adelaide Oval when Alec Bedser bowled him in our first innings.

I really did enjoy the best and worst of times with him in the centre. But I certainly can't complain. After all I first met him when I was eight years old and there I was partnering the great man in Ashes combat. When I was that young lad, Bradman was working for a sporting goods company and he visited my father, a teacher at Dungog. I walked up, without shoes or socks, put out my hand, said hello Mr Bradman, and shook his hand. Little did I know that some years later we would be playing cricket together for Australia.

My first real meeting with him was in 1946 when I played for an Australian XI against the MCC, scored a hundred and pretty much went straight into the Test team. Even then, you knew Bradman was great. Not like he was in the 1930s when he could put the ball anywhere he wanted, but still good enough to score two centuries in the 1948 series.

And this was an extraordinary time for Bradman. He was a living legend and the crowds were enormous and very generous. England had been bombed badly during the war, but the cricket gave everyone a chance to believe things would get back to the good old days - and the bonus was Bradman's farewell adventure. Contrary to some belief, this was not a five-star trip for us. We ate the food the locals ate and it was pretty tough going as that nation recovered from the ravages of war.

We were very lucky to be together for five weeks on the ship going to England because we bonded as a group. Going throughout undefeated didn't really come onto the radar until very late in the tour. We retained the Ashes after the fourth Test win at Leeds, and that was our objective. Ian Johnson and I headed to London immediately after that to watch the Olympics, but from what I gather we were lucky to win the next game because most of the blokes were extremely hung over from the Ashes win celebrations.

It was only late in the tour, the last couple of games, that we set our sights of going through undefeated. It was a wonderful achievement: 34 games in all sorts of conditions, uncovered wickets, no helmets and plenty of challenges from some quality opposition. But we were a great team. We had the batsmen and the bowlers, and the fieldsmen. Neil Harvey was the best all-rounder fieldsman I've ever seen - on the fence, in the slips or at silly point. Sam Loxton had a great arm from the outfield. Bradman was a superb outfielder as a kid - he ran so fast, and had a great arm.

And he was a great captain. You could go to him with a problem and trust him implicitly. He was always there. He would discuss anything with you about cricket, although you had to approach him. He didn't want to interfere and reserved his thoughts until you sought him out.

Yet it was off the field that he excelled as a captain. A lot of people can captain a champion team, but it is how you handle yourself and other people off the field that is vital. He led by example, both on and off the field. He was tough on the field, make no mistake about that.

And he made sure the team was together and focused on our goals. Any suggestion that he was aloof is nonsense. He would always have breakfast with us and dinner, unless some of us went to the local pub.

Hassett, who was vice-captain, led the way. Don didn't come. However there were two reasons for that. He would stay back in his room answering hundreds of letters that arrived every day - he always answered every letter. And the most important thing was that he simply couldn't go the local with the rest of us because he would have been mobbed. He was a celebrity. He couldn't walk down the street without a crowd gathering, so imagine his chances of having an ale in peace with the boys at a local pub!

Don also spent a lot of time preparing for his seemingly endless speaking engagements. He gave a great speech. He was so proud to represent Australia, to be a role model.

Don had a photographic memory. One day he moved me about five yards finer at square leg when Ray Lindwall was bowling to Denis Compton, who immediately pulled a ball hard and fast straight to me. When I asked what had prompted him to make the adjustment to the perfect position for the catch, he said he recalled Compton hooked on that line during the 1938 tour when facing Ernie McCormack.

But he hated to be wrong. Years later I recalled the event, but Don said it was at Lord's and I believed it was at The Oval. Anyway there was a thought of a $100 bet, but I backed off because of his famed memory. I eventually settled on a $15 bet, being positive it was at The Oval, and sure enough I was right. A cheque arrived in the mail the following week - for $10.

DON SAYS HIS TEST GOODBYE

Greatest Of All Players

Bradman leads the Australian Team out for the very last time in English Test matches.

A GREAT INNINGS ENDS

"Nothing can alter the figures which will appear in black and white in the record books, but they cannot record the spirit which permeated the side, the courage and fighting qualities of the players, for those things cannot be measured. They were on a very high plane." (Bradman commenting on the 1948 Invincibles)

Bradman finished the Test series with 508 runs at an average of 72.57 - not bad for a man on the verge of 40.

During his Ashes career he scored 468 at 66.85 in 1928/29; 974 at 139.14 in 1930, 396 at 56.57 in 1932/33, 758 at 94.75 in 1934, 810 at 90 in 1936/37 and 680 at 97.14 in 1946/47 and 508 at 72.57 in 1948.

Overall he amassed 5028 runs at 89.78 in 37 Tests against England. In Australia, in 18 Tests he scored 2354 runs at an average of 78.46 with eight centuries, while he did slightly better in England in 19 Tests with 2674 runs at an average of 102.84 with 11 centuries.

Australian cricket side undefeated

SCARBOROUGH (Eng.), Sat. (A.A.P.).—The 1948 Australian Test team yesterday became the only touring side to go through an English season undefeated.

The team, which drew yesterday in its last match—against Leveson-Gower's eleven—is the most successful ever sent to England.

The team played 31 games for 23 wins and eight draws.

Australia, with eight wickets for 489 (declared), yesterday drew with Leveson-Gower's XI. 177 and two for 75.

The match was a personal triumph for Bradman, who finished his career in England with a brilliant 153.

This brought his aggregate for the tour to 2428, at an average of 89.92.

Yesterday's century was his eleventh of the tour and his 41st in England.

Bradman Bowls

The Australians yesterday treated the crowd to an entertaining display of hard hitting.

Barnes hit four sixes. Bradman, Bill Johnston, and Ian Johnson got two each.

Harvey, Hassett, and Morris did most of the bowling during Leveson-Gower's second innings.

Bradman finished the day's play by bowling an over of leg-breaks, off which two runs were scored.

Bradman headed both the batting averages and aggregate for the tour.

Ten of the 17 Australian players scored one or more centuries.

Opening batsman Arthur Morris failed to reach his 2000 runs for the tour by only 78.

Fast bowler Ray Lindwall headed the bowling averages with 86 wickets at an average of 15.68.

Don Bradman

When Don Bradman collected his 153 runs against Leveson Gower's XI. at Scarborough last Friday, he put "paid" to one of the most illustrious careers in cricket history.

Close associates wonder what his dynamic frame will tackle next. He has already won titles at tennis, golf and squash rackets and is a 100-break exponent on a billiard table. There have been veiled hints that the next recreation will be bowls.

Actually, Don started his bowls career at Victoria Park, Sydney, in 1932, when he took such a liking to the game that he turned out a week later at Petersham. If he turns to the game made famous by Drake he will have plenty of old-time company during visits to Sydney.

Arthur Mailey, Bill O'Reilly, Tommy Andrews, Alan Kippax are among the bunch of internationals who could, at a pinch, muster an "Ex-Aust. XI. side" of three rinks.

HOW TESTS WERE WON

FIRST, at Trent Bridge, won by eight wickets.

SECOND, at Lord's, won by 409 runs.

THIRD, at Old Trafford, was drawn.

FOURTH, at Leeds, won by seven wickets.

FIFTH, at The Oval, won by innings and 149 runs.

Test Averages

Batting

AUSTRALIA.	I.	N.O.	H.S.	Agg.	Av.	
Morris	9	1	196	696	87.00	
Barnes	6	2	141	329	82.25	
Bradman	9	2	173*	508	72.57	
Harvey	3	1	112	133	66.50	
Toshack	4	3	20*	51	51.00	
Loxton	3	0	93	144	48.00	
Hassett	8	1	137	310	44.28	
Lindwall	6	0	77	191	31.83	
Tallon	4	0	53	112	28.00	
Miller	7	0	74	184	26.28	
Brown	3	0	32	73	24.33	
Johnston	5	2	29	62	20.66	
Johnson	6	1	21	51	10.20	
Ring	1	0	9	9	9.00	
Saggers	1	1	5	5	5.00	
*Not out.						

DON TAKES HIS CURTAIN

LAST APPEARANCE. Don Bradman leads his unbeaten Australians on to the field against Leveson-Gower's XI at Scarborough. It was Bradman's last appearance in a first-class match in England.

The Don's last game in England

The fairytale may not have come true in the Test arena, but it did for Bradman in his final innings in England. He began four tours earlier in 1930 with a double century against Worcester, and he ended it all in England with 153 in his final appearance at Scarborough.

Barnes & Bradman coming out to resume his last 1st Class
Innings in Scarborough, England - Sept. '48.

THE DON HITS A FAREWELL 100

In his last match at Lord's

Evening Standard Cricket Reporter

After a duck—at the Oval Test—a century has come from Don Bradman at Lord's to-day. Such is the contrast of his farewell appearances on London's two big grounds.

As W. A. Brown also scored a century—the Bradman-Brown stand was 181—the Australians are already sitting pretty in their match against the Gentlemen of England. The runs were scored fast and attractively, too.

With only two wickets down, Australians were approaching 300 runs—and it seemed as if Bradman's first innings in this match might prove to be his last. The start of the Australian innings was impressive. Barnes and Brown making the bowling of Bailey, Wooler and Palmer look commonplace, and scoring 40 runs in half an hour.

Then Barnes sent a ball from Bailey whistling round the ankles of third slip and Wooler,

who was fielding there, held on to the ball as he fell and rolled over. It was the sort of catch which explained better than half a column of print just how and why Glamorgan are champions of 1948.

Another record

With the total 40 for one wicket Bradman joined Brown, walking in to applause from both crowd and players.

Bradman was soon off the mark, driving Wooler straight and Palmer to the mid-wicket boundary. Soon Bradman passed his 2000 runs for the season He is the first batsmen to do this in four tours of England.

Meanwhile Brown had been batting in the immaculate but unobtrusive manner that gathers runs so easily and steadily that you hardly notice how they come.

The Australians scored their first 100 runs in 75 minutes—a handsome start, especially as the light was none too good and light rain fell much of the time. The game was held up for ten minutes by rain.

By the Gentlemen there was much good clean stopping and picking up, in which Mann, Simpson, Brown and Donnelly were to be noted. Keen and accurate fielding.

Varied attack

Robins varied the attack enough to keep its edge fresh and the batsmen thoughtful. He had begun with Bailey and Wooler, but soon had Palmer on, and after that Wooler again, Edrich, Yardley and F. R. Brown.

After lunch Bradman, needing only one run for his 50, was soon past it, but Brown ran away with the limelight, scoring the 26 he needed for his 100 in just under 20 minutes.

He took 13 in one over from Bailey, who was sending down more half-volleys than any bowler with a regard for his average can afford. Brown and Bradman put on 40 runs in little more than 20 minutes, and their partnership of 150 took only 100 minutes.

Brown was out to Wooller at last—after a stand of 181 with Bradman. Brown was batting two hours and 25 minutes for his 120.

Bradman and Hassett maintained the handsome pace the Australians had set from the start, and Bradman completed the second century of the innings with a characteristic cover-drive. His time was two hour sand a half

BRADMAN HITS THAT LAST 100

He goes on to 153, then is out

From BRUCE HARRIS: Scarborough, Friday

Don Bradman, Australia's captain, scored here to-day what everybody wanted to see, a century in his last match on an English cricket ground.

Two hours and 25 minutes, with 13 fours, was the scorers' recording of this century against Leveson-Gower's XI. Barnes marched down the pitch with a congratulatory handshake, and the crowd yelled.

Bradman went on to 153 (two sixes, 13 fours) before he was third wicket down—caught off Bedser, once again by Hutton—after batting 190 minutes.

To Bradman, thanks for another slightly sedate century—his 116th in first-class cricket To Barnes, even more thanks for the display of hitting with which he celebrated the farewell triumph of his chief.

Before he was out, heroically, for 151, caught on the boundary by Yardley, Barnes took his own score from 100 to 151 in 25 minutes.

Best this season

Three sixes, seven fours—and five singles. It is not a record in fast scoring—P. G. H. Fender once had 50 in 19 minutes. Others have been about as swift ; but it stands probably as the best bit of hitting this season.

Brown and Laker were the two suffering bowlers—one over from Brown yielded 24—two sixes and three fours.

Barnes's wicket fell to Laker, though it might have gone either way.

Meanwhile the admiring Bradman was unbeaten at lunch for 109, an innings in which he never took the bowling as Barnes did—by the scruff of the neck and thrashed it.

The farewells were long and hearty for The Don. This celebration is at the Savoy Hotel, London.

Bon Voyage to Don Bradman

A newspaper fund to give Bradman
a parting gift generated so much
money that after costs were taken
out for a massive silver trophy,
known as 'The Warwick Vase',
Bradman asked that surplus money
go towards providing concrete
pitches for the youth of England.

*Presented to Don Bradman
by cricket lovers of Britain.

This trophy a tribute to
a great Australian sportsman
was subscribed for by people
through "The People" newspaper*

LONDON 1948.

DON BRADMAN TESTIMONIAL
SPORTS PARADE

Under the Auspices of the Victorian Cricket Association.

In the presence of His Excellency Major-General Sir Winston Dugan, G.C.M.G., C.B., D.S.O., Governor of Victoria.

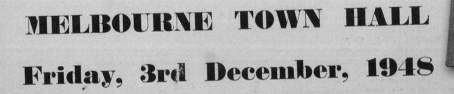

Melbourne
Cricket Ground

D. G. BRADMAN
TESTIMONIAL MATCH
SAT., 4th DEC.
(RESERVE STAND)

Block **C**

Row J 8

Keep this Portion

Melbourne
Cricket Ground

D. G. BRADMAN
TESTIMONIAL MATCH
FRI., 3rd DEC.
(RESERVE STAND)

Block **C**

Row D 9

Keep this Portion

MELBOURNE TOWN HALL

Friday, 3rd December, 1948

The Don Bradman Testimonial Edition of "Kia-Ora Sports Parade" will be broadcast from 3KZ, Melbourne, and a nation-wide network. Overseas transmissions, to all countries, will be from Radio Australia.

SOUVENIR PROGRAMME 6d.   № 1820

In early December 1948, more than 94,000 people flooded to the Melbourne Cricket Ground to watch Bradman in his Testimonial game. The match finished with the scores level after Don Tallon added 91 in the last hour with nine wickets down. Bradman scored 123 in the first innings, his 117th first class century.

ANOTHER RECORD TO THE DON

60,000 ROAR ADMIRATION

Back home, Bradman celebrated a century in his own Testimonial match at the MCG. He scored 123 in front of 53,000 fans on the second day in a match in which 1672 runs were scored in the four days - and the match finished in a tie.

When Don Bradman went out to bat at 3 o'clock this afternoon at his Testimonial match at the MCG, 60,000 people roared their acknowledgment of Australia's greatest cricketer. It was the greatest demonstration seen on the ground — and another record for the Don.

The Don — his head sunk into his shirt collar, edged his way down the aisle to the arena, faced a battery of cameras, and with his bat clasped under his elbow as if he were afraid of losing it, fidgetted with his batting gloves as he made his way to the wicket.

Don Bradman delights the big crowd with a cut for a single off McCool.

> "…..as a pavilion lover of the greatest of all games, I have balanced up the Bradman account and hereby acknowledge that, so long as my memory lasts, I shall owe him that which I can never repay."
> (Politician Sir Robert Menzies, on Bradman's retirement in 1949)

DON'S 123 IN TESTIMONIAL IS A THRILLER

MELBOURNE, Saturday.—More than 50,000 saw Don Bradman make his 19th century on the Melbourne Cricket Ground in his testimonial match today. His 117th century in first-class cricket, his innings was a fitting farewell to the majority of the Southern City's cricket fans.

When he was 97, Bradman skied a ball to McCool at mid-on, but the fieldsman started off late and was forced to try for the catch over his shoulder. Much to the satisfaction of the crowd, McCool dropped the chance and Bradman reached his century amid tremendous cheering.

While it would be foolish to say that the Bradman of to-day was equal to the Bradman of 10 years ago, it would be just as foolish to say that the Test captain was not still a great batsman.

For the first time, Bradman faced the bowling of Ray Lindwall, and apart from the first ball he received from the speed merchant—the delivery baffled him with pace and swerve—he played the fastest bowler in the world today with the utmost confidence.

Apart from the chance he gave in the nineties, Bradman's innings was deserving of the applause which greeted it.

With net gate receipts of £5673 19s 7d after two days' play and donations still coming in and to be counted, the financial success of the match is already assured.

It was reported that wealthy Mr. John Wren had promised Bradman £1 for each run the player made today.

From the time that Bradman's name appeared on the scoreboard the 52,960 people present cheered Australia's greatest cricketer.

The silence that descended upon the ground as McCool ran up to bowl the first ball to Bradman was eerie, and something never experienced at the M.C.G. before.

According to ex-internationals, players from various grades and spectators, the match to date has been one of the highlights in Australian cricket. Starting with the hand Barnes played yesterday and finishing with Bradman's century, the cricket has been bright and full of incidents.

Barnes has been the next best drawcard to Bradman over the last two days.

His six off Noblet's first ball started the crowd to begin reconsidering the ability of the Barnes who figured in such a dreary century against Victoria last season.

Today Barnes delighted everyone by his antics on the field. In fun he threw the ball on the ground when an appeal off his bowling was disallowed and when Brown, attempting to hit the wicket from the out-field, missed by a wide margin, Barnes tossed the ball back to him so that he could have another try.

Staid old onlookers in the Members' Stand were still talking of the great hand Lindwall turned on yesterday when play began today. They had to go back a long way to recall such a torrent of sixers in a first-class game.

FAREWELL THE DON!

MELBOURNE, Tuesday.—Don Bradman's testimonial match, which has provided some of the best cricket ever seen on the Melbourne ground, ended dramatically this evening when Don Tallon tied the scores from the last ball of the day.

Tallon made 91 out of 100 scored in the last hour and "stole" a century after it had seemed that Hassett's team had the game won.

DRAMA IN FINAL STAGES

BRADMAN 123

THE SCORES

BRADMAN'S ELEVEN
First Innings

K. MEULEMAN, c and b Johnson	100
A. MORRIS, c and b McCool	25
R. HAMENCE, st Saggers, b McCool	58
D. G. BRADMAN, c Harvey, b Dooland	123
K. R. MILLER, b Johnson	2
S. LOXTON, b W. Johnston	21
V. N. RAYMER, c Lindwall, b McCool	40
I. JOHNSON, c L. Johnson, b McCool	22
D. TALLON, lbw, b McCool	11
D. RING, c McCool, b Johnston	17
G. K. NOBLET, not out	4
Sundries	11
Total	**434**

Fall of wickets: 42, 138, 250, 254, 316, 348, 378, 398, 427, 434.

BOWLING.

	O.	M.	R.	W.
Lindwall	15	3	41	0
L. Johnson	12	1	46	2
McCool	19.4	1	101	5
W. Johnston	21	4	92	2
Dooland	16	0	95	1
Langdon	4	1	17	0
Barnes	4	0	16	0
Hassett	1	0	2	0
Brown	1	0	13	0

Byes, 6; Leg-byes, 4; no-ball, 1 (Langdon).

Colossus Of All Cricket's Giants

Bradman was a national selector at the time, and wasn't sure if he should play in a testimonial match for Kippax and Oldfield in Sydney in January of 1949. However, as his letter in this chapter explains, he was talked into it.

HOTEL WINDSOR

SPRING STREET
MELBOURNE

28th Decr. 1948.

The Secretary
NSWCA,
Sydney.

Dear Mr Heyden,

Following receipt of your letter of 22nd Dec. I advised my Co-Australian Selectors that the NSWCA had requested me to play in the Oldfield - Kippax Testimonial Match.

As you know I was reluctant to take part because my presence will mean that a potential candidate for South Africa must be left out.

However in view of your request, my Colleagues are prepared to agree that I should play therefore with much pleasure I am advising you that I shall play.

2

As I am not playing any cricket at all I fear my form will be far from satisfactory but I can only do my best.

In order to clear up any misunderstanding which may already have arisen in the minds of the public, and because I think an announcement now may be beneficial to the match, I am informing the press of this decision.

My kindest regards with best wishes for 1949.

Yours Sincerely

Don Bradman

Donald George Bradman, South Australia.— World's greatest batsman. Born, Cootamundra, August 27, 1908. Scored first century at 12. Holds world's record score—452 not out, v. Queensland, and highest Australian Test innings, 334 v. England. Has hit 2,596 runs in Tests v. England.

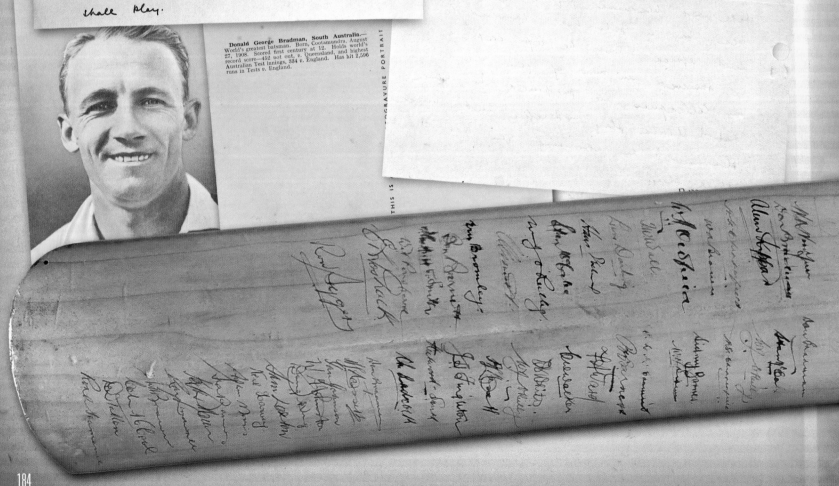

Bradman makes
his way onto the MCG
for his testimonial match.

"When Bradman
was gone the light seemed
to go out of the game."
(The Observer, London, 1949)

WORLD'S GREATEST BATSMAN

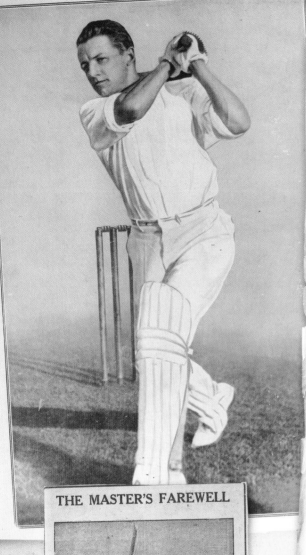

THE MASTER'S FAREWELL

THIS is the final picture of Don Bradman in action in a first class fixture. He is shown pulling a short ball from W. Johnston in the South Australia—Victoria Shield game to the square leg fence. The next ball he was bowled. Bradman trod on a ball while fielding and injured his ankle. He did not bat in the second innings.

Now Sir Donald Bradman, the world's greatest cricketer attracted 41,575 people to the Sydney Cricket Ground between February 25 and March 1 of 1949 for a final glimpse of his mastery in his native city. He scored 53 in the Kippax-Oldfield Testimonial in only 65 minutes.

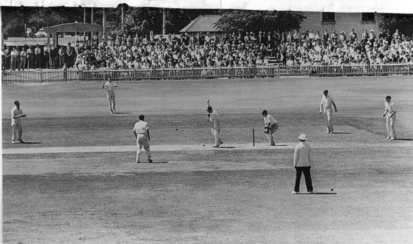

Bradman played his final first class match, for South Australia against Victoria at Adelaide Oval, in March of 1949, scoring 30 in his only innings.

SIR DONALD BRADMAN

"For Services Over Many Years As Cricketer And Captain" New Year Knighthood

55, Westminster Gardens,
London, S.W.1.

3rd January, 1949.

My dear Bradman

My wife and I were so pleased to see the distinction which His Majesty has conferred upon you. It is a recognition of great services which will cause much pleasure to all your friends.

I see you have modestly said that it is really a recognition of the great game for which you have done so much. I regard it as something more than that and as a recognition of the great services you have rendered to inter-Imperial relations by your tact and outstanding personality. Perhaps I am better able to appreciate the value of what you have done in this direction, owing to the long period for which I acted as Australia's representative in Great Britain.

I realise that you will be completely overwhelmed by the congratulations that will be poured upon you. Please do not trouble to send me any acknowledgment of the good wishes I want to convey to you.

With kind regards, and all good wishes for 1949.

Yours sincerely

Bruce.

Sir Donald Bradman.

Lord Stanley Bruce, an Australian government representative in England, congratulated Bradman on his Knighthood and applauded his "great services" to inter-Imperial relations "by your tact and outstanding personality".

CHAIRMAN'S ROOM.
THE STOCK EXCHANGE.
LONDON, E.C. 2.

3rd January, 1949.

Dear Mr. Bradman,

On behalf of the Council and Members of the Stock Exchange it gives me the greatest pleasure to send you a message of cordial congratulations on the Honour of Knighthood which His Majesty is conferring upon you.

Yours sincerely,

D. Bradman, Esq.,
Adelaide Stock Exchange,
ADELAIDE,
Australia.

Congratulations flowed from around the world upon the official announcement of Bradman's Knighthood, including from the London Stock Exchange.

SIR DONALD BRADMAN

The 1949 New Year's Honours List included Don Bradman as Knight Bachelor recognising his services to cricket and to Commonwealth sporting links. He was invested as Australia's first cricket knight in March 1949. He became the only Australian cricketer ever to be knighted.

DON BRADMAN KNIGHTED
South Australian Honors List

His Majesty the King has honored seven South Australians in the New Year Honors list issued last night. Mr. D. G. Bradman, who receives the only knighthood, heads the list.

The long service which Professors J. McKellar Stewart and J. B. Cleland have given to the University of Adelaide has been recognised, and Dr. E. A. H. Russell has been honored for his work with the St. John Ambulance Brigade.

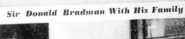

Sir Donald Bradman With His Family

Sir Donald and Lady Bradman with their two children, John and Shirley.

DRAWN BY ARTHUR MAILEY.

AUSTRALIA'S GREATEST BATSMAN

188

SIR RICHARD HADLEE

(Champion New Zealand all-rounder with 431 wickets at 22.29 and 3124 runs at 27.16)

A framed letter, accompanied by a cartoon, holds pride of place in my house in New Zealand. The letter came from Sir Donald Bradman and I cherish it greatly.

Sir Donald sent the hand written personal letter to me within days of the announcement of my knighthood. Without doubt the highlight of my playing career was to lead the New Zealand team onto Lord's on the first day of the 2nd Test in 1990, known as Sir Richard. To be knighted for services to New Zealand cricket is very special indeed.

Sir Donald, who was the first cricketer to be knighted in 1949, obviously knew what an honour, and obligation, it was to receive such a title.

So imagine my delight when, within days of the announcement of my honour, Sir Donald sent me this letter.

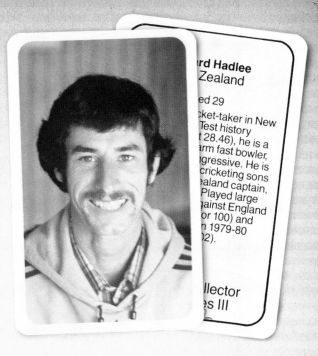

15/6/90

Dear Richard
Welcome to the club. It is with great pleasure that I read in this morning's paper where you have been honoured by a knighthood. Your exploits plus your exemplary conduct fully justify this elevation and I offer you my sincere congratulations.

From many years of experience I can tell you it will prove to be a mixed blessing. I know that as a modest individual you will be embarrassed when close friends of long standing insist on addressing you as Sir Richard.

But it will nevertheless be a source of pride in your standing as a very distinguished New Zealander and as recognition of your outstanding performance.

Apart from your personal honour I am sure this will also be regarded as a recognition of your family and as one who has had the pleasure in years gone by of working with your father in cricket administration. I am sure he will accept the reflected glory with much pride.

Knighthoods are not given lightly. They are awarded in cases when the recipients have exhibited and continue to uphold the finest traditions of cricket and your future influence in this area will remain of great significance.

New Zealand will always remember you as the first N.Z. cricketer to bring such an illustrious sporting award to your country and I trust you will long be spared to enjoy the honour.

The enclosed cutting from The Australian may amuse you.
With warmest regards,
Yours sincerely
Don Bradman

I was absolutely thrilled to receive this letter. The cartoon cutting that appeared with the letter from The Australian newspaper was also a tribute in a funny sort of way. It would be fair to say that my run in with Australian crowds was legendary during my playing career. Apparently, I was the first cricketer to be a called, 'a wanker'. Not a nice compliment, however it spurred me on though, because I took more Test wickets against Australia than against any other country I played against!

In the cartoon I am depicted taking off from the end of my run up near the boundary edge. A bloke in the crowd has a sign on his chest saying; 'Hadlee is a wanker'. I have turned round to this fellow and said: "Sir Wanker to you sport…"

Perhaps there was some respect from the Australians after all!

Sir Donald also went on record in 1989 when he honoured me in my autobiography Rhythm and Swing saying: "Richard was the Master of Rhythm and Swing."

"Richard Hadlee ….. Richard did not have enough pace to be classified as genuinely fast, although he was certainly beyond medium pace. No bowler I have seen, had better control of seam and swing, and he was a wonderful model for young players to emulate, in that he showed everyone what could be done, with a lovely action and proper body control, without resorting to an exaggerated run."

That was a wonderful appreciation of my trade. Unfortunately I only saw Sir Donald Bradman play cricket on film. Those pictures told a story of poise, elegance, control, quick footwork and wonderful stroke-play. Statistics will always be convincing and cannot be argued with. The fact that people still talk about him suggests he has survived the 'test of time' and is truly regarded as a great player – Wisden rated him the number one player of the 20th Century – no one would dispute that.

The word great is often overused – to me 'great' means a player will have succeeded in any era – he would have been good enough to adapt to any type of game or match situation. Few players would have been awarded that accolade.

My encounters with The Don were brief. I recall on one of my tours to Australia in the 1980s, he was sitting in the committee room by himself at the beautiful Adelaide Oval watching the game. I had the opportunity to be introduced to him – I cannot recall the conversation – I was in awe of the man. What could I say and how could I engage in a conversation with a legend?

Memories stay with you for life – The Don's accolades are very special to me and he always will remain a legend in my eyes.

THEY RELAXED AFTER INVESTITURE FORMALITY

NOW IT'S SIR DON BRADMAN

ARISE, SIR DON!

Bradman Knighted In 'Sportsmen's Honours'
F.A. SECRETARY BECOMES K.B.

THE New Year Honours announced to-day pay tribute to notable sporting personalities at the close of a year that has been memorable in the world of sport. Knighthoods are awarded to Don Bradman, captain of the Australian Test team, to Mr. Stanley Rous, secretary of the Football Association, and to Mr. Harcourt Gold, the rowing coach, who is chairman of the Henley Regatta stewards.

The 1948 Olympic Games are commemorated by the appointment of Viscount Portal, President of the Games, as a G.C.M.G., and four other honours, including a C.B.E. for Colonel Evan Hunter, secretary of the British Olympic Association.

A knighthood is also awarded to Mr. Will Lawther, President of the National Union of Mineworkers, and Dr. Edith Summerskill, Parliamentary Ssecretary to the Ministry of Food, becomes the fouth woman Privy Counsellor.

The list.—the 25th Honours List of the reign—confers three baronies, three Privy Counsellorships, 30 knighthoods in the home list, and appoints two new Companions of Honour.

The new barons include Sir John Boyd Orr, the nutrition expert, until recently Director-General of the United Nations Food and Agriculture Organisation. Mr. H. A. Marquand, M.P., Minister of Pensions, and Lord Hailey are other new Privy Counsellers.

Express Staff Reporter

DON BRADMAN, 40-year-old captain of the Australian Test Team, gets a knighthood in the New Year Honours today.

The accolade can be conferred by the Governor-General of Australia. Last night Bradman watched a cricket match in Melbourne.

Sir Don Bradman

WITHIN his own sphere "The Don," who as I forecast first and exclusively in this column, became Sir Don, undoubtedly heads the list.

The fame of his name in cricket playing countries has never known any equal, and has extended even to countries not knowing the difference between a cricket bat and a shillelagh.

It is arguable which name is best known in the British Empire, Churchill's or Bradman's, and a French industrialist who, when interviewed in London, declared he had never heard of Bradman and was astonished when told that Bradman's name was as famous as Mr. Churchill's, received more publicity than a Bradman double century.

French journalists thereupon endeavored to interpret Bradman's activities to the French people, and United States journalists sought to translate Bradman into terms of Babe Ruth.

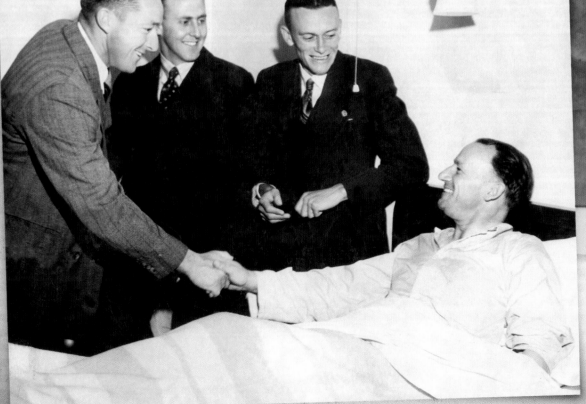

Bradman being congratulated on the announcement of his knighthood.

Bradman remarked on receiving the Award: "This was an honour that I never sought or dreamt about. If there had been nobody else to please but myself I would have preferred to remain just plain mister. But it was an honour for the game of cricket and in that context I accepted the responsibility of the title conferred by knighthood but one thing I do feel very proud of and that is that few people have ever carried the title of 'Lady' as graciously as my wife has and that if ever a woman deserved to be called a 'Lady', she did."

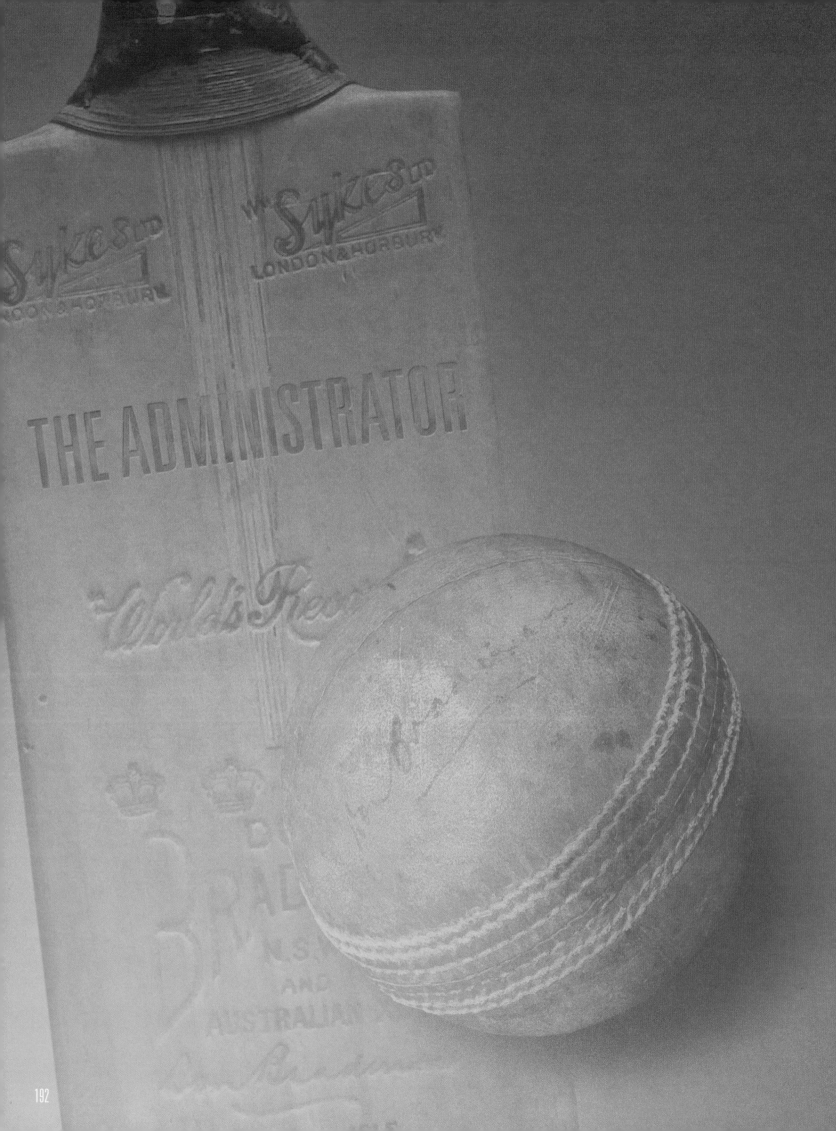

SUNIL GAVASKAR

(Incomparable Indian opening batsman who in 125 Tests scored 10,122 runs, with 34 centuries, at an average of 51.12. A media commentator he also was for eight years until recently the chairman of the International Cricket Council's cricket committee)

My fondest memory of Sir Donald Bradman is a compliment he paid me when I equaled his 29 century mark. I say mark, because unless someone can score 29 centuries in 51 Tests (he did it in his 52) then it is only reaching a mark, not setting a record.

Anyway, Sir Donald sent me a message and he said some very nice things about me.

He made a public statement that "Sunil is an ornament to the game." For Sir Donald, that was a wonderful compliment and one I shall always treasure from the great man himself.

The first time I met Sir Donald was at Adelaide airport during a transit visit during the Rest Of The World series in 1971-72. I was only 21 and Sir Donald asked to speak to 'the little fella from India' as everyone mingled at the airport. I was really proud to talk with him.

Gary Sobers, the captain of the team, noticed the two of us chatting away and he came over and said it was interesting that the 'little fellas' were hanging out together. Sir Donald laughed and then said as an aside: "The big fellas have the power but we little fellas have the footwork."

He was charming and engaging and it gave this young player a tremendous boost. To think that many years down the track I would be blessed with his kind remark about being an ornament to the game was most satisfying.

Everyone was in fine spirits at that airport meeting. I remember Pakistan's super batsman Zaheer Abbas joining Sir Donald and me and then West Indian Rohan Kanhai piped up and said: "Look, there's the Karachi Bradman, the Bombay Bradman and the real Bradman".

I hung on every word Sir Donald said. And it almost caused me to have an accident. On India's tour of Australia in 1977, I was seated on Sir Donald's right and captain Bishan Bedi on his left at a dinner in Adelaide, which went for more than three hours. He talked about India's 1947 tour of Australia and all sorts of other engrossing topics and I was spellbound. I was really busting to go to the toilet, but I wouldn't dare leave for a second in case I missed some of his conversation. It was only after he left that I ran, literally ran, to the toilet!

Dr. Don Beard always held a party at his home whenever we were in Adelaide, with Sir Donald and three or four Australians and three or four Indian players invited along. I always managed to get an invite, even before I was captain. Sir Donald was most relaxed at these evenings. He had a great sense of humour, always with a twinkle in his eye, and you had to be alert to know if he was serious or having a joke with you.

I visited Sir Donald on all my tours to Australia, up until 1999. He kept himself abreast of the cricket scene, and he was always prepared to talk tough topics. He suggested to me that night Test matches would come in sooner or later because people simply didn't have the time to attend because of work during the day. And he had firm opinions on the LBW law and the front foot no-ball law. We discussed such matters often, especially when I became the chairman of the International Cricket Council's cricket committee.

He was an outstanding administrator and who better to listen to an opinion of potential law changes than Sir Donald.

I tried to persuade him to attend the 1987 World Cup final in India. I called and offered a special flight, an accompanying doctor and the lot. However he politely declined the invitation. I only wish he had seen India put on such a great show.

It is not to be. However for me, I had wonderful times with Sir Donald and I will hold them dear to my heart forever.

An ornament to the game... and that from THE ornament to the game.

Don Bradman will be remembered eternally for his deeds as a cricketer, but he also was an outstanding contributor to the game as a selector and administrator. He was an astute and progressive administrator; an expansive thinker, philosopher and writer on the game. Indeed, in some respects, he was as powerful, persuasive and influential a figure off the ground as he was on it.

He was appointed an Australian Test selector in 1936 upon the death of selector Dr Dolling, a post he held until 1971 - aside from two years in the early 1950s, giving him a 33 year period as a national selector.

Bradman was a committeeman of the South Australian Cricket Association between 1935 and 1986. It is estimated that he attended 1713 SACA meetings during this half century of service. He served as President of the SACA from 1965 to 1973.

Bradman was elected to the Australian Board of Control in August 1945. He had not played cricket for five years and did not expect to play for Australia again because of severe muscular spasms. However he accepted the Australian captaincy in 1946 against Wally Hammond's English team in an effort to help a post-war recovery.

In 1960 he became the first former Test player to be elected chairman of the Australian Board of Control. He served as chairman from 1960-63 and again from 1969-73.

During the first period he dealt with the growing prevalence of illegal bowling actions in the game, a problem that he adjudged, "the most complex I have known in cricket, because it is not a matter of fact but of opinion". The major controversy of his second stint was a proposed tour of Australia by South Africa in 1971–72. On Bradman's recommendation, the series was cancelled and instead he instigated a multi-national Rest Of The World team tour.

Bradman remained a member of the Australian Cricket Board of Control until 1980 - giving him 35 years as one of the nation's premier administrators.

In the late 1970s, Bradman played an important role during the World Series Cricket schism as a member of a special Australian Cricket Board committee formed to handle the crisis.

At all times, he fought for what he believed was good for Australian cricket, and therefore world cricket.

You do well to love cricket for it is more free from anything sordid, anything dishonourable than any game in the world.

To play it keenly, generously, self-sacrificingly, is a moral issue in itself, and the classroom is God's air and sunshine.

Foster it my brothers so that it may attract all who find the time to play it. protect it from anything that will sully it. so that it may grow in favour with all men.

Lord Harris - (English captain - 1877-1884)

Don Bradman

Bradman often recited these words from Lord Harris and did so in his last public appearance in 1996.

Bradman always seemed destined to become an influential administrator. His knowledge of the game, from a playing perspective, was an inherent gene.

As early as January, 1933 - a day after playing for NSW against the touring MCG and between the 3rd and 4th Tests of the infamous Bodyline series, the young Bradman wrote to cricket's controlling body, the Marylebone Cricket Club at Lord's.

He "dared" write the letter and suggested he may have been presumptuous in doing so. However write it he did.

Copy

11 Lower Bayview Street,
McMahon's Point.
SYDNEY. 30th.Jany.1933.

The Secretary,
M.C.C.
Lords Cricket Ground.
LONDON.

Dear Sir,

Only after considerable thought have I dared to write this letter to the controlling body in cricket. In doing so however, I have but one thought in my mind which is "the betterment of our glorious game of cricket".

I have taken the liberty of presuming my letter will be read to the members of the M.C.C. Should my presumption be correct then it is quite possible that, after hearing the contents, the members will think it preposterous of me to have the temerity to even dream of making a suggestion to them. Should they take this view no harm will be done. On the other hand if they are prepared to listen to my suggestion I would feel very honoured.

At the present moment a rather unfortunate state of affairs exists. The Australian Board of Control and the M.C.C. are somewhat at variance over the tactics employed by theEnglish bowlers on their present tour of Australia. On such a subject I wish to make no comment except this. For some years past there has been a growing feeling amongst those in control of affairs that the task of bowlers, year after year, has become more difficult. As evidence of their belief in this fact the M.C.C. recently passed leglisation increasing the size of the stumps and altering the L.B.W. rule, thereby making the bowler's task slightly easier. Surely then, with the present controversy at its height, there could not be a more opportune moment than the present, for passing further leglisation which would materially assist all bowlers for all time and also, if my reasoning is correct, would make cricket better and brighter with scarcely any arguments against it.

My suggestion is one which may have been made before. On that occasion however the necessity of any further addition to the rules was probably not so apparent. Being purely a batsman myself, this new rule would affect me just the same as it would affect every other batsman. I wish to stress this fact. My suggestion, if ever carried, would not be to my advantage in any way whatsoever.

In addition to the existing rule covering a Leg-before-wicket decision why not add the following:-

"If with part of his person the striker stops the ball which in the opinion of the umpire at the bowler's wicket shall have been pitched on the off side of the wicket as to the striker and would have hit the wicket, the striker is out "Leg Before Wicket".

Pardon me for further presumption but I would like to add my reasons for believing in the success of this experiment.

Batsmen's leg-guards have been considerably improved to withstand knocks from the ball.   This was done to protect the batsman's legs, not to allow him to protect his wicket with those pads.   To-day we find batsmen so proficient in the art of using their feet, that a bowler, pitching the ball off the wicket, has no chance whatever of hitting the stumps.   The new rule as suggested, would force the batsmen to play at the ball.   Allowing the ball to pass outside the off stump merely by covering the wicket with the pads, would be a thing of the past.

In addition to the wickets bowlers would obtain by L.B.W. decisions under the new rule, slip catches and such like would become much more frequent because of the batsman being forced to play at the ball.   To-day a man bowling off breaks has an extremely difficult task obtaining wickets so that new bowlers coming on, are inclined to turn to a more successful type which is leg break bowling. Under the new rule an off break bowler would probably be more successful than a leg break bowler and yet no advantages whatsoever would be taken away from the leg breakbowler.   In fact the leg break bowler would gain considerably too. With a right hand leg breakbowler operating to a left hand batsman the new rule would definitely assist the bowler.   No batsman would suffer any more disadvantage than another and there is no type of bowling which would not receive assistance.

Unquestionably teams would make less runs.   To my mind it would be in the best interests of the game if this was so.   And yet none of the skill in handling a bat is taken away from the batsman.

The decision which the umpire would be called upon to make, should not be any more difficult than the present decisions, especially the L.B.W. decision after the ball has snicked the bat.   As always the player would accept the umpire's decision without quibble.

I cannot see anything against the suggestion.   Apparently many arguments may be used in favour of it.

As previously stated my love of and devotion to cricket where men should use a bat and a ball, causes me to offer this humble suggestion at a time when the predominance of bat over ball has become the subject of so much comment.

Compared with the members of your Club I am but an inexperienced youth but in a short space of time I have learned to love our grand game and if I have taken up your time with an impracticable idea I apologise.

                          Yours Sincerely,

While ensuring he did not buy into the raging Bodyline controversy, he set about suggesting an alteration to the LBW rule, and supporting it with arguments.

The letter is a classic example of a confident, lateral thinking young man of 26 who was prepared to lock horns with officialdom - even in the midst of a hostile Ashes series.

Cricket Australia, in 2008, unearthed a batch of priceless Bradman letters written during his days as an administrator and beyond when he was in regular contact with officialdom. The following letters in this chapter are extracts of his correspondence.

2 Holden Street,
Kensington Park. S.A.
10-2-69.

Dear Bob,
        Pressure of other matters has delayed my devoting any time to the question of throwing and what we should do about the next I.C.Conference but at last I am able to get around to it.
        There is no need to go back over the more recent history, i.e. from about 1960 onwards, because it is well known to you and to most legislators.   And I suppose going back to 1880 odd would be regarded as tedious.
        BUT I think it germane to say that throwing has been a re-curring evil for nearly 100 years and if the modern legislators can devise ways and means of curing this evil once and for all, they will do cricket a great service.
        Moreover I think ~~I think~~ it is powerful evidence in support of my view that we would be crazy now to revert to the old situation where we had no definition.
        Those who claim recent events have rectified the trouble may well be right - IN THE SHORT TERM.   But in 10 - 20 years it would certainly return and be a bogey once more, and I think our responsibility is to provide now against such a contingency.
        The thing is pretty well under control - let us make sure we keep it that way.
        Looking back over your 1967 Conference report I find where you said "it would appear that most member countries supported Australia's definition".
        The fact that it did not go through was because M.C.C. objected, and because, after seeing certain films, you, quite fairly, did not press the matter and asked for it to be deferred pending those films being brought back to Australia.
        Since then I have received the films and have shown them privately to you and to Gubby Allen on my projector, which is ideal for this sort of thing....

        ...The only true test is to take a bowler in a match when he is flat out and when he does not know he is being filmed....

        ...I think it correct to say that both Allen and yourself, after seeing the films on my projector, were not at all convinced that they were evidence to substantiate M.C.C.'s objection....

        ...I don't need to tell you the heated arguments that went on about Griffiths and Meckiff and I'm sure you agree that there ought to be some yardstick whereby such arguments can be settled....

        Here we are trying to settle a principle - something vital to cricket in all countries for all time.   Nobody doubts that our definition is clear cut and that anyone obeying it would bowl fairly.   BUT IT IS REFUSED BECAUSE ENGLAND HAS FOUND JUST THE ODD CASE WHICH THEY SAY JUST MIGHT BE JUDGED UNFAIRLY.
        Laws are altered from time to time because the legislators feel it wise.   A case in point is the present front foot no-ball law.   All his life Wes Hall, who does not drag, was adjudged as absolutely fair so long as his back foot landed behind the bowling crease.   Suddenly the law was altered to catch draggers and Hall was caught up simply because he is tall, has a big stride, and his front foot lands over the batting crease (which did not matter previously). He now has to change where he puts his back foot and this for Hall, and many others, is no laughing matter.

There are a vast number of great players, both past and present, who strongly disagree with this front foot rule but M.C.C. has been adamant in supporting it.   They are apparently unconcerned with any previously innocent bowlers whohave had to change.

In the throwing case the evil is infinitely worse, and if only a couple of bowlers can be located who get anywhere near breaking the definition which we all agree is foolproof, why shouldn't these bowlers too be expected, if need be, to make a small correction to obey the law in the same way that cricketers have had to do for other laws.

Tony Lock did it, and did it so successfully that he again played for England, bowling with a perfectly straight arm which would completely pass under the new proposed definition.

I find nothing whatever to alter the conviction so many of us have, namely that the wording of the present rule is open to a variety of interpretations by individuals, unpires and officials, and it has encouraged sectional interests (e.g. clubs etc) to question the validity of umpire's interpretations when their particular interests were affected....

. . . These people shelter behind the fundamental weakness of the rule that it is open to differing interpretations.

This is all because nobody can say exactly what is meant by "IMMEDIATELY PRIOR TO the instant of delivery".

I may claim it means the last 2 feet.   But if you argue it means the last 6 inches, who can say you are wrong?

It is interesting to repeat what I have emphasized before, namely that in 1960 the new experimental law adopted by M.C.C. defined "IMMEDIATELY PRIOR TO", as "ANY TIME AFTER THE ARM HAS RISEN ABOVE THE LEVEL OF THE SHOULDER IN THE DELIVERY SWING".

No legitimate bowler was called in County cricket under that definition so why is M.C.C. afraid one might be called now?

It is well known that Griffiths was accused of throwing but his supporters denied the accusation on the grounds that his arm was perfectly straight as he delivered the ball.   Photos clearly proved this point to be true.   But it was irrelevant.

Photos also clearly prove that the greatest javelin throwers have their arms absolutely straight at the point of release.   In many cases they are also straight at the horizontal.   The damage is caused by the bending and straightening between the horizontal and the delivery point.

I would like to meet M.C.C.'s objection if there was some reasonable way of doing it.   For instance I thought of saying "the arm must be fully extended at the horizontal or immediately thereafter", but that would be falling into the very error I am objecting to.   It might be an improvement nevertheless.

Frankly I think M.C.C. are being very pig headed and pernickety. They should have the guts to define a law that will work and can be interpreted, even if they gave existing bowlers a period of grace.

My view is that we should have another crack at what we put up before, using the arguments set out herein.   Maybe Gubby will be more reasonable after his visit to Australia.

Your comments will be appreciated and then perhaps something can be produced for the I.C.C.   As before, I would like to see our case set out in detail and sent to other countries well before the Conference.   If this is not done I doubt if you will get independent thinking.   You'll have a lot of yes men.

I also wondered about the efficacy of making a tape recording of our arguments and for same to be played at the I.C.C. It might be more effective than reading a screed.   Or does your conservative mind boggle at such a thought?

Haven't had time to work on the LBW law yet but hope to do so within a few days.

Kind regards,

Sam

This letter, dated February 10, 1969, expresses his concerns about throwing.

"BUT I think it germane to say that throwing has been a recurring evil for nearly 100 years and if the modern legislators can devise ways and means of curing this evil once and for all, they will do cricket a great service," he writes.

October 21, 1969 (l-r) Australian cricketer Barry Jarman, Gavin Stevens, Les Favell with Sir Donald Bradman.

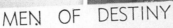

MEN OF DESTINY

THE AUSTRALIAN TEST SELECTORS watching the play on the last day of the match, England v. An Australian XI, at Sydney Cricket Ground yesterday. Left to right: W. Johnson, D. G. Bradman, E. A. Dwyer.

1970: Australian cricket captain Bob Simpson (l-r) with former cricketer Les Favell, Sir Donald Bradman and Richie Benaud at Adelaide Oval 1970.

The Australian Selectors - E.J. Dwyer, W. Johnson and Bradman.

RICHIE BENAUD

(Former Australian captain and all-rounder and doyen of cricket commentators)

Assume nothing is the best way to go in life, certainly if you are about to begin a working relationship with Sir Donald Bradman, Chairman of the Australian selection committee who was formerly the greatest batsman the cricket world has seen. More so perhaps if your own elevation to the captaincy had only happened because the current captain, Ian Craig, had withdrawn with a very nasty bout of hepatitis and the current vice-captain, Neil Harvey of Victoria, had moved house and business to Sydney. A week before the First Test, Tony Lock threw everyone into confusion by bowling out 'An Australian XI' at the SCG. He was unplayable, bowling left-arm over the wicket into the very deeply gouged footmarks left by Fred Trueman at the Paddington End of the ground.

Bradman chats with former Australian captains Richie Benaud and Bill Lawry as well as the Nawab of Pataudi of India.

Old Trafford, 1961, was light years away! There was though, another aspect deeply disturbing for the Board of Control; I was a working journalist.

Australia won the opening Test at the 'Gabba' a week later, but it was a dirge of a match relieved only by a splendid 71 not out from the brilliant youngster Norman O'Neill on the final day. The most important thing I did was say to the media that they would be welcome in the Australian dressing-room after each day's play. The voting on the captaincy had apparently been close, and those who had looked on me with a very wary eye were now convinced I was mad. No pressman, under any circumstances, had ever before stepped across the white line at the Australian team's dressing-room door.

In later years, over a glass or two of Riesling, I broached with Don the matter of our different attitudes to the media. He conceded he had been, because of circumstances, far too careful, even suspicious of journalists. He laughed and added that I was years ahead of my time and, most certainly, of the administrators' time.

We didn't always agree on the tactical side of things. In the Fourth Test in Adelaide in 1959 we were 2-0 up in the series against Peter May's team. We made 476 and bowled out England for 240 and on the way off the ground I saw Don waiting at the top of the steps leading to the dressing-rooms. I knew it would be to do with the 'follow-on' and he said: 'You know the only way you could get into trouble is to enforce the follow on.' I turned left to the England dressing-room and replied, "Yep, I'm just going to tell Peter to do it..." We won by ten wickets.

One of my favourite photographs is of Bradman, Alan Davidson and myself sitting in front of the 'Gabba' dressing-room at tea time. This one was taken on the last day of what was to be the first 'tie' in Test history. After Don's pre-match speech to the team, it had been a splendid match but we were in trouble on that last afternoon. At the tea interval we still needed 123, but had only 4 wickets in hand. Don always came down for a cup of tea each day of a Test and this time he had one question: 'What are you going for Richie, a win or a draw?' I replied: 'We're going for a win of course.' All I received was a dry 'I'm very pleased to hear it.'

Most brilliant selection I have known? My phone rang in Sydney in February 1963 and it was Don from Adelaide. 'Got some news for you,' he said. 'We'll be naming Neil Hawke in the Fifth Test team tomorrow. Thought you'd like to hear it first, rather than read it in the papers. We want to take him to England in 1964 where we think he could be a great success.' So he was, but what brilliant forward planning.

Apart from the serious bits on the field, there was always a good dry sense of humour with most things Don did. My last Sheffield Shield match was in Adelaide in February 1964 and, in making a presentation, Roy Middleton, Chairman of the SACA, emphasised mine was a household name in Australia and indelibly imprinted in the minds of cricket lovers the world over. He then proposed the toast 'to Richie Benny....' Three days later at the SCG I found pinned up behind the dressing-room door a newspaper story of the impending arrival of the great American comedian Jack Benny. In Sir Donald's handwriting were the words, 'Your brother I presume...?'

THE BRADMAN HONOUREE
Neil Harvey
Wednesday 31st October, 2007

"When considering the stature of an athlete, I place great store on certain qualities which I believe to be essential, in addition to skill. They are that the person conducts his life with dignity, with integrity, with courage and perhaps most of all modesty. These virtues are totally compatible with pride, ambition, determination and competitiveness."

BRADMAN
FOUNDATION
www.bradman.com.au

Sir Donald Bradman AC

Neil Harvey used this bat to score 112 in his first appearance in England, during the famous Leeds Test victory when Australia chased down 404 on the final day to secure the Ashes, with him hitting the winning boundary.

He used this bat for the first and only time in the historic Test. Years later Don Bradman wrote on the back in fountain pen ink: "This bat is a symbol of the great innings of my friend Neil Harvey during Australia's greatest ever test victory: Leeds 1948 - Don Bradman".

NEIL HARVEY

(Left-handed batsman who scored 6149 runs at 48.41 in 73 Tests for Australia and a national selector for 12 years. Member of Australia's Team of the 20th Century)

Don Bradman was an outstanding mentor to many, especially me: firstly as the 19 year old baby of the 1948 Invincibles tour of England, and later as a selector sitting by his side.

One of my prized possessions is the bat I used when I scored 112 in my first appearance in England, during the famous Leeds Test victory when we chased down 404 on the final day to secure the Ashes, with me hitting the winning boundary.

I didn't have a bat in Australia, so I borrowed one from my district club Fitzroy for the tour. When we arrived in England, Slazenger gave us two bats each. They were Don Bradman autograph Sykes bats. I used one against the counties and kept the other in case I played a Test.

When I was given the nod for the fourth Test at Leeds, I used the new bat. It had not even been used in the nets. After my century and the winning blow, I never used it again. Some years later, Sam Loxton asked if he could borrow it, and to never mind why. He took it to Don who wrote on the back in fountain pen ink: "This bat is a symbol of the great innings of my friend Neil Harvey during Australia's greatest ever test victory: Leeds 1948 - Don Bradman".

It is a marvellous reminder of that great tour, and the great man. We had one, and only one team meeting, and that was on the ship en route to England. He told us he didn't care what we did as long as we were fit and ready for action at the start of each day's play. He said he wanted us to play bright and exciting cricket - and enforced that was what we would do! And that was it.

Bradman led from the front and was a great captain. He had a tough job in 1948. He spoke on behalf of the team at all the functions, luncheons and dinners - he was outstanding at it and, of course, nobody wanted to hear from anyone but Bradman. He worked hard on those speeches to ensure he represented himself and Australia with total professionalism. When we were on the ship for five weeks going to England, he never appeared before lunch. It wasn't, as some originally thought, that he suffered from sea sickness - he locked himself in his cabin each morning preparing his speeches. This was his final tour and he knew what would be required. He was a freak at whatever he did, and he was a first-class speaker.

The English loved him. He was the No 1 sportsman there, revered more than even their own soccer or cricket heroes. I don't think I know a bloke who was so feted, as indeed he is in Australia with grandstands named in his honour at Sydney and Adelaide, and statues almost everywhere. He still maintains his position as the No 1 sportsman this country has produced. And I'm not sure anyone will ever take that honour from him.

For me, it was an experience of a lifetime. I was there on that eight month adventure to learn as much as I could and there was no-one better to learn from than Bradman and that group of senior champion players. I watched every ball of the 34 matches, whether I played or not. I even watched every ball the day we scored 721 in a day at Essex, and I sat in the dressing rooms after every day's play and listened to the senior players talking cricket. I was a non-drinker in those days and I would sit in the corner and leave with the last players - and all that education made me the cricketer I became.

Don was a good mentor. He wasn't one to offer much advice, as I discovered early. I had an average of seven after four county matches and I asked Loxton to visit his mate and ask how I could overcome my batting problems in these dramatically different conditions. Sam returned with the message: "You tell your little mate that if he keeps the ball along the ground he can't get out." I stopped trying to loft the ball after that and the runs started to flow.

But he was never one to curtail a batsman's freedom. I remember years later during an Adelaide Test that I joked to Sam that Bradman had given me almost no advice during my playing days unless I approached him. Of course, as expected, Sam put it to Don who said that maybe there was one thing he might have suggested along the way.

"That shot from just short of a length, when Neil steps back and gives himself room to smack past point for four.... maybe I would have said that he could do better to push it for a single and diminish the risk. But how disappointing it would have been to those people to whom he gave so much pleasure with that shot."

Bradman always wanted you to succeed and score runs, but at the same time he wanted cricket to be entertaining and he preferred you played exciting shots than poke around.

I played only one game against Don Bradman, for Victoria against South Australia in Adelaide in 1946/47, and I played only four Tests with him (and was 12th man five times).

I joke these days that I out-scored him in three of those four Tests (13 to 201 and 153 to 58 against India and 112 to 33 and 17 to 0 against England) so I must have been a better player at the time! Gee, I was only 19 and he was 39 and he obviously wasn't the dominant player he had been in the 1930s, but he was still outstanding. I could only imagine how good he was at his prime.

His second innings at Leeds when he and Arthur Morris shared that 301 run partnership was just exhilarating to watch. He scored 173 not out, and I took plenty of ribbing down the years for hitting the winning boundary.

We joked later that I was to blame for depriving Don from finishing his Test career with an average of 100 because I should have allowed him to collect that final boundary.

Of course, I respond that I wasn't to know he was going to get out for a duck in his final innings. The irony of all that was that nobody knew that he needed only four runs to finish his Test career with an average of 100. It is not like today with all the statistics available. The players didn't know, and neither obviously did the English media, as it was never mentioned at the time. He just went out to bat as usual. I am convinced the rousing reception he received from the crowd got to him emotionally, and he had tears in his eyes. He came back in after the duck and none of us knew what to say. He sat down and said: "Fancy doing a thing like that!" It was some time later we discovered his final average, which made it all the more remarkable.

While Bradman let the players pretty much do their own thing, he was still a tough leader. They knew their limits and made sure they toed the line: nobody wanted to let Don or the team down. But if he felt it necessary to provide a gentle reminder, he was not afraid to let a player know, in his own way, that he needed to step back into line. After we had secured the Ashes at Leeds we jumped straight on a train to Derbyshire, where we had to front up to play the next day. We didn't get to the hotel until close to midnight, and Ray Lindwall celebrated our success with a session of beers off his long run. He wasn't feeling too well the next morning but Bradman threw him the ball and made him bowl for an hour and a half and then said: "Ray, you will not do that again, will you?" Bradman had his way of making his point.

Bradman was a champion bloke, as I discovered later when I was a selector. He was 20 years older than me, which was a big difference when I was a teenager but not so dramatic when I was a retired Australian vice-captain. I got to know Don a lot better when we were selectors. I started alongside Don and Jack Ryder, and there were no better blokes to learn anything about cricket and selection than that pair. They were two great Australian captains, two outstanding cricket minds. It was a privilege to sit and listen to them and see how they sifted through players to come up with a team.

It was a privilege to go to Don's home to pick teams. He was a great entertainer, a wonderful host. And he was not a wowser, as many believed. He wasn't a bloke to walk into a public bar, and I never saw him have a beer. But he enjoyed the best wines and a sherry.

His contribution to the game was enormous. When you look back and think that he was Australian captain and a national hero when I was eight years old says a lot about his sustained contribution to cricket as a player, selector and administrator. He knew everything about the game, from absolutely every angle.

And in his no fuss way he passed on his wisdom - and I was one of the great beneficiaries.

These pads were worn by Bradman
on his last tour to England in 1948.

THE
LAWS OF CRICKET

(1947 Code 1st Edition)

W. A. OLDFIELD LTD
OFFICIAL DEPOT

The "Classic"
CRICKET SCORING BOOK

WITH LATEST RULES
AND SUMMARY

Bradman was always keen for entertaining cricket and looked at all angles when assessing the laws of the game. In this letter, written on May 26, 1969, he ponders the LBW law. His suggestion is aimed at giving more encouragement to leg-spinners.

Copy for
Information

26th May. 1969.

Mr. Alan Barnes,
Sec. Aust. B. of Control,
SYDNEY.

Dear Alan,

Yours of 19th May to Emergency Committee to hand....

.... (a) Excessive pad play. I wrestled with this for ages. It takes quite a deal of digesting.

We can be very gratified at the measure of agreement between M.C.C. and Australia. At least we have the same intent, which is very good.

It took me a long time to really appreciate the difference between the M.C.C. proposal and ours. I'm not absolutely certain I have it right now but I believe it to be simply this:-

Under our proposal (among other things) a man could be out LBW to a ball pitched outside the off stump, even though he makes a genuine attempt to hit the ball, providing the obstruction takes place between wicket and wicket and the ball would have hit the wicket BECAUSE THAT IS INCLUDED IN THE PRESENT LAW TO WHICH WE PROPOSE TO ADD A NOTE.

Under their proposal this proviso in the present law is cut out. A man may be hit on the pad between wicket and wicket by a ball pitched outside the off stump and which the umpire believes would have hit the wicket, but, PROVIDING HE ATTEMPTS TO PLAY THE BALL, he is not out.

Two things about it. One is that I don't think the wording of the M.C.C. proposed new law is as clear as it might be. I am inclined to think the rank and file umpires will have some difficulty in deciding what it means. (My wife says I'm wrong about this. Am I?)

The second thing is that I hesitate to take away from bowlers their existing advantage that they can at present get a man LBW to a ball pitched outside the off stump even though he plays at the ball.

However the withdrawal of this benefit seems to centre entirely around the criterion that forcing a batsman to play at the ball should be the paramount objective; and that has merit.

Boiled down to its simplest terms it means we go back to the old LBW law, EXCEPTING WHEN A MAN DOES NOT PLAY AT THE BALL AND IT IS PITCHED OUTSIDE THE OFF STUMP.

I have considerable reservations as to whether this will prove adequate. But it has set me thinking.

If we now accept this new criterion, then I think we have got to re-think the law as a whole. If we go back to the old LBW law (EXCEPT WHEN NO ATTEMPT IS MADE TO PLAY THE BALL), there is surely a very strong case for adding the leg side.

My previous objection to including the leg side (at this stage anyway) was on the grounds that a man could be given out to a ball pitched outside his leg stump, EVEN THOUGH HE PLAYED AT IT. (I won't enlarge here on the reasons I advanced).

But if he can't be out LBW to a ball not pitched between wicket and wicket PROVIDING HE ATTEMPTS TO PLAY THE BALL, this is a different matter.

Why not give him out on the leg side as well as the off side (where the conditions are fulfilled) providing he makes no attempt to hit the ball.

This would be a great encouragement to the leg spinner.

At this late hour Alan I can scarcely expect that this latter view will find majority favour but at least I feel it ought to be put forward for very serious and detailed discussion.

Whilst I have reservations about the M.C.C. proposal in that it will restore certain LBW protection to batsmen which today they don't possess, I am mindful of the views apparently unanimously expressed by English captains on Page 2, and of the aim which we both have to encourage strokes - even though I still fear the strokes of the Cowdreys will be as negative as ever.

To sum up, I would be willing to accept either change, theirs or ours, according to the majority view of the Conference, but, if the M.C.C. view prevails, would like to press for a full debate on the aspects of the leg side and its possible effect on the development of the leg spinner.

Yours faithfully,

Don Bradman

Bradman was a conservative administrator and was especially keen to ensure that funds were available for grassroots cricket. This letter, written on October 22, 1973, confirms $20 per day was "ample remuneration" for players for expenses. He also queries the prospect of players being paid more for a one-day international than a day of Test cricket.

2 HOLDEN STREET.
KENSINGTON PARK.
SOUTH AUSTRALIA 5068

SIR DONALD BRADMAN

22nd October 1973.

Mr. R. Parish,
G.P.O. Box 2000,
MELBOURNE.

Dear Bob,

Yours of 19th Inst. reached me today. Before dealing with the prime matter therein you may be interested to know that the S.A. delegates voted unanimously that (a) with great reluctance they would agree to our team starting in N.Z. on the Friday (15th), (b) they were firm in their view that $20. p.day was ample remuneration, and (c) they thought the allowances to manager and captain were adequate.

In regard to (b) we pointed out in particular the remarks of Mr. Jacobs in his final report on allowances on the W.I. tour, and the probable precedent we would set and the problems we might create for ourselves when the next and much more important overseas tour took place.

Now back to the Wills sponsorship. Here we all agreed that we should accept the offer of $150,000 for the two years and we don't feel disposed to argue about the split up of $50,000 and $100,000.

I assume the last paragraph on page 1 of your letter is intended to refer to the N.Z. tour of Australia this summer. There is of course no International one day match on that tour, so therefore we are at this stage only talking about the 3 test matches. I am assuming you do not intend to recommend any sponsorship prize money for matches between a State and N.Z.

Whilst I am very tempted to say that would be the right attitude, I just wonder whether we are not setting up an anomaly by paying our players bonus money for a Shield game and nothing for a State game v N.Z.

The next thing is that I assume we would have to get the concurrence of the Board of the visiting country for any payments to be made so far as they were concerned and that this money should, in the absence of any other arrangement, be paid to their manager.

With that brief pre-amble I think I would agree to the figures you suggest - namely $3,000 per test, divisible in the way you mention.

I guess the above matters should be decided quickly.

So far as the English tour is concerned, I believe the whole Board could decide this matter in January. In the interim, I lean to the same for tests, but for the 1 day Internationals I'm a little inclined to think $1,000 to the winner and $250 to the loser and $100 to the "man of the match" on each side would be ample (i.e. $1,450 per game). On your basis you are really proposing $600 per day for tests and $2,000 (or $2,200, I'm not sure which) p.day for the 1 day games. The difference seems out of proportion. But as I said there is time for the Board to decide this in January.

For Sheffield Shield matches I think your suggestion is as good as one could devise. It is a big slice to give the players 50% of the cake but if it saves us paying more or establishing a fund, it may pay off. If this eventuates, God only knows what will happen in the first season afterwards when or if sponsorship is withdrawn. The players will still expect the same and they won't be worrying about where the money comes from. But I guess we have to leave some problems for our successors to grapple with.

I hope my comments may have been helpful. I've not sent a copy to Barnes or Tim because I preferred you to have a look first, but if you have no big disagreement perhaps you could send a copy on.

Kindest regards,

Don

DON BRADMAN
Australia's Champion Batsman

STARS OF THE TEST MATCHES

This Wallet belongs to......

Bradman was a stickler for proper behaviour on the field and was concerned in April of 1976 about an incident involving wicketkeeper Rod Marsh. While Marsh was severely reprimanded, Bradman wrote that "I'm certain that no Board member feels that Marsh has been adequately dealt with." He suggested a code of behaviour with the national body, not state bodies, to be in control.

"In addition to skill I value character in any sportsman, specifically dignity, courage, integrity and above all, modesty." (Bradman and what he valued in a sports person).

SIR DONALD BRADMAN

2 HOLDEN STREET.
KENSINGTON PARK.
SOUTH AUSTRALIA 5068

12th April 1976.

Dear Bob,

        ... I now understand that the Board members as a whole have agreed that Marsh be severely reprimanded.   No doubt this decision was arrived at simply because under all the circumstances the Board could not, in practical terms, do anything else.   But I'm certain no Board member feels that Marsh has been adequately dealt with.

        We have become victims of a system which does not provide the machinery to cope with the happenings which regrettably took place last season.   In switching from Interstate Conference to Board controlling everything, this little matter inadvertently got under our guard.   I believe we must rectify the position by altering our machinery and this requires very careful thought.

        It will, I think, mean altering the Board's Constitution, probably getting uniform legislation adopted by each state in its own by-laws and probably altering the format of umpires report forms and their destination. Possibly also players agreements to play.

        I don't really see any insurmountable problem providing the legislators have got the guts to agree that we are going to stamp out bad behaviour by our cricketers.   However it does worry me that, as things stand, the issue looks like being left until the September meeting of the Board when obviously a very long and wearisome discussion would ensue, with agreement on all points unlikely.

        Then, as I see it, any agreement which might be reached, would need to go back to the States for ratification and there would possibly be further delays in getting State legislation adopted.

        Whilst all this was happening the season could be half over, whereas I believe we should aim to have any change operative from the start of the season.

R.SP. (Cricket Tele)

My preliminary thoughts are that (a) the Board should get umpire's reports and be responsible for taking action in all Test matches.

(b)   That umpire's reports in all matches between states and between an international team and a state should go to the State or States concerned, and that the State of the player involved should be responsible for inflicting a penalty (if any) on such player, but obviously such penalty could only extend to (i) Club matches under the control of that State and/or (2) to interstate games in which that state was engaged.   In other words they could suspend a player from selection from Shield Matches, but not tests.   The Board however could easily adopt a clause that no player shall be approved for tests whilst under suspension by a State and so the position would automatically be covered.   The States could then adopt "in reverse" legislation, so that an offence in a Test could bring about automatic suspension from State games.

Frankly I think it is absurd for the Board to have the responsibility of say determining the sentence on a W.A. player who misbehaved in Perth in a game S.A. v W.A., and of course no State can have authority to impose a sanction on another State's player.

As for Barnes' idea of some "uniform" penalty as between States, I think this unworkable.   The multiplicity of offences that can be committed is such that the penalties must always remain a matter of discretion, from "no action" to "life".   Moreover the background is very important and here is where the State knowledge and control is so vital.

We have at least one, I think two senior players, who have been reported for serious offences in grade cricket three times, and they've been warned that next time will bring suspension.

Clearly an offence at Shield level by one of these players would be much more serious than a "first offence" by some youngster in his first ever moment of heated confrontation, perhaps brought about by provocation.

Anyway thats a brief run down on my thoughts Bob.

I feel we should not let the matter rest until September but should start getting our teeth into it now, and who else can start the ball rolling but the Emergency Committee?

How do you see the situation?

Kind regards,

Don

BILL JACOBS

(Manager of the Rest of the World and Australian touring teams, a Victorian selector, Fitzroy wicket-keeper and media commentator)

Sir Donald Bradman always looked outside the square as an administrator: he was a man of vision, a man who could turn crisis into triumph.

There was never a better example than in 1971/72 when, as chairman of the Australian Cricket Board, he was forced to cancel the tour by South Africa because of raging apartheid in that country. Rather than take it as a defeat, he organised a Rest Of The World team to show that cricket was above politics. The side was multi-cultural - it brought together English, West Indian, New Zealand, Indian, Pakistani and South African cricketers to show the world that apartheid (racism) had no place in cricket, or, indeed, sport.

The Herald & Weekly Times sponsored the tour, I think for $70,000. The players received $200 a week, and they were rapt. And Bradman gave me the challenge, on 24 hours notice, of managing the group. It was the experience of a lifetime.

Gary Sobers was captain. He came only because of his great admiration for Sir Donald, who personally approached him. When the team gathered in Melbourne, I called a team meeting and told them we would have a ball - there would be no curfews or whatever, so long as they did what I asked. If not, I would tell them.

There were challenges galore. For example, in the December there was a seven day war between India and Pakistan. I called Sunil Gavaskar, Farookh Engineer and Bishen Bedi from India to a meeting with Intikhab Alam, Asif Masood and Zaheer Abbas from Pakistan and asked what the situation was, and if we had any problems.

They said all was well between them and the only thing to be wary of was having their photos taken together, because if that went home their families could be in strife.

So we played ducks and drakes, even when the players walked on to the field. Gavaskar would walk out behind Sobers, a Pakistan player would be a couple back, followed a few back by an Indian and so on down the line. We never had an Indian and a Pakistan player together in case of a photograph.

Sir Donald's influence on this group - they were the best in the world and playing a wonderful Australian side - was amazing. When they were thrashed in two days in Adelaide by South Australia, I ordered them to stop packing their bags and to be at training the next day. I wasn't too popular, and certainly no more so when I insisted they did it again the following day.

To put a fire under them on that second training morning, I told them that Sir Donald was coming to watch them in the nets. You have never seen a training session like it! Even Sir Donald said he was amazed by their enthusiasm and skills and looked forward to a great series. The boys really lifted, simply because of the presence of the great man.

At the end of the tour I organised a dinner and Sir Donald was our only guest. It was a night to celebrate, not one for speeches. However after I thanked all the players for their efforts, Sir Donald asked if he could say a few words. He went through every player as a mark of his appreciation for them coming to save the Australian summer and to show the world that cricketers could mix with immunity to racial or religious bias.

When he arrived at Richard Hutton, the son of Sir Leonard, he told him to forget about his ordinary tour and that his time would come. Then he said: "I have an appreciation of what it must be like to be the son of a famous father because I can tell you that in the space of the next few days my son is changing his name by deed poll."

That was in February 1972. He was not critical or anything. He just mentioned it because he was making a point to Richard. It was a stunning end to a stunning tour.

The players presented me with a pair of boxing gloves that night. It was appropriate because we had our moments on tour and I didn't mind stepping in to sort things out. I figured Sir Donald had chosen me to manage this team because, I'll admit, I could drink and smoke and stay up all night with the best of them - we got on famously for that reason.

That probably was one of Sir Don's strengths: he could see who might best handle a particular job. I reckon we proved that on this farewell night. I knew a bit of Afrikaans from my trip to South Africa - and we had Tony Greig, Hylton Ackerman and Peter and Graeme Pollock in the troupe - and the Indians had taught me a bit of Urdu along the way. So during a speech I mixed a bit of the languages with forthright Aussie speak and later Sir Donald asked what I'd said in a foreign tongue. Intikhab told him and he said; "That is not very becoming of an Australian manager!" We all had a great laugh.

From what was a crisis in world cricket, with Australia at the pointy end, Sir Donald had conjured a counter-attack with a world team. He was the master, and cricket was the winner.

My time with Sir Donald went back to 1966/67 when he paid me a great compliment by asking me to manage the Australian team to South Africa. That was the first time someone who wasn't on the Australian Cricket Board was made a tour manager. At the end of that tour, Victoria was ravaged by bushfires and the Board organised a Bushfire Test between the tourists to South Africa and an Australian XI that had toured New Zealand. I spent three or four days of that match at the MCG talking to Sir Donald - especially as we had been humbled in South Africa. And I later was manager of the Australian team to the West Indies in 1973.

Sir Donald's vision was not restricted to cricket. We now have a national AFL competition but it was way back in 1969, years before the national expansion that Sir Donald thought of spreading the code under one umbrella.

After I had interviewed Sir Donald at my home in Pascoe Vale one day, I drove him to the Windsor Hotel. On the way he told me he was going to speak with the president of the Melbourne Cricket Club, Sir Albert Chadwick, about the prospect of forming a southern states football league, comprising ten teams from Victoria, two from Western Australia and two from South Australia. Of course these days the national competition does have two teams from both WA and SA. His idea failed at the time. He told me later that Sir Albert rejected the idea because it meant that two teams from Victoria would have to be dumped. When you think that was in 1969 and South Melbourne didn't go to Sydney until 1982 to start the expansion to a national competition, it just showed how far ahead of the times he was.

SIR DONALD BRADMAN

2 H.   EN STREET,
KENSINGTON PARK,
SOUTH AUSTRALIA 5068

10th April 1978.

Mr. R. Parish,
G.P.O. Box 200C,
MELBOURNE.

Dear Bob,   S. Africa - Varachia.

Yours of 3rd April on the above subject is to hand.

As you are aware, I had been informed by Joe Pamensky
that he was going to London with that delegation.
Freddie Brown's letter is a masterpiece of telling us
nothing.   There is no indication whatever of the U.K. views.
But of course he seeks ours.
In reply to Pamensky, back on 29th March, I said
"inter alia", -

"I shall be anxious to hear what happens when you go to London
with that delegation.   Unfortunately I am despondent in believing
(as I always said) that although your cricketers have done everything
you can in S.A.,....

....countries will now come out with the verdict,
the political verdict, that they can't play S.A. so long as Apartheid
is Gov't policy.   Regrettable too, our Prime Minister, gives the
impression that he thinks the same way.   And I don't think the Unions
have changed their stance.
I believe you will get a good and sympathetic hearing from the
cricket fraternity in London, but what is the use of that if the powers
that be won't let tours take place....

.... That, as I see it, is a summary of the position....

....I gravely doubt whether our Board can do anything.
The subject is now so political that I can't see
us playing S.A.... we have the problem of our Gov't, the Unions and
the demos. If Varachia comes to Australia, maybe he should
seek an interview with the P.M.   In any event surely the next
positive step must come through the I.C.C.

Sincerely,

Don

Bradman wanted the tour by South Africa to proceed in 1971-72 but relented to political pressure
because of Apartheid. Instead he instigated a multi-racial team tour to show sport's solidarity against
apartheid. South Africa's ban from international cricket continued and in April, 1978, he wrote a
pragmatic letter to Board chairman Bob Parish explaining that the governments of the world, not
cricket officials, would determine when South Africa would be welcome back into the fold.

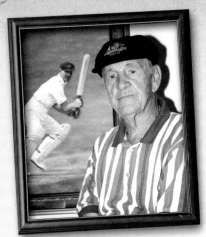

SAM LOXTON

(1948 Invincible and national selector between 1970 and 1981)

I will never forget the day I bowled my first ball to my hero, Don Bradman.

It was at the Adelaide Oval in 1947-48, just after lunch on the opening day of Victoria's match against South Australia. My captain Lindsay Hassett beckoned in my general direction in the covers. I looked around and only Neil Harvey was near, so I knew I was being called upon to bowl. Harvey just said " bad luck" as I marched to the bowling crease. I looked up and there was my boyhood hero, Don Bradman, at the striker's end.

You must remember that when Don was playing his first Test series in 1928-29, I was an eight year old playing cricket against a pine tree in the corner of the Yarra Park state school, just near the MCG. I told Hassett that I wanted two slips and he suggested I leave the captaincy to him and perhaps I should mark out my run. As I went to do so, he tapped me on the shoulder and suggested I might need what he had in his hand - the ball. Yes, I was a bit nervous.

Hassett then said: "We will do our very best to get the ball back to you as quickly as possible". Buoyed by the obvious confidence of the captain, I hurled myself into the task and the direction of my first ball was spot on and the length looked good. I had a vision of the ball passing through the bowler's gateway to heaven, between bat and pad, and into leg stump. Then something four and a quarter inches wide and weighing only 2lb 2oz got in the way and the ball hit the square leg fence at the speed of light.

Bradman probably hadn't been bowled at by a raving lunatic before, and we met half pitch and I said: "Turn it up, that was a pretty good nut". And, smiling, he replied: "But a better shot, Sammy." I was dumbfounded - more by the fact that he knew my name than by the shot or his comment. We stayed on the friendliest of talking terms for the rest of his life. I get tears in my eyes just thinking about the wonderful times we had together.

I had the pleasure of being part of Don's 99th and 100th first-class centuries. The 99th was when I first bowled to him in Adelaide, and his 100th came when I was his teammate in an Australian XI against India at the SCG soon after.

He just scored runs at will. I recalled a comment Don made to Norman May in a series of interviews in 1988, during which he talked about his playing days at the famous MCG ground. "I didn't like playing at The Melbourne. I found it a difficult ground to play on."

Well, I looked up his Test record: 1671 runs at an average of 128.5, with one double century, eight centuries and three half-centuries in 17 innings. God help us if he had liked the ground!

I saw every innings he played there from 1931-32, having missed only three earlier Tests. I was there when he got out first ball, and you could have heard a pin drop.

However the highlight for me was the 1948 tour, which was a dream. Don pretty much had the perfect side: bowlers for all occasions, batting depth, excellent fieldsmen. It was on the way to England on the ship that I first started calling him George, his second name, and which I always called him after that. Ron Hamence, who had a beautiful voice, would go back to his cabin at night and sing away, while Don was in his cabin next door. One night Ron suddenly yelled out: "What did you think of that, George?" I figured if Ron would get away with George, I'd try it. Don never objected and that's the way it was to be from then on.

I guess I got away with a lot more than most with Don. Like the time on that 1948 tour when I asked, loud enough for everyone to hear, what you had to do to get a bat in this side. It was at Manchester and, as usual, Don put up the batting order on the back of an envelope behind the dressing room door. Lo and behold, I was at No 4. I batted with Don that day and he was out to Malcolm Hilton. I spoke with Don in the rooms later and said: "That wasn't very nice of you this morning. I don't get a chance to bat with you very often and you get yourself out to that ordinary conveyance."

Well, he did the same in the second innings. Now to dismiss Bradman gave any bowler a chance of Test selection, and to do it twice in a match was a huge boost. I figured Don was trying to con the English selectors into picking Hilton for the next Test, but they didn't fall for it.

The only 'sledge' on that marvellous tour came during our innings of 721 in the day at Essex, and it was nothing like you hear these days.

Don was in scintillating touch when Essex introduced spinner Frank Vigar for the final over before lunch. After looking at the first ball, Don belted the next into the white tin fence forward of square leg, making a small impression, the following ball into the same spot to make a dent, and the next into the exact same spot to embed the ball in the hole.

The wicketkeeper, Frank Rist, walked up to Don and said: "Sir, is that the only shot you've got!"

After a gent used the heel of his boot to release the ball from the fence, Don hoisted the next delivery, which again pitched outside leg stump, high over mid-off into the fence. "That's another one," he said.

Being a selector with Don was a wonderful experience. There was never an argument, only discussions. We talked about the coming game or tour, what was required, who the candidates were and what they had done and could be expected to do. It all flowed from there. The days of Don, Neil Harvey and myself at the selection table were truly memorable. He would pick me up at the Adelaide train station and drive me home to his place, where I would stay with he and Jessie.

I was a very lucky bloke to know Don Bradman - and to have known him as a friend.

MALCOLM GRAY

(Former chairman of the International Cricket Council and Cricket Australia and now patron of Cricket Victoria)

The first time I met Sir Donald was in Sydney in the early 1980s when I attended an Australian Cricket Board meeting as a proxy for Victorian Len Maddocks. Sir Donald was in the second of his three year terms as chairman of the ACB. I remember ringing my wife Nerida and commenting that only two people at the meeting weren't using Brylcreem (a hair product that kept combed hair in place and gave it a shine or gloss) - her father, Ray Steele, who was bald, and her husband, who was too young to slick back his hair like the rest, being only 40 at the time.

Anyway, I didn't really know many people at the meeting and I sat on my own at lunch. Don Bradman, quite deliberately, joined me, sat beside me and made me feel most welcome. Of course, he was keen to find out more about this young bloke from Victoria, and I was overjoyed to meet the legend.

When I became chairman of the then Australian Cricket Board in 1986, it was the start of a new era. The board had consisted of some wonderful servants of the game, including Bradman, Tim Caldwell, Fred Bennett, Bob Parish and Ray Steele. They had all moved on, and the new board was from a new generation, facing new challenges in rapidly changing and volatile times.

It did not take long before there was a potential crisis. Because of his exalted position within Australian cricket, and his worldly knowledge, I asked if I could call on him for counsel.

In typical Bradman fashion, he organised afternoon tea at the Hilton Hotel in Adelaide and we discussed the situation for a couple of hours. I believe it was about the time that the players were urging for a bigger slice of cricket's finances.

I requested advice and he gave it to me. He was always more than happy, if I asked for help, to provide advice, but he would never interfere in the operations of Cricket Australia or the International Cricket Council.

His advice always was logical, well-reasoned and gratefully accepted. He would not argue a particular line or take a specific side, but instead would suggest that I consider this point or that, make allowances for any potential ramifications and the like.

He added an historical impact, often saying I should remember an episode in the past, look at the outcome, and perhaps see if there was a parallel to be drawn with the modern era problem. He brought his extensive knowledge and experience to bear, and his advice was always sound.

I was chairman of the Australian Cricket Board from 1986 to 1989 and then chairman of the International Cricket Council between 2000 and 2003. Throughout all my travels it was obvious what an influence Bradman had within the game, and the esteem in which he was held, not only by cricket folk but the wider community. He was admired universally as a sportsman, recognised as the international face of cricket, and feted as a national icon by cricket lovers, all sports people, politicians, religious leaders: all and sundry. And his impact on this nation was hailed internationally.

There is no doubt he made a massive contribution to cricket administration in Australia, and influenced the way fellow administrators looked at their duties. Bradman always considered what was good for the game, both within Australian and globally. Bob Parish was one administrator who followed Bradman's doctrines to the letter, and he too was regarded as one of the world's outstanding administrators. I admit to copying his administrative tact, a trait I learned from two others he mentored, Parish and Steele.

Yet it was the extraordinary influence, and esteemed position, that Bradman held overseas that amazed me, particularly in India and England. In fact, many senior administrators from those countries, even though they didn't know him, would come to Australia to get an audience with him. To have met the man, the cricketing god, the doyen of cricket administrators, was to have bragging rights for life for many of them.

I must confess there were times when being in Bradman's company seemed odd for me, a man whose life in cricket's family was as an administrator with an aggregate as a Melbourne University fourth XI captain probably about the same as Bradman's Test batting average. I was always destined for administration, and how fortunate I was to meet so many wonderful people along the way, and enjoy so many marvellous experiences.

That occurred to me when Australia returned home after winning back the Ashes in 1989. It was the first time since 1930 that a team had reclaimed the Ashes on foreign soil and a ticket-tape parade was organised through the main streets of Sydney.

Sir Donald, who was involved in the previous milestone series win (he scored 232 in the deciding Test at The Oval to clinch a 2-1 series win), and Malcolm Gray, as chairman of the Australian Cricket Board, sat in an open horse-drawn carriage along the parade route. Just the two of us together as tens of thousands cheered home our victorious modern day heroes. I wondered at the time what I was doing there. And so, perhaps, did Bradman.

The public cheered him all the way, as you would expect, and I just went along for the ride. It was a unique experience and the only advice he gave me was to smile and savour it all.

So typically Bradman.

Kerry Packer's World Series Cricket caused upheaval in cricket ranks from 1977 until the compromise in 1979. Bradman, who was on a sub-committee dealing with the issues at the time, wrote to Parish in March of 1978 about several concerns, including TV rights, the media, an impending visit by South African Cricket Union head and his opinion of comments by young Australian batsman David Hookes on a hopeful end to the cricket hostilities.

SIR DONALD BRADMAN

HOLDEN STREET,
KENSINGTON PARK,
SOUTH AUSTRALIA 5068

21st March 1978.

Dear Bob,

Thankyou for yours of 15th March.

Re T.V.   I would not willingly support any move to have government interference in T.V. rights which may control Packer because, as I have said many times before, it would inevitably bring control of the fees that may be paid.

On the other hand, your assessment of a "realistic" fee for T.V. can only be judged in the future when we know what is offering following the conclusion of our present arrangement.

Re The Media.   I agree your remarks.   There is no doubt the Packer protagonists are cleverly using the press for propoganda purposes.   I see no clear cut solution but I believe the only hope is for you, personally, to see the executive heads of all these papers, privately, and explain the position to them and ask for their support in the interests of national cricket.   And I think it ought to be done well in advance of next summer....

...Varachia.   I knew all about his impending visit.   Of course you must see him.   But I see no way that you can avoid telling him that with all the goodwill in the world, despite all the efforts of the S.A. cricket fraternity, that India, Pakistan and W.I. will not have them back in the I.C.C. until "Apartheid"nis abandoned by their Gov't.   Also that the Aust. Gov't is opposed to apartheid and would not support a visit by us to S.A. or vice versa.   If he doesn't understand that I'm afraid you might have to ask him to see Fraser for himself to get confirmation of our Gov'ts views.

This reply will be galling to him.   He will ask what else must the S.A. cricket community do?   They've done all they can. I'm afraid the answer to that is that cricket has been removed from the sporting basket and put in the political basket - not of our wish or doing, but by fate.   Difficult and unpleasant, but we can't mislead Varachia.   He must be told the situation as we see it.

David Hookes won the "Sportsman of the year" award here last night on channel 9.   He was interviewed and asked direct by Michael Charlton "With hindsight, would you do the same again"? David replied "I can't very well answer that - I am on Channell 9". But he went on to say the "younger" members of the Packer troup sincerely believed there should be a get together between the parties and clearly he is feeling his position very keenly....

Kind regards,

Sincerely,

Don

Former captains of their respective countries who have all been knighted - (L-R) Sir Leonard Hutton, Sir Garfield Sobers & Sir Donald Bradman at luncheon, 06/12/84.

Bradman and Len Hutton, 1954.

Frank Worrell, Don Bradman and Richie Benaud.

RANJAN MADUGALLE

(International Cricket Council chief referee and former Sri Lankan captain)

Sir Donald Bradman has incomparable statistics to confirm he is the benchmark for all cricketers. I doubt another of his ilk will come along again. If one however does come along the game of cricket would be the lucky beneficiary.

However, and most importantly, his legacy is not just statistics. He impressed on all cricketers to enjoy the game, to play it hard but fair and be humble with success and gracious in defeat. He firmly believed the game was a noble sport, a character building exercise - in short a way of life.

And at the end of the day, the end of a career, you should look back and think of the enjoyment, the friendships and the achievements, and make sure you have handed the game on to the next generation with its good name and spirit enhanced.

That was what Sir Donald wanted, and he has inspired me and, I dare say, my fellow referees to help the players of the modern era to understand his wishes and the bonus of enriching the game's traditions and its values.

I have read what Sir Donald has said and written and researched his works to the best of my ability and I think I have the drift of his ideals and principles. He had a steely determination, played superbly at the highest level and played it hard. But nobody has anything bad to say about him. He received only tributes throughout his playing days, and he was an ambassador for the game then and later as a selector and administrator.

That is something that every cricketer should seek to emulate, to take a leaf out of the life book of the game's greatest player. You would hope that whenever a player's name is mentioned in the media it is about his skill and on field brilliance played in its correct spirit. That should be their goal. No cricketer should seek attention for any other reasons.

The role of the referee has changed during the past 10-15 years, certainly since I began in 1993. At first we looked to inject a sense of responsibility, respect and introduce minimum standards from playing conditions to practice facilities. These days, at the top end, players play it hard but with a better and fairer sense of understanding of how the game needs to be presented as a total package.

Sir Donald Bradman and cricket are synonymous. He has a presence everywhere in the cricket world, even today. I hear him talked about in revered tones in all my travels, and from my earliest days I can recall people talking about the great man visiting our country when the Australians were en route to England in 1930, 1934, 1938 and 1948.

People talked about the 1930 trip when the Australians played in Colombo against the All Ceylon team and Bradman was out hit wicket from the first ball bowled by N.S. Joseph in his debut match. This is supposed to be the first and the only occasion that Bradman got out hit wicket.

Although he did not play in the 1934 and 1938 trips, a massive crowd of more than 20,000 was at the Colombo Oval for his last visit. He scored only 20 runs before being caught by R.L. de Krester from the bowling of B. Russell Heyn. The bowler gained hero status after that. Such was Sir Donald's status that just to dismiss him gave anyone iconic status. I have heard the story about this dismissal from the bowler himself later to be Major General Russell Heyn when he was our manager on a few tours. Of course the flavour of the dismissal varied from tour to tour and according to the audience!

Unfortunately I never had the opportunity to meet him. I was in South Australia a few times but unfortunately he was not in the best of health and I couldn't meet him. That was disappointing because I have heard so much of him since I was a toddler.

I began playing the game when I was about three years of age. I made the Trinity College, Kandy under 12 team when I was 10 and went through the school system, playing most of my cricket later at Royal College in Colombo. In our formative years we were taught that you should never impinge on any of the traditions and values of the game. If anyone stepped out of line he was no longer part of the team. Such principles were deemed and advocated by Sir Donald as paramount and the bedrock of the game.

I have always thought of Sir Donald as the greatest cricketer to play the game. He was a batsman way beyond anyone who has ever played, but sadly there is limited film footage available of his expertise for us to see and learn.

Yet his image remains as strong as ever. I am proud to help uphold such principles - if they were good enough for Sir Donald, they must surely be good enough for others.

Australian cricketer Sir Donald Bradman with Neil Harvey, Alan Davidson, Phil Ridings, Ray Lindwall, Sam Loxton and Bill Johnston.

Len Darling, Bill O'Reilly and Sir Donald Bradman Adelaide Oval 1988.

Former cricketers Neil Harvey (L) & Sam Loxton at the MCG in Melbourne during wake for legendary cricketer Keith Miller.

COLIN EGAR

(Test umpire (29 tests between 1960-69), International Cricket Council delegate, chairman of Cricket Australia, tour manager and friend of Bradman for 50 years.)

Don Bradman was a huge influence on cricket administration in Australia, particularly South Australia, and indeed the world.

He led by example when he was an administrator. He was no man's fool and although he enjoyed a busy life, he wouldn't miss a meeting either at state or national level.

Don always was abreast of issues and he saw their potential impact on the game of cricket - not just a blinkered view for South Australia, or Australia. He was always mindful, and impressed this on all administrators, what ramifications any action could take on an international front. His fight against throwing, the apartheid issue and law changes such as the front foot rule were examples. There was never a case when he would say something might suit Australia but not the rest of the cricketing world - they were one in the same to Don. If something was good or bad for world cricket, it was the same for Australia, and vice versa. His vision was for the game worldwide, not sectional interests.

He took control of meetings, both at state and national level. Everyone listened to every word he said, and he spoke only when he had something important to say. He used commonsense for what was good for cricket, somehow using a vision to comprehend impacts years down the track.

He had vision and he was forthright. I knew him really well as a friend, but in a committee meeting he adopted a stern appearance: business was business and he ran a meeting in an efficient and professional manner.

When I became chairman of Cricket Australia, he often would ring to ask about progress on important issues. He loved to be, and really needed to be, informed and kept up to date on all matters cricket. He never gave any directives or was overbearing, but he would occasionally put forward a suggestion. He had retired, but he knew what was good for the game and he wanted to ensure those currently in control also were thinking along those lines.

Bradman was a man of his word, and he expected anyone who said they would do something to follow through. I remember one occasion when I was on the International Cricket Council. Don had asked a person to raise a certain issue and he didn't. Don had not asked me to do so, and when he casually asked one day if a certain issue had been raised at the ICC meeting, and I said no, he was furious. He related the story and I don't think he ever spoke to that man again.

When I retired as an umpire in 1970, I was out of cricket for only a month before I joined the finance committee of the South Australian Cricket Association. Don was a wonderful influence on my development in administration. He was a champion cricketer, a champion administrator and a champion bloke, and I was lucky enough to be his friend for half a century.

Bradman was a high level administrator: a man of high integrity. He could be very short, but deep down he was a real character, a great story teller.

He also was a master of business, very astute. Although he left school very young in his education, he was smart. When we were alone one day, I asked if he was a good student. He looked around to ensure nobody was listening, and said simply: "yes". He said it with such an air of confidence that it left me in no doubt he was indeed a very intelligent person, but one who didn't care to let the general public know the depth of his wisdom. I discovered over the years that he was an avaricious reader. He didn't read fiction, but would consume biographies and historic material and rarely spent a day without reading a new book.

I remember seeing him play in 1938 when I was 10. That was a memorable thing for a lad and I've never forgotten it. He was playing for South Australia and my father had enrolled me as a junior SACA member and I loved going to the Adelaide Oval to see The Don play. I can close my eyes and still see him playing shots.

It wasn't until 1952 that I actually met him, when I was umpiring an intervarsity cricket match. Don was a selector at the time, and like everything else he did, he did it efficiently. He would go to matches all over the place to look at the talent on show - grade games, school matches, intervarsity matches, state matches and tests. I remember the varsity matches because they had future Test players on show such as Colin McDonald and Bob Cowper, and Bradman went along to cast his eagle eye over any young talent.

He came over to speak with me on the ground. It was my first year as an umpire. I had umpired League football, a couple of grand finals and interstate matches, and when I was talked into being a cricket umpire I went straight up the ranks. That chat with the most important man in cricket began a friendship and association from which I gained so much pleasure for the next 50 years.

Becoming a cricket umpire was the best move I ever made, although a regret I always harboured was that Don finished playing in 1948 so I never got to umpire a match in which he played. That would have been something special!

Bradman never talked about how good he was as a batsman, or captain or administrator. In fact, he rarely talked about himself, other that to relate stories about tours which involved other people as the main character in the tale.

He was a strong-minded and a resolute person, strong enough to overcome everything that was thrown at him. He was a country boy who went to the big city and took the world by storm as a sportsman. He was a stockbroker who took over a business in Adelaide in controversial circumstances and overcame a lot of negative reaction. And nobody can appreciate what he put up with as a public figure. He couldn't go anywhere without people wanting to talk to him, to get an autograph or a picture.

In the end, that drove him away from going to the Adelaide Oval to enjoy a day watching the cricket. Everyone wanted to sit and talk to him about cricket, or about him. He had no interest in talking about himself, and he went to the game to watch it, not to listen to what others thought of it or to explain what he thought of the play.

It drove him away in the end, and he preferred to play golf rather than sit through another afternoon meeting people he didn't know or want to know. We in the committee room - including SACA president Phil Ridings - did our best to protect him, but people were so brash they would just walk up and sit next to him and start yakking away.

Golf was a marvellous outlet for Don, and he played regularly. One day on the golf course he totally mishit a drive on the fourth tee. He was extremely embarrassed as he turned to Phil Ridings and me and said: "Never done that before in my life." Phil never said a word at the time, but whenever he mishit a shot after that, for years to come, he would turn to Don and declare: "Never done that before in my life." They said it in chorus after a while as they laughed about a poor shot.

Don, in fact, was an excellent golfer who regularly beat his age and won tournaments. He had an extraordinary hand-eye co-ordination. He was brilliant at cricket, golf, tennis, squash, billiards, and piano, absolutely anything he turned his hand to.

Don was a traditionalist, but he knew also that times were changing and that nothing should be set in stone. I recall umpiring at Adelaide Oval and after the day's play I was exhausted. When the Board's umpires' department head Bob Parish, later to become chairman of the Australian Cricket Board, dropped in to our rooms, I told him that it was too hot to wear the white butcher's coat and tie in the heat in the centre, and that if it was as hot again the following day I wouldn't be wearing them. Parish said he hoped he would never see the day that umpires didn't wear the white coat and tie, and left in a somewhat uneasy mood.

Not long after, Bradman visited our room and asked if I had had a clash with Parish. I told him what I had said and he told me to use my commonsense - if it was too hot and we couldn't properly concentrate, leave the coat and tie in the rooms. And when it was sweltering the following day, that's exactly what happened. When Bradman gave you the green light, you knew there would not be any repercussions.

Don was basically a conservative person. However one of the funniest things to happen was when he was caught speeding when driving. It made headlines and he was so embarrassed. He always drove so carefully and within the limits so this was really out of the blue. Naturally all of us gave him hell about it. "Never done that before in my life" and all that.

He had a lot of attributes. He was most hospitable and would always have drinks waiting when people arrived at his home - and he knew what everyone preferred. To listen to him playing the grand piano in his lounge room was a highlight of any visit.

He was a great story teller. One night we went to dinner, Don, myself and Test umpire Lou Rowan and our wives. I had to fly to London the following morning, but Don was still telling stories at 12.30am until Jessie insisted he let me go to bed to be ready for my flight. Don told me later he thoroughly enjoyed the night - although he got lost driving home!

Jessie was wonderful for Don. One evening at a dinner party, he was going on about a particular theory he had, and obviously was bouncing it off Ridings and me to see our reaction. Suddenly Jessie piped up and said: "Don, even you don't believe that!" He immediately dropped the subject. She was the one person I believe had his measure. He adored her, and vice versa, but she held a special spell over him throughout their wonderful marriage.

Don truly was a champion for the game of cricket. He was the hero everyone needed in the Great Depression and after World War II, and he was the administrator who steered the game after his playing days. He sometimes was bemused by change, but he accepted every era was different. When an England team arrived and were put through training drills on the field, doing all sorts of unusual exercises, I asked Don why he was quietly smiling at the exhibition. I asked what he did to get fit for a match. "Just batted" he said.

And when the betting scandals arose not long before his death, I asked what impact he thought it would have on the game. He suggested it would be a slur on the game for a short period, but the game would prosper again and be the great sport it had been for centuries.

There will always be challenges for the game, but the game will conquer all in the end, he said.

Just as Don did during his brilliant life.

SIR MICHAEL PARKINSON
(English television great)

This is the story of how, after a lifetime devoted to interviewing the most famous and talented people in the world, I failed in my ambition to meet the greatest batsman of them all, Sir Donald Bradman. This is an article chronicling my failure written in 1996 during a visit to Australia. After Sir Donald died I was asked to give the Bradman Oration. It was the nearest I got to him and it made me feel very proud.

I have travelled long and far in my search for Donald Bradman. It started nearly fifty years ago when I rode on my bike the thirty miles to Leeds to see his Australian team slaughter our lot.

Since the first glimpse I have been seeking an audience. I have telephoned, telegrammed (remember?), written, faxed, pleaded, ranted and cajoled. The answer has always been no.

I have offered money, attempted to lure him with limousines and expensive hotel suites, persuaded mutual friends to use their influence, even tried incense and prayer. I still haven't interviewed Sir Donald. Not even got close.

On the odd occasion when I have glimpsed him in the distance he vanished before I could reach him, like a mirage. Once or twice I have been somewhere only to be told he had just left. One time the host showed me the teacup he had been drinking from. The liquid was still warm. I felt like an explorer who had just found a fresh footprint of the Abominable Snowman.

Why so persistent? Because he was the greatest cricketer who ever lived and a significant man both in the history of the game and the development of his country. In cricket there have been two towering figures, two people who more than any other wrote the history of the game. They are W. G. Grace and D. G. Bradman. One was still with us and any journalist worth his salt had a duty to try to talk to him.

The other reason is much more selfish. In a lifetime of interviewing people I have talked to most of my heroes.

The two big ones who escaped were Frank Sinatra and Donald Bradman. I got closer to The Kid from Hoboken than I ever did to 'The Boy From Bowral'.

But let us suppose that dreams come true and the interview has been arranged. What do I ask The Don? Well, all else apart, what fascinates me about Bradman is his fame. Generally speaking, being famous is a bit like having measles.

It is a minor affliction and the rash soon disappears. But for some it never goes away. It dictates their life and shapes their circumstances. They and their family are forever on display.

They are isolated by a special kind of celebrity and become icons of their time. Sir Donald Bradman belongs in that category.

I went looking for him on Australia Day in Adelaide. Adelaide is his lair, the cricket ground on the first day of a Test match one of his regular watering-holes and therefore offering the best chance of a sighting.

A man I met said he would take me to have tea with Sir Donald in a box in the Bradman Stand. Overcome by emotion I clasped my new friend by the lapels and told him of my search for the Holy Grail.

A short time later he took me to one side and said he would have to ask Sir Donald if he minded having me in the box. I had obviously frightened him with my exuberance. He must have thought I was going to kidnap The Don or film him with a hidden camera picking his nose.

I told him not to bother Sir Donald with such petty problems and settled instead for a drink in the Bradman Bar looking at pictures of the great man and wondering if they sold such a thing as a Bradman Burger. How close did I get to Sir Donald? Well, eventually I sat at one end of a box and he was fifteen people away.

I know. I counted. In profile he looked like a kookaburra. It was interesting observing people's reaction to his presence. Some sneaked photographs of him, while others blatantly turned their backs to the cricket and surveyed the great man.

Mooching around the ground I came upon my old friend Keith Miller making one of his rare public appearances.

He had just been to see Sir Donald. How was he? "Looks fit enough to be still playing," said Keith. Life is never dull in his company. People are attracted to him like iron filings to a magnet. His personality embraces everyone from bookmakers to conductors of great orchestras, barmaids to brain surgeons, people who sell newspapers on London streets and men who commanded armies in time of war.

His meeting with Sir Donald was a significant one. It might be the last time the two of them got together. Keith is in his mid-seventies, Sir Donald ten years older.

They played with and against each other and it was, at times, a fairly turbulent relationship; they were very different men. Miller was the maverick, Bradman the authoritarian.

Conflict was inevitable. In Sir Donald's last first-class game at Sydney, Miller greeted him with two bouncers. The first, of the harmless variety, was hit for four. The second, preceded by a gesture to the press box declaring, 'If you think that was funny you ain't seen nothing yet', nearly decapitated Sir Donald, who at the time happened to be the chief selector.

Differences apart, what the two men have in common is a celebrity that travels far beyond the shoreline of Australia and represents much more than a reputation gained as flannelled fools.

What they symbolised in their prime, and still do today, is the Australian character at its very best. Bradman was the gifted Aussie battler, the man of few words but great deeds. Miller was the handsome, sun-kissed playboy who laughed at life and didn't give a stuff.

Bradman was the Outback and the fight against nature, Miller was Bondi Beach and a celebration of the good life.

The Bradman legend is built on stories underlining the prowess that set him apart from other men, demonstrated by the encounter with George Macaulay, the feisty Yorkshire seam bowler, in 1930. It was Bradman's first tour of England and there was a popular rumour that the English wickets would sort him out. As an ardent subscriber to this theory Macaulay couldn't wait to get to Bradman.

When Yorkshire played the Australians early in the tour Macaulay demanded loudly of his captain, 'Let me have a go at this bugger'. His first over was a maiden. Bradman then hit him for five fours in the second over and took 16 from the third. A spectator yelled, 'George, tha' should have kept thi' bloody trap shut'.

I once interviewed Jeff Thomson, the fast bowler, about Bradman, and Jeff said that in the 1970s he was at a social event organised by a man who owned a cricket field. During the afternoon, Sir Donald, then in his sixties, was approached by two young cricketers who were on the fringe of the state team. They asked Bradman if they could bowl at him. He pointed out he hadn't played for nearly thirty years, but eventually removed his jacket and picked up a bat.

At first, the young men bowled respectfully at him, aware both of his age and the fact he had neither pad nor gloves. But when Bradman started playing shots, they quickened up and eventually were bowling flat out. According to Thomson, the quicker they bowled, the harder Bradman smote them to the boundary.

Jeff said, "It was bloody magnificent. All my life I had looked at his record and thought, 'How can anyone be twice as good as Greg Chappell?' That day, I found out."

Governor-General Sir Zelman Cowen with Dame Enid Lyons and Sir Donald Bradman after their investiture ceremony at Government House, Canberra, 19/03/80.

RMR/gmc

20th June, 1979

Sir Donald Bradman A.C.,
2 Holden Street,
KENSINGTON PARK. S.A. 5068

Dear Sir Donald,

It gives me great pleasure to write, on behalf of the President and Members of the Association, and indeed on behalf of the hundreds of thousands of cricket lovers in the State of New South Wales, in order to offer our sincere and hearty congratulations on the occasion of the very high honour - Companion of the Order of Australia - recently bestowed upon you.

At a full meeting of this Association held last night a unanimous vote of congratulations to you was carried amid acclamation and it is thus my pleasant duty to advise you of our delight.

As the citation states, your record both as a player and as an administrator is quite without parallel in the history of Australian cricket.

No honour could be more richly deserved or more overdue. It recognises your eminent and gargantuan contribution to the game we all enjoy so much and more importantly it shows that people in high places in this country are aware of your service to Australia in general, cricket in particular.

Your very many friends here send their kindest regards to you and Lady Bradman at this happy time.

Sincerely,

R.M. RADFORD
Secretary

Sir Donald Bradman had long finished his
illustrious playing days but accolades, tributes
and memorials continued to flow. In 1974 he
was honoured at a dinner at Lord's.

In 1979 he was made a Companion of
the Order of Australia.

He was feted throughout the nation and
at all times replied to the hundreds of
letters that arrived daily.

Photograph-Patrick Eager
Sir Don Bradman A.C.
90 YEARS YOUNG - 27/8/98
A TRIBUTE
Limited Edition of 600 sets of which
50 sets are being donated to the
Bradman Museum, Bowral, New South Wales

SIR DONALD BRADMAN

2 HOLDEN STREET,
KENSINGTON PARK,
SOUTH AUSTRALIA 5068

22 . 6 . 79

Dear Sal,

Thankyou for your congratulatory telegram
on the occasion of my recent honour.

I regard it as a tribute to our great national
game & it seems that I am the fortunate medium
through which this recognition is channelled.

Over 50 years I've tried to maintain a
standard and it has not been easy in an age
when virtually everything has become debased.

Even in cricket as I watch 6 men fielding on the
boundary, and no slips, I wonder. Changing
values & changing values are a challenge not only to
our thinking but our characters; and who knows that
better than you.

Regrettably this occasion was marred by my wife
having to undergo another operation but once again
she is bravely & cheerfully on the mend.

Our warmest regards

Sincerely

Don Bradman

223

Dame Pattie Menzies with Sir Donald Bradman.

In 1962/63, Bradman made one final appearance: representing the Prime Minister's XI against the MCC. To the great disappointment of the large crowd - and to the MCC players - he faced only five balls, playing onto his stumps via his foot from a delivery from Brian Statham.

Prime Minister Sir Robert Menzies, Sir Donald Bradman and England captain Ted Dexter walk down the stairs at Manuka Oval in Canberra for the Prime Minister's XI match against the MCC. This was Bradman's last cricket appearance, in 1963, when he came out of retirement at age 54. He scored four runs.

Sir Donald was at the top of everyone's guest list - and the who's who of Australia attended any function he held. Prime Minister Bob Hawke was on hand at a dinner in 1987.

Bradman said as a child in 1921 that he would never be satisfied until he played on the SCG. Fifty three years later, in 1974, he played a mock drive in the centre of the ground as fans cheered the unveiling of the Bradman Stand.

"It is strange, but I think true, that all the time, day and night, somewhere in the world somebody is talking about Bradman." (Jack Ingham - English Sportswriter)

Sir Donald Bradman was inducted into the
Sport Australia Hall Of Fame in 1985.

SPORT AUSTRALIA
HALL OF FAME

honours

Sir Donald Bradman
as a
MEMBER
for
Excellent Performance
in
Cricket

Chairman
SPORT AUSTRALIA HALL OF FAME

Selection Committee Chairman
SPORT AUSTRALIA HALL OF FAME

New South Wales Cricket Association

CABLE & TELEGRAPHIC ADDRESS: "STUMPS"

TELEPHONE: 27 4053

TELEX: AA72734

FAX (02) 262 2728

EXECUTIVE DIRECTOR: R. M. RADFORD

1ST FLOOR
47 YORK STREET
SYDNEY. N.S.W. 2000

28 June 1988

Sir Donald Bradman A.C.
2 Holden Street
KENSINGTON PARK   5068

Dear Sir Donald,

I have been somewhat remiss in not writing earlier to congratulate
you, on behalf of all of us at the Association, on your having been
named for the best single performance by an Australian male athlete
in the 1988 Bicentennial Sport Australia awards.

Bradman received the ultimate individual accolade in the Sport
Australia Bicentennial awards in 1988 when he was honoured
for the best single performance by an Australian athlete - his
309 in a day against England at Leeds in 1930.

Sir Donald Bradman played his final first-class match for South Australia at Adelaide Oval in 1949, and 41 years later he walked the famous ground again after the unveiling of the new grandstand named in his honour. He officially opened the stand in January, 1990.

The modern stand was a fitting tribute to his involvement and promotion of the game in South Australia.

ADELAIDE OVAL.

First used for first-class cricket in 1884. Dimensions of playing area, 207 yards by 140 yards. Record cricket attendance, 50,962, during 3rd Test, January, 1933. Venue of 12 England-Australia Tests. Five won by England, 7 won by Australia.

Although long retired as an administrator, this speech by South African ambassador demonstrates the esteem in which Bradman was held throughout the cricket world.

AMBASSADOR DAVID TOTHILL'S REMARKS AT A SOUTH AFRICAN COMMEMOR-ATIVE DINNER HOSTED BY THE CHAIRMAN AND TRUSTEES OF THE BRADMAN TRUST [Burradoo Room, Resort Hotel Heritage Park, Bowral, 23 February 1992]

Don Bradman was not just a cricketer. Even in his playing days he was a national icon and for reasons which transcended the world of cricket. Indeed, future historians may well conclude that Sir Donald's greatest contribution to his country's national life lay outside the sport he graced. His record shows him to have been the greatest batsman who ever lived. But in the trying times when he held sway, he helped give a sense of national identity and purpose to his fellow Australians. We South Africans are now engaged in the arduous task of nation-building. We need a Don Bradman to give impetus to our efforts. I wish we could borrow the original.

SACHIN TENDULKAR

(India's champion batsman and former captain who until July 2008 had scored 11,821 runs in 148 Tests at an average of 54.98)

Sir Donald Bradman gave me the greatest compliment I have ever had and the most wonderful and memorable moment of my cricketing life.

The greatest batsman the world has ever seen, and surely will ever see, remarked in 1994 that I was his like image as a batsman, the player who reminded him most of his own batting genius.

I remember clearly when I first heard it. We were in Sharjah and a television crew asked for my reaction to Sir Donald's comment. I didn't know how to react. You never expect such a compliment, certainly not from the great man himself.

If someone else, anyone else, had suggested such a thing it would never have meant as much. But for Sir Donald to say it himself was just such a tremendous honour, a tribute that I will cherish forever.

Like every other kid in India who picks up a cricket bat, I was aware of the name Don Bradman from a really early age. His name is known throughout the cricket world and every kid marvels at his feats, how consistent he was and how he averaged 99.94 in Test cricket.

For such a man to liken your style and attitude to batting, to entertainment and seizing the initiative in a match with his very own is more than any player could dream of.

Then, as if to put icing on the cake, I was fortunate to meet him and to be with him at his 90th birthday celebrations in Adelaide in 1998. I was invited by Cricket Australia and the Board of Control of Cricket in India graciously gave me permission to take a day off a training camp and fly to the celebrations.

It is a day I will never forget. To meet Don Bradman, the maestro, was a wonderful moment, the highlight of my cricket career.

It was a fabulous experience and we spent about an hour chatting privately on a range of topics, including golf, but generally about the standard of cricket in the modern era. He was casual and charming and certainly knew what was going on in cricket even then.

I asked him about his pre-match preparations. He told me he didn't have time for that sort of thing. He worked before the game and he went back to work immediately after.

He told me he just loved to bat and that he played cricket for the love of the game, because the game was something special. And every time he went out to bat he didn't want to get out. He wanted to savour it for as long as he could in the centre in every innings, every game. When you consider that he was almost 40 when he toured England as captain of the 1948 Invincibles team that went through the tour undefeated, he certainly enjoyed the game from start to finish of a 20 year career. And to think that on that tour he scored 11 centuries, including 138 in the Nottingham Test and 173 not out in the Leeds Test when Australia chased down 404 on the final day to win. That's the sort of stuff you see in movies or read in fairytales.

Bradman stands out from the best of the rest. There is such a big margin between him and anyone else statistically that he will always stand out. You cannot ignore his statistics, no matter what era you play in, or for what country.

It is remarkable that almost every time he went to bat he scored handsomely. He not only scored at a fast rate to entertain the crowd, he averaged 99.94 in Test matches which is just unreal.

And to perform at that level under the pressure of all the adulation of the time and the expectations of a nation is a remarkable achievement. Bradman was a national hero at 21 years of age. Even at that early age, he was expected to make hundred after hundred, to win Tests, to set record scores. He had the pressure of lifting the spirits of his country during the Great Depression and then World War II. And he did. To think that he averaged a century every third time he batted in a Test is truly incredible.

I have an appreciation of similar pressure, and you must deal with it. It is not easy with the adulation and public's expectations. But there comes a stage when you forget about the pressures and play to live up to your own expectations. If you do that you surely will satisfy the people.

Bradman did, and he did it on uncovered wickets and without all the protective gear of the modern era. Any cricket lover must just shake his head coming to terms with that, and any batsman knows it is virtually asking the impossible to average a tick under 100 in such conditions and under such sustained pressure.

Bradman did. He simply was the best. Unchallenged.

Mrs JUDY GRIBBLE

Kensington Gardens

(Adelaide, bridge partner of Sir Donald Bradman for 26 years.)

My husband, Michael, and I were extremely privileged to have been close friends with Don and Jessie Bradman, and to have spent so much time with them. We feel honoured as he is an icon of Australia, not just in sport but as part of our national history and the fabric of this nation.

We often asked ourselves: why us? Perhaps it was because, although we enjoyed cricket, we were not real cricket buffs, and that our interests (especially the game of bridge) were a necessary and desirable distraction for Don. We rarely talked about cricket, and for that I think Don was most grateful. Don evidently felt he could relax with us away from the pressures of being the face of cricket and enjoy playing bridge, sip and discuss wines, relate stories, for example, about a 1923 Buick Jessie's father bought. It did 400,000 miles and then had the engine taken out and used on the farm. And they would tell us about the many interesting people they had met in various parts of the world. He loved telling jokes and always laughed heartily at them. That freedom was probably the key to our long and close friendship.

For 26 years, until three months before his death in 2001, I was his bridge partner and until her death Michael would partner Jessie. We had dinner and played bridge on average about once a fortnight until 1997. After Jessie died Don came to dinner Sunday evenings and David Kirby or Pat Kiemich or my sister Helen made up the bridge four.

I first met Don as I had looked after the granddaughter of a friend of his, Lord McGowan, when I was nursing in England. Years later I took my 6 year old nephew David Crouch to the cricket here and he wanted Don's autograph. I said to him "Look there's Keith Miller" to which he loudly replied "Who's Keith Miller?" Keith Miller overheard this question, turned around, and said "Why don't you educate the kid?" Don, who was with Keith, thought it was a great joke.

Shortly after this we bumped into Don and Jessie at a restaurant and Jessie suggested we had dinner with them the following week and a game of bridge and that was the beginning of a friendship which was to last 26 years.

Bridge became an integral part of our lives. Don and Jessie would visit our home or we would play at Holden Street or our beach house which was then at Victor Harbour, or occasionally, we would dine at a restaurant and then play bridge later. Don would always sit with his back to other diners so we wouldn't be interrupted by people wanting his autograph. Don enjoyed his wine, preferably a good red wine and was quite a connoisseur. If playing at our home he always arrived with a bottle of wine. One night he bought a bottle of Henschke Hill of Grace to celebrate his and Jessie's 60th wedding anniversary. We also celebrated their 65th wedding anniversary with them. On another occasion he bought a 75 year old bottle of Para Port which had been given to him on his 75th birthday. "You realise that each sip is costing a fortune" he joked as he poured the drinks. Another time he came around 24 hours before expected and said the bottle of red he was bringing needed to be opened then as it was very old and had to breath for 24 hours. He was absolutely correct. It was dreadful when he brought it but delightful the next evening.

We were amused one evening. That afternoon Don had wanted to open another account at a bank in King William Street where he had banked for years and they asked him for his ID. He said you know who I am, and they still insisted they had to physically sight his ID. As he had left his wallet in his car he was a bit put out that he had to go and get it. He came in grumbling "Do they think I am, Ned Kelly?"

There was an occasion when Don was really grumpy and that was when they changed the name of the Sheffield Shield to the Pura Cup. That really upset him and he kept talking about it the entire evening.

One day I answered our door to find Don standing there holding a very large container. He announced he had spent the morning fishing and then explained that he had filled in their fish pond which had been at the front of their home and as we had a fish pond his fish were coming to join ours.

Publicity was something that Don shunned and he couldn't really go anywhere without being noticed. He received letters, bats, and all manner of things sent to him to autograph. For much of his life he would do as requested but it irritated him that he had to then take them to the post office and post them back. One day while at the Post Office a stranger walked in, looked at Don and said "Do you know you look quite like Don Bradman." Don said he replied "Yes I have been told that" and promptly left.

Don's bridge was a little different. He used to play auction bridge on the ships in his cricketing days and he thought some of the bidding for contract bridge unreasonable, especially asking for aces. I could never get him to do that, but when he played a hand, he was brilliant. If a contract was there he would always get it, and he loved winning. On one occasion he made a mistake and was still apologising for it, and remembered every card, a week later. If Jessie and I were talking too much about other things, for example, the club of which we were both members, he would say to Michael: "Michael are we here to play bridge or is this a ladies meeting?" Jessie would wink at me and we would go on playing.

During dinner we talked topics of the day, music, the stock market, and politics or anything but cricket. Occasionally he would question Michael on various medical problems. He always seemed to have some acquaintance with something wrong with them and he wanted to know all about it. He had a fabulous memory, which doubtless helped when playing cards. He could look at the stock market listings in the newspaper in the morning and for the rest of the day he seemed to know exactly what all the prices were. On one occasion when playing bridge he said to me "Now concentrate, this is serious, not like those speculative shares you bought today!"

An example of how thoughtful Don was, when Michael and I went to England, he got in touch with Gubby Allen (ex English captain) to show us over Lords. Gubby was a charming man and obviously he thought the world of Don and Jessie. He met us at the gate and we were taken everywhere. Even shown where he lived through a gate beside the ground.

During Don's time as a director of Rigby's he claimed to have read every book they published in that period and he and my husband continually lent each other books, many being biographies. One Christmas we gave Don a Brewer's Dictionary of Phrase & Fable, which is a collection of almost every obtuse and seemingly offbeat fact in history. He loved it and nothing gave him more pleasure than being able to catch out Michael, who has several degrees from Oxford. Don would say: "Don't know what they taught you at that university" and have a hearty laugh.

It was a pleasure to hear Don play the piano. He was a brilliant self taught pianist playing mostly classical music, and consequently, he was immensely proud of his granddaughter Gretta who has a lovely voice and had inherited his and Jessie's musical talents. He also said she looked like Jessie.

He loved nearly all sport. He would leave our home on a Sunday evening and go home and sit up until four o'clock in the morning watching soccer from England on television. Jessie told me she thought, had he concentrated on tennis rather than cricket, he would have won Wimbledon.

One evening I asked if he had ever played squash and he politely muttered that he was a five time South Australian champion. He was amazing as he had also played billiards with Walter Lindrum, and in his eighties regularly broke his age at golf having previously been a scratch player. His stories were a constant source of entertainment, and you marveled at the people he had met, the places he had been. I am sad I didn't ever make a note of them.

We tried without success to get him to buy a new TV and typewriter as the ones he had were very basic. He said it was easier to get me to record anything he wanted on our TV! He did, however, have an automatic door fitted to his garage and he was so thrilled with it we were taken out to see how it worked.

He always retained a dislike of planes, trying to get out of any travel that involved flying. Late in his life, British Prime Minister John Major rang to invite Don and Jessie to England, all expenses paid, for a function. Don hated flying so he apologised, hinting that Jessie was unwell. The fact that Don couldn't attend because Jessie was unwell made it into the London newspapers, whereupon Jessie began receiving flowers and get-well cards from friends in England. This embarrassed her as she was longing for Don to accept so they could both go.

Don had a lot to put up with at times, for example, on one occasion a gentleman rang from India saying he was coming to Adelaide on a certain date and would Don autograph a book for him. Don consented if the gentleman came to his city office door at 5 p.m. The fellow turned up with 20 other tourists who had paid him for the honour of seeing Don! Don was annoyed at the time but laughed about it afterwards.

Don had to put up with people knocking on his door all the time, all the fan mail and all those who wanted to interrupt him for an autograph. He really wanted peace, so when his 80th birthday arrived, he shunned the media which was looking for him and according to the news reports "went into hiding at a secret location." That secret location was at our beach house at Victor Harbor.

Most people would not realise that Don was a very emotional man. I recall the Les Favell Testimonial match, Les Favell XI v Sir Donald Bradman XI, when Don wore his Australian blazer for the last time. It was a tribute to Les, who was only 57 when he died, and who, Don said, represented everything that was good in cricket. One evening I showed him some photos of the testimonial day and he said: "Do you want to make me cry?" as tears filled his eyes. He thought the world of Les Favell.

It was terribly sad when Jessie died. She was incredibly brave during the 2 years she was having treatment. I had accompanied her to the hospital on these many occasions and all the nurses and doctors adored her. When she died Don rang us and asked us to take him to her funeral and Memorial Service which we were honoured to do.

Some years earlier after my mother died, my father had a wonderful carer called Mrs Betty Joseph. After my father died I introduced her to Jessie and she became the Bradmans' dependable and much appreciated housekeeper and friend known to many visitors as the friendly face who opened the front door. Mrs. J, as Jessie called her, was with the Bradmans for 14 years right up to a fortnight before Don died.

Don was a stickler for punctuality. Even after Jessie died we knew at exactly 6.30 every Sunday evening our door bell would ring. We are sure he would drive around the block if necessary, or pace up and down the street, just to ensure he wasn't early and that he was precisely on time.

One of the things that kept Don going after Jessie died was the welfare of the Bradman Museum. He signed many hundreds of things to be sold there. Even when he was really ill he would sit in his study signing to raise money so young cricketers would have a chance to further their careers. He had explained to us that he had legally given the Museum the use of his name to ensure its financial future. He told us he had discussed this with Mr Vin Kean, one of his regular luncheon friends and Sir Ron Brierley amongst others who had the interests of the Museum at heart. He was very fond of Richard Mulvaney who was the then director of the Museum and told us how he had told Richard to pack up and take his collection of Wisdens to the Museum but Richard had said "You keep them while you enjoy them."

About three months before Don died, when he was diagnosed with pleurisy and pneumonia, I took him to St Andrews Hospital for an X-ray. He refused to let me get a wheelchair to go inside the hospital and insisted he walked. We battled for about 20 paces from the car until we got to the hospital door and he turned and said: "Well, if you insist (which I hadn't) I'll use a wheelchair..."

27.8.96 DON'S 88TH BIRTHDAY

From the portrait by Reg Campbell

Don Bradman

With Best Wishes for a Merry Christmas and a Happy New Year

from

Don & Jessie

2 Holden Street,
Kensington Park,
South Australia 5068

231

Sir Donald yearned for peace and quiet in his latter years and found solace with Judy and Michael Gribble as friends and bridge partners. They shared many evenings together and a lot of laughs - including jokes about Sir Donald's moustache.

CONTRACT SCORE PAD

INDIVIDUAL SCORES

PLAYERS					
1ST RUBBER	Don's Bridge				
2ND RUBBER	score				
3RD RUBBER	On his 88th BIRTHDAY				
TOTALS					

WE	THEY	WE	THEY	WE	THEY
		6		12	
				11	
		75			
		180			
		20	30	30	
70	7		50	150	
20					
40	60	60		30	
40		800	100	200	
30				760	
		120		70	
570	60				
	120	130			
170				40	
580					
24					

SIR DONALD BRADMAN

2 HOLDEN STREET,
KENSINGTON PARK.
SOUTH AUSTRALIA 5068

Wednesday

Dear Judy,

Rigbys have produced a novel book on bridge. To take advantage of it one needs time, patience & intelligence; three attributes which I lack. As you have the intelligence you only need time & patience and maybe you can find them.

Anyway I am sending it to you with my compliments and am sure you will at least get some fun out of it.

If you study it well and make sure you are my partner, maybe we can take the Gribbles for a fortune.

Cheers

Don

232

Sir Donald Bradman wore his Australian blazer for the last time in 1987 at an emotional tribute to former South Australian captain Les Favell, one of Bradman's favourite cricketers. The Bradman XI played the Favell XI at Adelaide Oval in a Testimonial match Sunday, April 5th.

Les Favell with Sir Donald Bradman.

The Lord's Taverners

Presenting

The Les Favell Testimonial

Souvenir Programme

Les Favell XI v Sir Donald Bradman XI

Sunday, 5th April 1987

at

The Adelaide Oval

FAVELL XI			V	BRADMAN XI			
BOWLERS	WKTS	RUNS	BATSMEN	OUT	B	RUNS	FALL OF WKTS
1 FREEMAN			RICHARDS				1
2 HORSNELL			LILL				2
3 CUNNINGHAM			HOOKES				3
4 GIBBS			HARVEY				4
5 CHAPPELL			LLOYD				5
6 HOLE			DAVIDSON				6
7 MACLACHLAN			CAUSBY				7
8 DANSIE N			SLEEP				8
9 PHILLIPS			CORNES				9
DARLING							
SORELL							

The State Library of South Australia in the heart of Adelaide is home to an exceptional collection of Bradman material, including bats, caps, souvenirs and the famed Bradman Collection of the icon's life.

THE WEEKEND AUSTRALIAN

BRADMAN BATS ONCE MORE

OCTOBER 14-15 1989   Printed and published by Nationwide News at the office of the company, 2-4 Holt St., Surry Hills 2010

"Bradman 99"

Sculptor Stanley Hammond MBE

This bust was commissioned by the State Library of South Australia Foundation to commemorate the establishment of The Bradman Collection Exhibition at the State Library of South Australia and Sir Donald Bradman's 90th year January 1998

The State Library Of South Australia became the custodian of Sir Donald Bradman's personal collection of cricketing memorabilia in the early 1960s when he gave the first items from his valuable collection. Beginning with the creation of 52 scrapbooks, a substantial archive grew as more items were donated leading up to the opening of the Bradman Collection at the State Library on January 29, 1998. And the news of the day celebrated it.

THE **AUSTRALIAN**

BRADMAN

90 not out

4-PAGE LIFTOUT

Thursday, August 27, 1998. Printed and published by Nationwide News at Main Rd, Chullora, 2190

Bradman's message

MY DAYS DRAWING TO A CLOSE

FRIDAY, AUGUST 18, 2000
MAIN

Sir Donald was busy as ususal on his 90th birthday, congratulated by friends and neighbours. He entertained India's Sachin Tendulkar and Australian spin legend Shane Warne at his home during the day, and attended a gala celebratory dinner that night. Everyone was keen to wish him well - including the Governor General - but Bradman warned his great innings was coming to a close.

Bradman gets a kiss from a fan on his 90th birthday at his Adelaide home.

SIR DONALD BRADMAN, A.C.

2 HOLDEN STREET,
KENSINGTON PARK,
SOUTH AUSTRALIA 5068.

66

2 September, 1998

Sir William Deane
Governor-General of the Commonwealth of Australia
Government House
CANBERRA   ACT   2600

Dear Sir William

I was very touched that Australia's No. 1 citizen should recognise my birthday and I thank you most sincerely for your greetings.

It was an exhausting but memorable day.

Yours sincerely

Don Bradman

Lady Jessie

Sir Donald Bradman enjoyed many outstanding partnerships during his cricket career, but the partnership he cherished most was with his childhood sweetheart and wife of 65 years, Jessie.

He confessed he loved her as soon as he saw her - when he was 12 and she was only 10.

Jessie Menzies, the daughter of the local landed gentry of Scottish descent, was a girl with wavy auburn hair and bright hazel eyes who was to captivate Don and become the First Lady of cricket as his major supporter and confidante.

Jessie Menzies first saw her future husband when he wafted in the flyscreen door on a Sunday afternoon, bandaged and embarrassed about being knocked off his bike by a car.

Their parents were old friends. When Jessie started her first year of school in Bowral, she lived with the Bradmans during the week so she did not have to travel 12km each day on horse and buggy from their dairy farm at the hamlet of Glanquarry. They were playmates when he was hitting a golf ball against the brick base of a water tank with an old cricket stump, or begging his mother Emily, a left-hander, to bowl to him.

Jessie was also a fine athlete, a horsewoman and tennis player. Don was also a talented tennis player He carried her books to school, across the Bowral park and beside the oval which later would be named after him in 1976.

He admitted. "I wanted to marry her in my later teens but I was too shy to ask" She admitted it took her a little longer to be convinced he was the one. When he asked her to marry him 12 years later, she told him to sail off to England on the 1930 tour and to see if he felt the same way when he got back. He did.

She eventually said yes in November 1931, when Don Bradman was already an international sensation. Crowds burst through barricades to be part of their wedding at St Paul's Church in the Sydney suburb of Burwood on April 30, 1932.

After a brief honeymoon in Melbourne, the newlyweds travelled to North America with a private cricket tour organised by former Test cricketer and sports journalist and cartoonist Arthur Mailey. They arrived in Vancouver, Canada, on 16 June. In 75 days, the Australians travelled almost 10,000 kilometres across Canada and the USA and returned to Sydney on September 23.

When Bradman was captain of the Australian cricket team she gave wise counsel and he always credited her sound opinions. She was known for her humour, strong will and ability to put people at ease, especially those in awe of her husband.

The Bradmans mixed with royalty, Hollywood stars and high society all over the world. She was regarded as shrewd, reliable, selfless and, above all, uncomplicated - the perfect foil for an international hero.

They moved from Sydney to the Adelaide suburb of Kensington Park in 1934 and were, apart from major cricket engagements, inseparable. Bradman described her as "the most marvellous woman that ever lived" in "the best partnership of my life".

She would record his scores and often knit while watching her husband from the ladies lounge enclosure at the top of the members stand at Adelaide Oval. They were collaborators in all things, whether she was helping him to write newspaper articles, writing speeches for other cricketers or working as a bookkeeper in his Adelaide stock broking business, Don Bradman & Co.

Bradman fought for her, clashing with the Australian Cricket Board of Control when they refused to allow her to join him in England after the 1938 tour. She and other wives eventually went.

Their family life contained tragedy and hardship. Jessie nursed her husband through many illnesses. He had such serious appendicitis at the end of his triumphant 1934 tour of England that there were reports of his death. She flew to his side. During World War II, Bradman was 34 when he was discharged from the military with fibrositis so painful that Jessie had to shave him.

Their first-born son, Ross, died after only two days in 1936. Their daughter, Shirley was born in 1941 with cerebral palsy and is always referred to as not having had the good health her parents would have wished for her. Their son, John, born in 1939, contracted polio at the age of 13 and was in a frame for a year. But he fought back so strongly he set the State 120 yards hurdles record at Adelaide Oval.

John Bradman, who went to Adelaide's prestigious St Peter's College, forged a distinguished academic career in law but, at 32, changed his surname to Bradsen, such was his frustration at being identified only as the son of Sir Donald Bradman.

Those who knew Jessie Bradman never heard her complain about their family's misfortune. The couple shared many interests, music, gardening, golf and bridge among them.

She became Lady Bradman when her husband was knighted in Melbourne in 1949.

When she died on September 14. 1997, Prime Minister John Howard said "the warmth of Lady Jessie Bradman was infectious". She had been treated for cancer for 18 months without complaint.

In 1989, Sir Donald remarked at the Bradman Oval in Bowral:

"It was while Jessie and I were walking across this lovely ground together on our way to school that I decided to marry her. I was only twelve at the time... I didn't ask her then, but after another ten years I had the courage to ask her... And so formed the best partnership of my life".

In 2001, in a moving dusk ceremony at the Bradman Oval, Sir Donald was reunited with Lady Jessie Bradman as their ashes were spread across the ground that bears his name.

—Dayne.

Miss JESSIE MENZIES, daughter of Mr. and Mrs. J. Menzies, of Burwood, whose marriage with the well-known young cricketer, Mr. Don Bradman, will take place on April 30, at St. Paul's Church, Burwood. Canon E. S. Hughes, of Melbourne, will come to Sydney to officiate.

1932

Don proposed to Jessie before touring England in 1930 and she eventually accepted upon his return.

MARRIAGE OF FAMOUS CRICKETER.

Don Bradman and his bride, formerly Miss Jessie Menzies, leaving St. Paul's Church, Burwood, on Saturday night. *1934*

Home Study of Don Bradman and his bride after last night's ceremony at St. Paul's Burwood.

1934

THEY HAD TO SEE DON BRADMAN MARRIED

Crowds burst through barricades to be part of their wedding at St Paul's Church in the Sydney suburb of Burwood on April 30, 1932.

Leaving the church.—Don Bradman and his bride found difficulty in forcing their way through the crowd after the ceremony at St. Paul's, Burwood, last night. *1934*

Don and his new wife Jessie enjoyed a drive from Adelaide to Melbourne to start their honeymoon. The newlyweds then travelled to North America with a private cricket tour organised by former Test cricketer and sports journalist and cartoonist Arthur Mailey. They arrived in Vancouver, Canada, on 16 June. In 75 days, the Australians travelled almost 10,000 kilometres across Canada and the USA and returned to Sydney on September 23.

Don and Jessie were considered an ideal couple, a pair of country childhood sweethearts who conducted themselves impeccably in public but were unpretentious in private. They were young, photogenic and admired by both the male and female population.

With all my love
Jessie

— Dapne
Sydney

Jessie Bradman was indeed a pin-up girl. Beautiful, graceful and
the perfect foil for her internationally acclaimed husband, she
was universally admired. Bradman declared her "the greatest
woman who ever lived", such was his admiration for her.

John Bradman playing backyard cricket in front of his school-mates.

Jessie and the children spent many hours listening to Don Bradman's performances in England on the wireless.

The Don's longest partnership

South Australian cricket legend Sir Donald Bradman celebrated his most successful partnership yesterday — his 65th wedding anniversary.

Described in 1932 as the "perfect couple", the great batsman and the great beauty, Sir Don and Lady Jessie married at St Paul's Church in Burwood, Sydney, on April 30, 1932.

Admirers crowded inside the church, and blocked traffic outside, to witness the "wedding of the year".

Sir Donald, who retired from first-class cricket after scoring 28,067 runs with an average of 95 — and a Test average of 99.94 — told Channel 9's *A Current Affair* last night he fell in love with Jessie when she moved into the Bradman family home while attending a nearby school when he was just 12.

"That's when I fell in love with her, the first day," he said

"I don't think she fell in love with me (at that time) because I was a terrible sight, they used to tell me."

They considered getting married in 1930, however Lady Jessie postponed it until 1932, after an Ashes Tour to England.

"I said we would postpone it until he got back, so he would go a free man and enjoy his trip to England," Lady Jessie said.

Sir Don said he would not have achieved his success in life without Lady Jessie.

"She is the most marvellous woman that's ever existed," he said.

Sir Don and Lady Bradman have two children, a son John and daughter Shirley.

Sir Donald and Lady Jessie: fell in love with her when he was just 12 years old.

Celebrated with dinner on 29th & at our home playing Bridge on 30th

Sir Donald and Lady Jessie retreated from public life to live quietly in their Kensington home in Holden St. However they were delighted to appear at the opening of the Bradman Meseum in 1989, and (right) in a stunning portrait in 1993 at their home.

The death of Lady Jessie was a body blow to Sir Donald. Lady Jessie
died on September 14, 1997 after a protracted fight with cancer.

JAMES SUTHERLAND

(Chief executive officer, Cricket Australia)

Bradman was, reluctantly in his case, an early mass media celebrity, although, unusual by today's standards, his fame was based on substance and lasted longer than a twinkle of the eye.

Such was his household status that legend holds he once received a letter addressed with nothing more than a photo of his face clipped from a newspaper and a line saying: "Somewhere in England".

Modern posties would struggle with such an envelope.

Wander into an Australian school yard today and you will find very little sport being played and a new generation of physically inactive Australian children who are not familiar with the Bradman legend.

Does it matter that kids today don't know the Bradman story?

Time moves on and each generation has its own interests and heroes relevant to them.

For the most part, this is natural.

But every now and then, a nation has a hero who stands above the rest and who has the ability to have an enduring positive influence, not just on his or her calling, but on the nation's sense of identity.

Bradman was such a hero.

The estimable cricket writer Peter Lalor recently reported that, statistically, it is likely to be another 6000 years until an athlete somewhere in the world will dominate an international sport to the extent that Bradman dominated cricket.

Bradman inspired countless thousands, including many women, to take up the game as players or fans – and not just in Australia. His name creates passionate responses today among keen students of the game around the world, but particularly in England and India, as well as in Australia.

His exploits also encouraged confidence and even cockiness in a young nation, then only two or three decades into its new political existence, scarred by the shocking casualties of and cultural upheavals from the Great War, and shaken by the Great Depression.

In my own case, his name still resonated in a cricket-loving household in which I grew up as a sports mad kid in the late 60s and through the 70s.

I had the good luck to develop in an environment where a school master ran a Bradman trivia quiz over many weeks which I was fortunate enough to win.

The treasured prize: a copy of the classic Bradman book: 'The Art Of Cricket'.

But by then I was probably in something of a charmed time warp. I am sure most of the students in class rooms around Australia in that era were more focused on the merits of more contemporary cultural heroes, sporting or otherwise.

I never had the good fortune to meet Sir Donald, although, in a sense, I work with his presence every day as a large print of a 1989 Bill Leak portrait of the Don overlooks my meeting room table at Cricket Australia.

But I have been lucky enough to meet many who did. There are not too many now who saw him play, and the technology of his era does not leave us with the comprehensive film and video reminders that keep images of modern champions alive.

There are also a declining number who worked with him as an administrator through earth-moving cricket issues such as the cancelled South African tour or the birth of World Series Cricket and the modern cricket TV era.

I feel something of a connection, albeit distant, with the great man through those who talk of their experiences seeing or working with him. But the time will come, too soon, when even those first-hand experiences are gone.

Importantly, using various initiatives the Sir Donald Bradman legend will be kept alive to inspire future generations.

At Cricket Australia, my predecessor, Malcolm Speed, and his chairman, Denis Rogers, created the Sir Donald Bradman Oration in 2000, designed to be a presentation by a prominent public figure which honours Sir Donald's name through a presentation on the importance of cricket to the Australian way of life.

John Howard, Michael Parkinson, Richie Benaud, Alan Jones, General Peter Cosgrove and, on 2? August 2008, Australian captain Ricky Ponting, were the first six Bradman Orators selected. Their varying approaches to their brief can be seen in the Spirit of Cricket section of the Cricket Australia website www.cricket.com.au.

The annual Allan Border Awards towards the end of each Australian Summer include the Bradman Young Cricketer of the Year Award and most recipients so far have gone on to national honours. And Bradman trophies and function rooms can be found within cricket all around Australia.

The Bradman Foundation is also doing great work to keep the legend alive.

Its Bradman Museum and Oval at Bowral in NSW, where the young Bradman famously practised hitting a golf ball rebounding off the brick base of a corrugated iron tank with a cricket stump, offers a world-class display capable of leaving true students of the game with goosebumps.

Importantly, in my view, the Bradman Museum is working to broadcast the Bradman story to a wider global audience via the internet and enhanced displays in Bowral to show how that story remains perfectly relevant to aspiring young cricketers today.

Bowral, despite its charms, will not attract the whole world to its doors so it is, via the ubiquity of the 'net', taking its exhibition to the whole world.

But the true answer to keeping the Sir Donald Bradman legend alive probably lies with the children of Australia.

As a cricket administrator, and as somebody who was a kid enchanted by the Bradman story, I applaud the work to include the legend of Sir Donald Bradman, both as a cricketer and an acclaimed historic Australian figure, in school curriculum material that helps all Australian children of all backgrounds and global birthplaces understand the various strands that collectively weave our national culture and character.

Australia's culture has many elements, including the artistic, sporting, political and other contributions of the diverse people who populate Australia.

Bradman's influence on what it means to be Australian is a worthy part of that, and the Bradman Foundation's emerging success in developing school curriculum material about Sir Donald Bradman could be the most important current initiative that will help keep the legend alive.

News that Sir Donald Bradman had died, aged 92, on February 25, 2001 evoked national mourning and triggered an avalanche of tributes.

Bradman had been convalescing with home-based nursing care after treatment for pneumonia and pleurisy.

His son John described Sir Donald as "a wonderful father, grandfather and friend". "His love, generosity, humour and strong good sense will be very much missed," he said.

Members of the Australian cricket team touring India observed a minute's silence during training. Sports people who gathered at the 2000 Australian Sport Awards in Adelaide also paid silent tribute.

An emotional Prime Minister John Howard, who was joined by New Zealand politicians in a minute's silence at a state lunch in Wellington, said millions globally would share his personal grief. Mr Howard had flown to Adelaide 10 days earlier to present Sir Donald with an Australian Sports Medal.

Mr Howard described his sporting hero as "the greatest" and declared "nobody will be anywhere near him."

"He had an enormous impact, not only on the cricketing world but on the sporting world generally. More than that, he had a great impact on Australian life, especially during the desperate years of the Depression when his prowess on the cricket field lifted the hopes and the spirits of a people who at times felt they had little else."

Governor-General Sir William Deane said Sir Donald was the best-known and most admired Australian of his time.

"His wonderful qualities as a man combined with his absolute pre-eminence as a cricketer to make him the best-known and most admired Australian of our times."

Opposition leader Kim Beazley said Sir Donald's death would "be like a death in the family" for many Australians. "He was an icon, an exemplar, a hero, but he was accessible," he said.

Kim Beazley recalled how Sir Donald helped his own recovery from polio at the age of five. "My parents had never met Don Bradman. Nevertheless, he had seen the fact that I had polio and he sent my father a list of exercises for me to pursue."

Treasurer Peter Costello described Sir Donald as "our tallest poppy, and he was never cut down".

"I too can recall as a six-year-old boy standing at the back of my house with a stump and a golf ball, hitting the golf ball against the weatherboard house. If I could only do it long enough, I'd be another Bradman. But most of us were not destined (for) the heights of Bradman."

Labor deputy leader Simon Crean said Bradman's tcontribution to national life equalled that of George Washington, Abraham Lincoln, Sir Winston Churchill and Charles de Gaulle.

"Perhaps it says something about the culture of our nation ... it says a lot more about the person who filled the position: The Don."

Australian captain Steve Waugh declared: "Everyone loved Sir Donald Bradman."

Sir Donald's death was felt around the country - in streets, offices, homes and on the airwaves, people talked about The Don and his legacy.

John Bradman declined a state funeral for his father to fulfil his father's wishes. As well as John, Sir Donald was survived by his daughter Shirley and three grandchildren, Greta, Tom and Nicholas.

Sir Donald's funeral on March 1 gave Australians a final chance to salute him, and the final procession was fit for the most noble of kings. More than 5000 people lined the funeral cortege route to pay their own last respects.

During the 15km journey through Adelaide's southern suburbs in the early evening thousands of people, some up to five deep, lined up outside the Greenhill Rd funeral home and Centennial Park cemetery. As the coffin and hearse, led by Sir Donald's son, John, left on its journey the crowd broke into sustained applause.

Elderly people stood at attention; children were held aloft by their parents; even a young cricket team, in freshly pressed creams, formed a line of respect and saluted with their bats as the hearse passed.

Giant screens were set up at Adelaide Oval to accommodate the thousands of people unable to attend a memorial service on March 25 at St Peter's Anglican Church in suburban North Adelaide.

Then, according to Sir Donald's wishes, his and his beloved late wife Jessie's ashes were scattered at the Bradman Oval in his hometown of Bowral.

Newspapers around the nation announced the death of Sir Donald Bradman on February 25th, 2001 and the entire nation stopped to read tributes and to watch television news and listen to radio broadcasts.

The Advertiser

Adelaide, Tuesday, February 27, 2001 · State Edition · Phone (08) 8206 2000 · 90 cents* including GST

SIR DONALD BRADMAN
1908~2001

INSIDE:
12-PA

Classifieds Ind

R.I.P Don Bradman

1908 – 2001

FAREWELL TO THE DON

PAGES 2 & 3 · PLUS 8-PAGE SPECIAL TRIBUTE

The Daily Telegraph
SPECIAL EDITION
BRADMAN IS DEAD
Nation mourns greatest hero

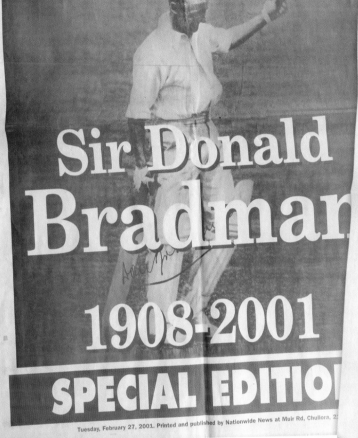

THE AUSTRALIAN

Sir Donald Bradman

1908-2001

SPECIAL EDITION

Tuesday, February 27, 2001. Printed and published by Nationwide News at Muir Rd, Chullora, 2190

The West Australian

Farewell to The Don

SPECIAL 12-PAGE SOUVENIR

TUESDAY FEBRUARY 27

KRYGSMAN

The nation stopped when news of the death of Sir Donald Bradman, aged 92, broke on February 25, 2001. Newspapers around the nation published posters and page after page on his life and influence on the nation. The news also dominated radio broadcasts, while television devoted days of special programs to his illustrious cricket career and his memory.

Sir Donald Bradman's son John led a funeral procession through the streets of Adelaide which were lined with thousands of mourners paying their last respects.

Funeral Service
for

DONALD GEORGE BRADMAN

Thursday 1ˢᵗ March 2001
8.00 pm

The Heysen Chapel
Jubilee Complex
Centennial Park

RICHARD MULVANEY

(Former director of the Bradman Museum who gave the following eulogy for Sir Donald Bradman on March 28, 2001)

In 1949 the Observer newspaper remarked after Bradman's retirement "when Bradman was gone, the light seemed to go out of the game".

It was probably how many of us felt as the news broke with the announcement of Sir Donald's death on 25 February. Having said this, I believe there is no one else who has contributed more to the game and that throughout his life he kept the flame of cricket burning.

I am very honoured today to be asked to say a few words about Sir Donald. It is a somewhat daunting task after the very moving comments made by family and friends at the memorial service, in Adelaide, only a few days ago. He had a long and meaningful life, which is very hard to encapsulate in the time allocated to me.

When I think about Sir Donald the only regret I have is I wish I had met him sooner. Many of you gathered here today will have known him for much longer or have known him at an earlier age. I hope I can speak for all of you. We come together to celebrate a life that was very much influenced by his family, friends and upbringing.

There is no doubt that the young Don enjoyed growing up in Bowral and as he got older would often reflect on his early life. He once reminisced with me of sitting on the back of the gaslighter's horse and helping him light the Bowral street lamps. He remarked in his autobiography 'Farewell to Cricket', published in 1950, that his Bowral days were "completely happy". I think as we all get older, our formative years gather greater significance and special meaning. Bowral was always important to him and was one of the reasons why he gave his support to the development of the Museum.

"From the very first, my name was linked up with the town of Bowral and I was dubbed the 'Boy from Bowral'." We are gathered here in the church where he sang in the choir, his school with the famous bellpost is across the road, the cricket ground and his former homes only a few blocks away. There is a special synergy with this world figure and this small country town.

Cricket was an integral part of country town life in the first half of the 20th Century. From a very early age Don began serving the game. He became the Bowral team scorer before he could play and at twelve attended his first Annual General Meeting of the Bowral Cricket Club. By the time he was 14 he was elected to the social committee and later became the assistant secretary and treasurer. It was this early experience that later served him so well in his cricket administrative life.

His cricketing exploits have been well chronicled. We would be here all day if I were to recount them. A quick tour through the Museum can do that for me.

In summary, he was selected to play for Australia in November 1928 and so began twenty amazing years where 'The Don' would dominate the world of cricket. He became the greatest run-getter of all time, averaging a century in every three innings he played in first class cricket. He retired from Test cricket in 1948 with an incredible batting average of 99.94 from 52 Test matches. He scored 6,996 Test runs with 29 centuries and a highest Test score of 334.

As Sir William Deane so eloquently remarked on Sunday evening, he gave this country pride in itself at a time during the 1930s when we most needed it. He became one of the first Australians to be regarded as a world figure. During the 1948 tour Winston Churchill observed that when in his company no one paid him any attention as the public rushed to greet The Don. He was an ambassador for Australia and a statesman for the game. He was as much respected overseas as he was here.

In 1949 he became the only Australian cricketer to be knighted. He remarked on receiving the Award: "This was an honour that I never sought or dreamt about. If there had been nobody else to please but myself I would have preferred to remain just plain mister. But it was an honour for the game of cricket and in that context I accepted the responsibility of the title conferred by knighthood ... but one thing I do feel very proud of and that is that few people have ever carried the title of 'Lady' as graciously as my wife has and that if ever a woman deserved to be called a 'Lady', she did". Sir Donald continued to serve cricket for many years as a selector and a member of the Australian Board of Control, including the position of Chairman, for two terms. We tend to concentrate on his playing days, but in many ways he gave much more as an administrator. He helped influence the development of other cricket playing countries and in doing so enhanced Australia's leading role. He did not seek attention, preferring that the captain and players represent the game as it had been during his time on the field.

In a retrospective of the twentieth century Sir Donald was selected as 'Australian Sportsman of the Century', 'Wisden Cricketer of the Century' and in the Top Ten of world sports figures of the century by the World Confederation of Sport. He was also only one of two Australians to be selected in the top 100 world figures of the twentieth century. No one had dominated a sport in the way Sir Donald did cricket. This was a theme we explored at the Museum in our new exhibition, which was opened on Sir Donald's 92nd birthday 'Sporting Greats of the Twentieth Century'.

Without taking anything away from the other great athletes selected Don still seems to stand out. This was a point stressed by Simon Barnes of The Times after the announcement of Sir Donald's death: "Each of these names represent an Everest. But the point about the Himalayan mountain range is that it is a family of giants ... Bradman is not only Everest, he is also K2 piled on top. Where other cricketers peak, Bradman had merely found his stride. When others gasped through lack of oxygen at these rarefied heights, Bradman is in his natural element. Where others get vertigo, Bradman simply looks up, not down."

Having recognised this we must be very mindful to heed the counsel of the speakers at the memorial service in Adelaide. With his death we must not turn him into an icon or a religious figure. He was only a man. The public response to his death has been astonishing when you consider that it is well over fifty years since he last played the game. Many Australians today would not have seen him bat but still appreciate his achievements. In all this it has been his values that have stood out and not his batting statistics. It is his honesty, humility and integrity that we now cherish. I am sure this is what he would have wished. He provides us with a will to succeed and inspiration to have a go.

I was very pleased to read Ian Thorpe's letter that was published in Sunday's Sun Herald. Sir Donald, a follower of many sports had keenly anticipated the Sydney Olympic Games and wrote a number of letters of support to athletes and sporting associations. He wrote one to Ian Thorpe which Ian claimed helped inspire him to win Gold. Last Sunday Ian wrote:

"I believe that The Don was one of those people who was placed on earth to challenge us to challenge ourselves, every day, to be better people. He taught us to be humble in our victories and to appreciate the performance of others. To be honest with ourselves and with each other. Thus living life without a question hanging over it." Curiously Don remarked in his autobiography, that swimming was the only sport that eluded him. In fact he once nearly drowned when a young boy.

I have similar views of Sir Donald although no comparable Gold medals. I do consider myself very fortunate to have spent time with him. He was a very special person. He had an ability to make you feel that your ideas were of value, he encouraged you to expand your thoughts and would often give a very considered and measured response. We developed a very close friendship despite being fifty years difference in age. He had a marvellous capacity to accept and value people of any age. He did not seem old to me because he seemed so progressive. He remained a very astute thinker and we would have many conversations about all manner of things well beyond cricket and the Museum. He would often remind me of things that had slipped my mind but not his. He possessed a strong work ethic and attention to detail. I don't think he was ever unprepared. He felt a real obligation to serve and received as much mail in his final years as he had during the peak of his playing days. Before retiring to bed in the evening those letters were answered.

It was not all work. He very much enjoyed the company of friends and family. He loved his golf and bridge. As his son John has remarked he played sport for the fun of it. He also had a wry sense of humour.

I remember Norman May telling the story when comparing Sir Donald to today's players. In short Norman asked him what did he think his batting average would be against the modern bowling? He replied that he thought it would be about 45. Norman remarked that while appreciating the speed, fitness and conditions of today's game surely his average would be better than less half his 99.94. Don replied that he was 82!

The Museum was very important to him and he gave very generously of his time to make it a success. He actively participated in its development and worked tirelessly for us. I remember during my earlier visits he would have a list of questions to ask me and no matter how hard I tried on occasions to skirt around the questions he always managed to get an answer from me. As we progressed he seemed more comfortable with the Museum and as my mind became older I was the one who had the list of questions, not him. We had many happy days together. Even in his final days he had that trademark sparkle in his eyes. He received marvellous support from the medical staff and his family especially his son, John.

As John remarked, Sir Donald keenly felt the price of fame. His career coincided with the development of radio and television which helped telegraph his deeds around the world in a way no other cricketer had experienced before. The fact that he kept his head level is testimony to the values that he possessed. We should also not forget Jessie Bradman. She did much to provide that balance throughout his life. He did describe their marriage of sixty five years as his greatest partnership. We cannot celebrate Don's life without Jessie. It is very pleasing to have so many members of the Bradman/Menzies families with us today.

It is their life together that we should celebrate and remember their very special qualities. Which I might add, have been passed on to their children and grandchildren. We should not put Don on a pedestal but reflect on how he lived his life and in some small way, try to do the same. That is his lasting legacy. It was a life of giving.

In 1928 Bowral hosted a reception for the visiting St George Cricket Team that included Don Bradman. The then Mayor of Bowral, Alf Stephens, gave Sir Donald, on behalf of the town, a gold watch and chain. On accepting the presentation Don thanked them all from the bottom of his heart and he hoped he would never do anything to make them regret they had given him this present. He was only 20. Throughout his life I do not think there is anything that he did to cause regret.

The Bradman Foundation has the responsibility to ensure that the Bradman name continues to have relevance in society and that we continue to do good things in the community. In a message read out at the opening of the Museum in 1996, he remarked: "In the twilight of a long and happy life I still think cricket is the finest character builder of all our sports. And in the years ahead I trust that the Museum in its lovely setting will be the catalyst to encourage and inspire the young people of Australia to serve their nation with courage, honour and humility."

We are all fortunate to have lived a time when Sir Donald was amongst us. As was his wish, we must above all else, remember him for his integrity.

We must make sure that that light still burns brightly.

"Sir Donald was much more than our great pre-eminent sporting person. His qualities as a man combined with his cricketing skill and on-field sportsmanship and decency made him a significant part of our Australian identity. In short he was the best known and most admired Australian of our time." (Former Governor-General Sir William Deane, a family friend, at Bradman's funeral).

Thousands of fans flocked to Adelaide Oval on March 25 to watch the giant screen and remember so many of Bradman's deeds at the famous ground. The fans watched the memorial service from St Peter's Anglican Church in suburban North Adelaide.

This statue by Louis Laumen honours Sir Don outside the Melbourne Cricket Ground. Bradman once commented that he found it difficult to bat at the MCG - despite scoring 19 first-class centuries there!

SIR DONALD BRADMAN

1908 - 2001

The Don played 52 Tests for Australia
from 1928 to 1948.
He was captain in 24 Tests scoring 6996 runs
at a world record average of 99.94.
His amazing first class batting record
of 117 Centuries included 19 at the MCG.

SCULPTOR: LOUIS LAUMEN

A GIFT TO ALL AUSTRALIANS FROM
TATTERSALLS

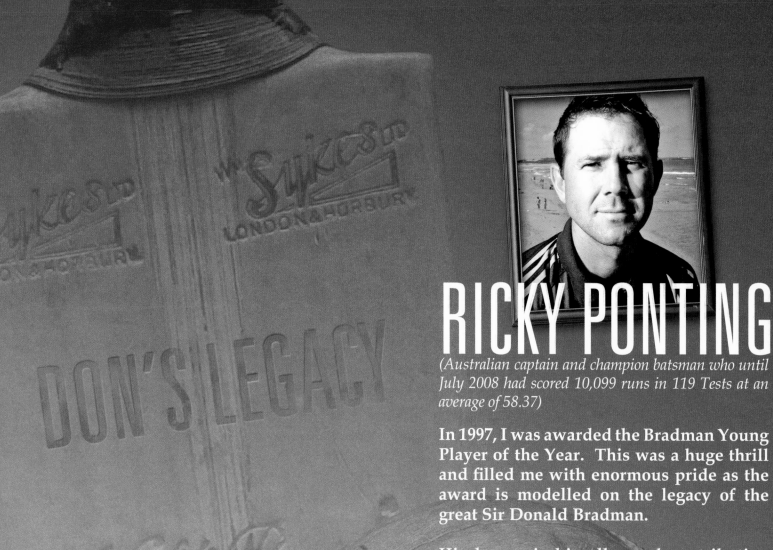

RICKY PONTING

(Australian captain and champion batsman who until July 2008 had scored 10,099 runs in 119 Tests at an average of 58.37)

In 1997, I was awarded the Bradman Young Player of the Year. This was a huge thrill and filled me with enormous pride as the award is modelled on the legacy of the great Sir Donald Bradman.

His legacy is his all-round contribution to cricket, the consistent, modest and responsible way in which he conducted his personal life, and the shining example he set for young sports men and women.

I was extremely proud to honour the world's best-ever cricketer at a special Centenary Dinner in Sydney in August, where I delivered the 6th Sir Donald Bradman Oration.

The centenary year enables all of us to celebrate Sir Donald's contribution to Australian society and the role he played in shaping how our nation defined itself.

As the first current international cricketer to deliver the Oration, it was a very special moment for me.

All Australian cricketers grow up learning about the achievements and contribution of Sir Donald, not just his raw statistics but also the way he influenced and contributed to Australian way of life throughout his lifetime.

Sir Donald built a platform which must be extended upon by today's cricketers - and indeed the wider Australian community. If we don't leave the game, or our country, better off for being part of it, we have clearly wasted our opportunity.

The Bradman name is the most powerful in international cricket history and to be a part in his centenary celebrations was incredibly humbling.

Even today more than 60 years after Sir Donald retired, every Australian growing up, quickly learns of his batting records, his standing in the game and the unbelievable contribution he made to the game as a whole.

His batting statistics are simply phenomenal - to play 52 Tests, score 6696 runs and average 99.94 is just unbelievable. Every modern Australian player aspires to emulate him, but even the best haven't got close.

I am pleased and proud to follow in the footsteps of other great players at No. 3 - obviously Sir Donald, Neil Harvey, Ian and Greg Chappell and fellow Tasmanian David Boon. I feel that I have carried on a rich tradition and enjoy the extra responsibility in the batting order.

And to captain a great side is also an amazing honour, just as Sir Donald obviously felt when he led the Invincibles.

Like Sir Donald, I have been lucky to be surrounded by a lot of great cricketers who, when you look back on their records when they retire, were also genuine champions of the game.

I have a particular interest in perpetuating Sir Donald's name and values promoted through the Bradman Museum.

In his speech at the opening of the Stage One of the Bradman Museum in 1989: Sir Donald said "In my eyes the Bradman Museum has been created to honour and strengthen the game of cricket and my name is merely a catalyst to give it birth and life…."

Then at the opening of Stage Two in 1996, he wrote: "The Museum was built primarily for the youth of Australia. It is a symbol of what cricket has meant and will continue to mean to the people of our nation. In the twilight of a long and happy life, I will think cricket is the finest character builder of all sports. In the years ahead, I trust the Museum, in its lovely setting, will encourage and inspire the young people of Australia to serve their nation with courage, honour and humility."

These words continue to have major influence on me and are always front of mind when I lead Australia on to cricket fields around the world. Sir Donald left a legacy for our sport and our country that I am extremely humbled to be part of and I hope one day that I will be remembered for continuing and building upon his legacy.

Such was the influence of Don Bradman even 60 years after he retired that Australian captain Ricky Ponting decided to replicate Bradman's 1930 captain's jacket.

For a decade under Mark Taylor and Steve Waugh the Australian blazer had vertical stripes, much akin to English college jackets.

However Ponting decided to revert to Bradman's style.

The Ponting picture, courtesy of Cricket Australia, shows that the only differences are that Ponting has his captain's number under the coat of arms on his breast pocket, and that he does not have side pockets. He also has only two buttons, while Bradman's jacket had three.

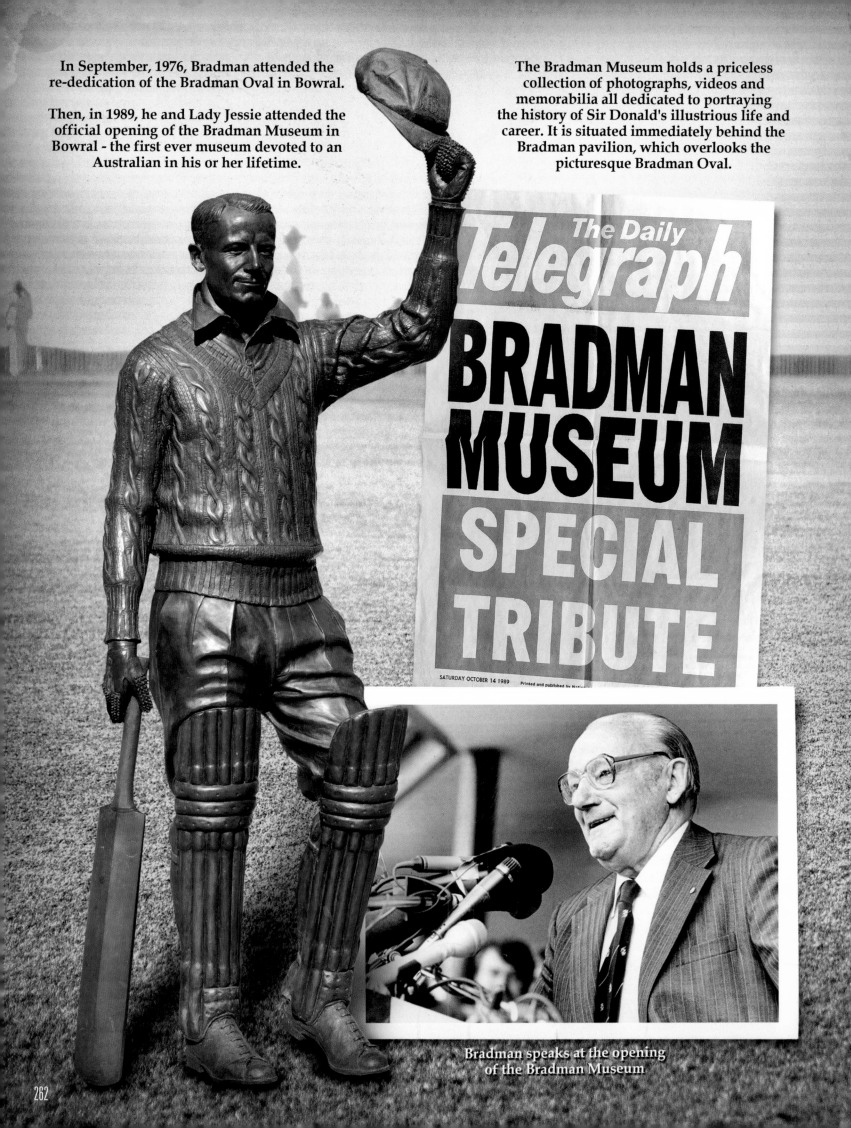

In September, 1976, Bradman attended the re-dedication of the Bradman Oval in Bowral.

Then, in 1989, he and Lady Jessie attended the official opening of the Bradman Museum in Bowral - the first ever museum devoted to an Australian in his or her lifetime.

The Bradman Museum holds a priceless collection of photographs, videos and memorabilia all dedicated to portraying the history of Sir Donald's illustrious life and career. It is situated immediately behind the Bradman pavilion, which overlooks the picturesque Bradman Oval.

The Daily Telegraph

BRADMAN MUSEUM

SPECIAL TRIBUTE

SATURDAY OCTOBER 14 1989   Printed and published by Nation...

Bradman speaks at the opening of the Bradman Museum

Former Australian teammate Bill Brown unveiled a statue and plaque "The Final Salute" at Bowral on February 24, 2002 in the presence of former Bradman Foundation Chairman and Australian captain Ian Craig and sculptor Tanya Bartlett.

THE FINAL SALUTE

Sir Donald Bradman AC
1908 ~ 2001

Donald George Bradman was born on 27 August 1908. He grew up in Bowral and became the greatest cricketer of all time. In 52 Test matches Bradman scored 6996 runs at an average of 99.94. Sir Donald died peacefully at the age of 92 on 25 February 2001.

"Future generations will regard him not only as a very great batsman, but also as a brilliant captain and, above all, as one of the truest gentlemen who has ever worn flannels"
Arthur Gilligan, England cricketer and commentator

This statue was unveiled by former Australian cricketer and Bradman team mate, Mr Bill Brown, 24 February 2002.

Mr Ian Craig
Chairman

Ms Tanya Bartlett
Sculptor

BRADMAN MUSEUM

Bradman and children at the re-opening of the re-constructed Bradman Oval in 1976.

Fifty years after they first met on the Bowral ground, Bill O'Reilly bowled his last ball (pictured below) to Sir Donald Bradman as part of the ceremony to mark major improvements to Bradman Oval in September 1976.

BRETT LEE

(Australian fast bowler with 269 Test wickets in 68 Tests, Bradman Young Cricketer of the Year and ambassador of the Bradman Foundation junior coaching scheme)

To receive the first Bradman Young Cricketer of the Year Award in 2000 was a really special honour to me, and I have tried to uphold his ideals and sportsmanship ever since.

I have always looked up to Don Bradman. He has been the benchmark as a batsman for everyone in the game, but equally he always played in the right spirit which is an inspiration to all players, not just batsmen.

Any young cricketer knows who Don Bradman is because his name is synonymous with cricket excellence, not just in Australia but around the world.

I was lucky enough to grow up 40 miles from where Bradman lived in Bowral, so that gave special significance to the Award.

The Bradman Young Cricketer of the Year Award is special because it gives a young person, as it did me, something to strive for. You don't have many opportunities as a young player to win an award that honours the great name of Bradman. And when your name is linked with Bradman through this award, you have responsibilities to uphold his name and ideals.

I know that in 20 years time someone else will be just as proud as I am to have received the award.

I have tried during my career to uphold Bradman's ideals of sportsmanship and how he liked the game to be played. I always try to play in the right spirit of the game and to give something to the public, which Bradman always did. When you look at how quickly he scored his runs, there was always an entertainment value for the public besides his own enjoyment of the game. If you do your best and you try to emulate Bradman's spirit and sportsmanship, you can't go wrong.

I have tried to give back to the game as the patron of cricket coaching of kids at the Bradman Museum.

I think Don Bradman always will be the greatest cricketer who ever lived. Simple as that.

Bowral Municipal Council

Civic Reception

Friday, 3rd September, 1976

To honour
Sir Donald Bradman,
Mr. Bill O'Reilly
and Jack Chegwyn's XI
on the occasion of the re-opening
of the re-constructed Bradman Oval

BOWRAL

Established 1863

DAVID WELLS

(Curator of the Bradman Museum)

Sir Donald Bradman assigned the intellectual property rights of his name and legacy to the Bradman Foundation to assist with the sustainability and viability of the Museum in the long term.

The Museum was never designed to be a shrine to the cricketer - indeed it was the last thing he wanted. In his own words, spoken at the opening of Stage One of the Museum in 1989 he said, "In my eyes the Bradman Museum has been created to honour and strengthen the game of cricket and my name is merely a catalyst to give it birth and life…"

The Bradman Museum pays tribute to his illustrious career and life, and the history of the game itself with memorabilia, historic documents, film and artefacts. The exhibitions are supported by the Bradman Foundation (www.bradman.com.au) and the Bradman Trail (www.bradmantrail.com.au), dedicated websites, which both chronicle the life of a legend and national treasure.

But the game of cricket is more than just one man. To remain relevant in our ever-changing world, the Museum must think of the future and a generation of cricket lovers who will look to us to display the global story of this loved game, and those of its many heroes.

In recognition of Sir Donald's Centenary, a funding grant of $7m has been made to the Foundation by the Federal government. The Centenary Project will establish the *'International Cricket Hall of Fame'* which will feature the world's best cricketer's with Bradman as the captain of the inductees. The achievements, personalities and cultures of the inducted members will be profiled to ensure the museum truly represents the global nature of modern cricket. These displays will be delivered using the latest technology, much of it interactive. Central to the narrative will be the interpretation of One-Day International and Twenty20 alongside the greatest challenge in the game - Test cricket. Through this initiative and its websites, the Bradman Museum, so proudly grounded in Sir Donald's legend, will take its story to the world and embrace the contemporary global game.

Sir Donald wanted every generation to appreciate how the game has evolved, to respect its wonderful traditions while enjoying its current influences and heroes. He believed cricket was the finest character builder of all sports.

The Bradman Foundation is a non-profit charitable trust and operates the Bradman Museum and Oval providing a unique "living centre of cricket".

In addition to the Museum and Oval, the Foundation also awards and manages the Bradman 99.94 Scholarships. Each year, an Australian student is funded in their University studies for a three-year period. They are chosen by an independent panel with the criteria being: highly promising academically, talented at cricket but not necessarily at the highest level, and a person who espouses to play and live his or her life as Don Bradman would have encouraged young people to live with similar values to his own.

The Foundation also conducts coaching clinics for resident and non-resident groups. Children from around Australia and overseas can come to learn how to play cricket in the very place Don Bradman grew up and learned the game. Accredited Cricket NSW coaches run the clinics for 12 to 17 year-old boys and girls. Creating an important link with the modern game, the coaching ambassador is Australian fast bowler Brett Lee.

Subsidised schools projects are also conducted to enable children in primary and high schools to learn more about Sir Donald as a person, rather than merely his statistics as a cricketer. This is important as it puts Bradman's contribution to Australia into perspective.

The Museum also conducts volunteer-guided tours of 'Bradman's Bowral' presenting his boyhood home adjacent to Bradman Oval where he first played cricket, Bowral Primary School - where he attended, the family's chosen church, and the site of his first employment. There are elements of the Bradman Trail that educate children about early Australia between the First World War and the Great Depression, and Bradman's national role within that.

The Museum depicts how he lived during one of the harshest economic times this nation has endured. How he continued to be a beacon throughout his life defined by his cricketing achievements, his dedication to sports administration and his mentoring role to many other great Australian sportsmen and women. For many it is revealing that he responded by letter to Prime Ministers and inquisitive children alike and equally.

The population of Bowral numbered only 3000 during Bradman's childhood. A pretty rural district, its industry was farming based. Bradman's father was a carpenter and Don left school at 14 as there were no educational opportunities beyond that age in his day. One of five children, he initially worked for Percy Westbrook's stock and station agency and took people out to the district surrounds to show them real estate.

He grew up during the First World War in hard times. His parents didn't allow him any privileges. Despite his early love of cricket, he received his first bat out of a kit at 12-years-old and didn't get a new bat until he was 16.

The Bradman family's life centred around work, community, music and cricket. The family would gather around the piano in the evenings, and Don taught himself how to play and he sometimes wrote his own music. A love of music continued to sustain him throughout his life.

In spite of his unglamorous childhood, destiny marked him and this quiet country boy went on to conquer the world of cricket and influence the passion and pride of our nation.

Sir Donald was instrumental in the creation and development of the Foundation and Museum. He took a deep and detailed interest in all its progress, from the original plans to the completion of Stage One to the official opening of Stage Two. It says so much about his stature in world cricket that the Museum receives many international visitors, particularly from England and India, who wish to pay their respects to Don Bradman.

Many come to see Bradman Oval. It is here that Sir Donald made his first century as a 17-year-old playing for Bowral against Wingello (with Bill O'Reilly bowling!!) Today the Oval, and the Bradman Foundation XI team, host players from all walks of life, from all corners of the world and every player level - international stars to gangly school children dreaming of their first century. To many it has become the spiritual home of cricket.

The Bradman Foundation is managed by an executive team, an Honorary board and more than 60 volunteers who assist the Foundation's day-to-day activities. It is testimony to the good intentions and hard work of so many passionate and motivated people over a long period of time.

The Museum relies heavily on the many benefactors and friends who consistently assist the Foundation through donations of both important cricket items and funds that go towards the Museum and our charitable programs.

The Foundation is also indebted to the continued support of the global corporate community in the realisation of the plans for the future of the Museum and the *International Cricket Hall of Fame.*

Without doubt, for everyone who has been a part of this wonderful organisation since its inception, there is great pride in the work done, marked by this Centenary year, and great anticipation for the goals to be achieved and the vision ahead. It is for the cricket-loving generations of the future that the Foundation now plans for.

(David Wells, Bradman Museum Curator)

Sir Donald Bradman A.C.
27 August 1908 - 25 February 2001.

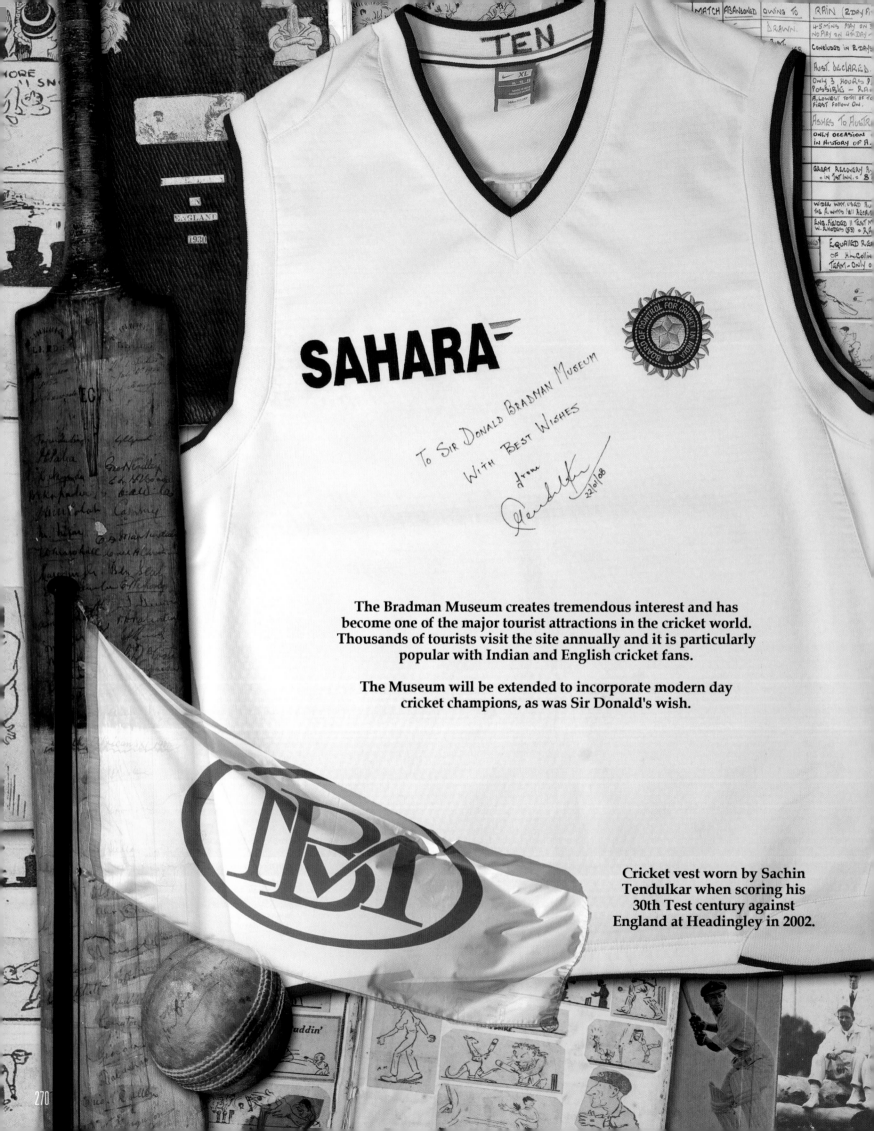

SAHARA

To Sir Donald Bradman Museum
With Best Wishes
from
22/01/08

The Bradman Museum creates tremendous interest and has
become one of the major tourist attractions in the cricket world.
Thousands of tourists visit the site annually and it is particularly
popular with Indian and English cricket fans.

The Museum will be extended to incorporate modern day
cricket champions, as was Sir Donald's wish.

Cricket vest worn by Sachin
Tendulkar when scoring his
30th Test century against
England at Headingley in 2002.

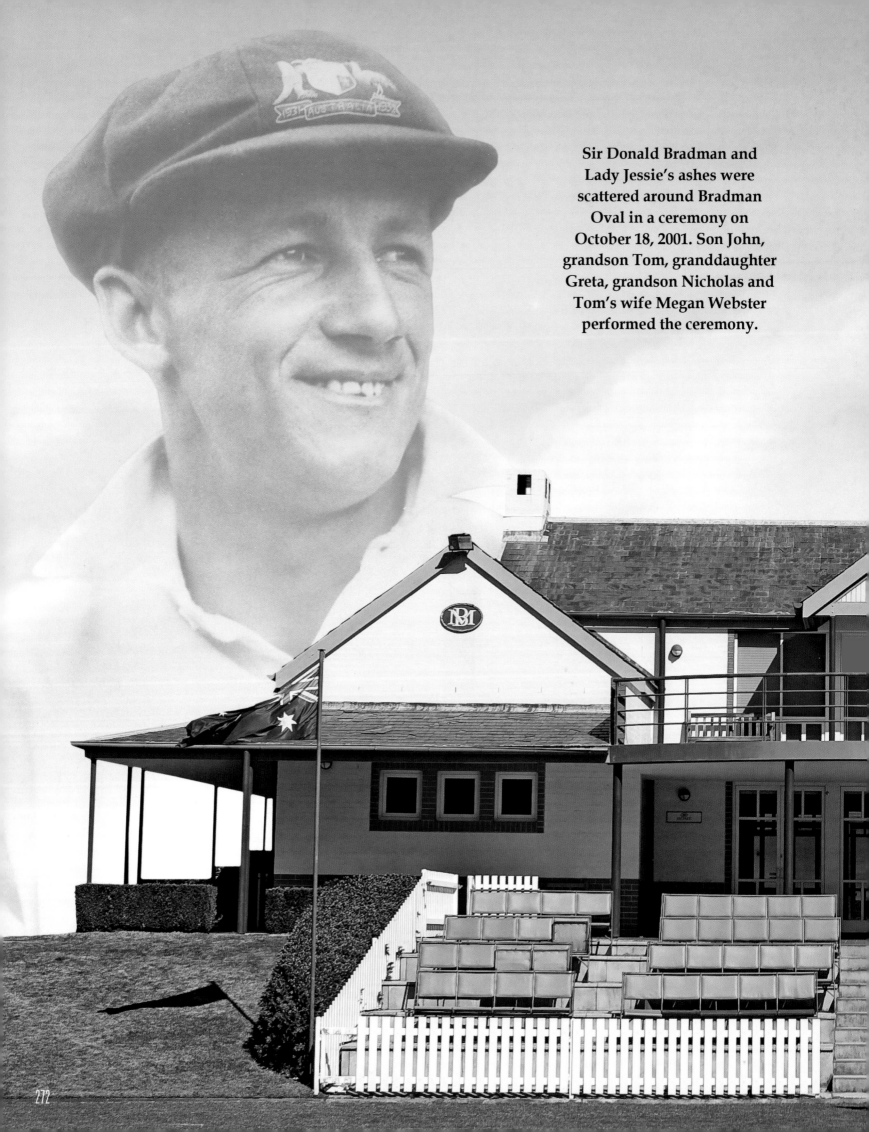

Sir Donald Bradman and Lady Jessie's ashes were scattered around Bradman Oval in a ceremony on October 18, 2001. Son John, grandson Tom, granddaughter Greta, grandson Nicholas and Tom's wife Megan Webster performed the ceremony.

"Mum and Dad loved this place. They loved Adelaide and were able to lead a normal life there but here they inhabited a world without expectations and pressure. Part of them never left this place. The down-to-earth values they learnt here never left them."

(Son John Bradman at a memorial service at Bowral)

BRADMAN STATS

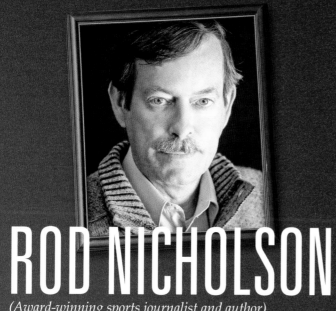

ROD NICHOLSON

(Award-winning sports journalist and author)

Sir Donald Bradman is incomparable as a batsman: sheer statistics confirm such an elevated status, but don't reveal the exceptional influence he had on the game.

He has a Test average of 99.94, about 40 per cent better than anyone who has played the game during the past 200 years. He scored a century every three innings, another dazzling feat. And, in quality teams, he scored 26 per cent of the runs.

He set standards beyond the dreams of ordinary mortals. He broke records, he set records. Bradman scored six centuries in consecutive innings during the 1938/39 season. C.B. Fry (Sussex 1901) and M.J. Proctor (Rhodesia 1970/71) are the only other players to have achieved this feat.

He scored at such a fast rate that even massive totals did not deprive the team from chasing victory. When Australia played during his 20 year span, The Don had an average of 130.08 when the team won. In drawn Tests it was 111.90, and in Test losses his average was 43.27. He was not a one player team, but his influence was emphatic.

Bradman scored 200 or more in a single day on 27 occasions, such was his thirst for runs and the speed at which he dominated the opposition.

He completed his 100th century in only 295 innings. The next quickest was Denis Compton who needed 552 innings. And he is the only player not to have competed in county cricket to boast that 100 first-class innings feat. He was so good that England adopted tactics known as Bodyline to curb his run making. Few sportspeople in history have been afforded such an honour.

More than the statistics that follow, Bradman was acknowledged in various walks of life for his cricket prowess, his administrative skills, his citizenship and his impact on a nation.

His score of 309 in a day against England at Headingley in 1930 earned him the honour of the best single performance by an Australian athlete in the history of the nation at the Sport Australia Bicentennial awards in 1988. He was ranked the No.1 Australian Athlete of the 20th century by Sports Illustrated magazine. In 2000 he was voted the greatest cricketer of the 20th century by Wisden Cricket Almanac. This decision was unanimous amongst the 100 judges.

Bradman was selected as one of only two Australians by International Who's Who top 100 people who have done the most to shape the 20th century. The other was Rupert Murdoch. Bradman was one of only three athletes selected, the other two were boxer Muhammad Ali and soccer player Pele. That's rarified territory.

He is the only Australian cricketer to be knighted (1949), and in 1979 he was created a Companion of the Order of Australia.

In 1960 he became the first former Test player to be elected chairman of the Board of Control. He served two three year terms. He was a national selector for almost four decades, and he was an administrator whose opinion was sought around the globe.

Australians loved Don Bradman and feted him throughout his life. He has grandstands named in his honour at the Sydney Cricket Ground, Canberra's Manuka Oval and Adelaide Oval, statues at the Melbourne Cricket Ground and Adelaide, as well as dining rooms and bars dedicated to his memory.

The Australian Broadcasting Commission's postal address in all capital cities is Post Office Box 9994, Bradman's Test batting average.

Australia Post has immortalized him with Legends stamps. Coins have been struck in his honour. The main street from Adelaide Airport to the city is named after the man who lived in Adelaide for the last 60 years of his life.

Records have been made to honour him, and books and calendars and all manner of memorabilia has been dedicated to him. The Bradman Medal is awarded to Australia's young cricketer of the year, and the annual Bradman Oration is given in his honour to promote sportsmanship and the spirit of sport.

In 1989 the Bradman Museum opened in Bowral. It was the first ever museum devoted to an Australian in his or her lifetime.

The list seemingly never ends. The statistics will last forever, and so too will fans of The Don as generation after generation comes to learn of his feats, his influence on a young nation, and his outstanding sportsmanship.

*Sir Donald averaged 99.94 in Test matches
and the next best, with 20 or more Tests, is
current Australian batsman Mike Hussey,
who in 22 tests before the recent tour of
the West Indies had an average of 78.14
with 2188 runs. Only three other players
average just over 60 – Graeme Pollock
(SA, 60.97), George Headley (WI, 60.83)
and Bert Sutcliffe (ENG, 60.73).*

First Class Career Record

M	Inns	NO	100s	HS	Runs	Ave
234	338	43	117	*452	28,067	95.14

Sheffield Shield Record

In Australia's domestic competition, then the Sheffield Shield, Sir Donald played for New South Wales from 1927/28 to 1933/34 and for South Australia from 1935/36 to 1948/49.

He scored a century on debut (118 - New South Wales v South Australia, Adelaide Oval 1927/28), and still holds the record for the highest first class innings in Australia, 452 not out for New South Wales v Queensland, in Sydney 1929/30.

Sheffield Shield Matches Record - v. Other States

For NSW	Matches	Innings	NO	HS	Runs	Average	Cent.
v. VIC	13	21	7	340*	2065	147.50	8
v. SA	11	20	0	258	1269	63.45	4
v. QLD	7	11	2	452*	1299	144.33	5
Total	**31**	**52**	**9**	**452***	**4633**	**107.74**	**17**

For SA	Matches	Innings	NO	HS	Runs	Average	Cent.
v. VIC	13	18	0	357	1577	87.61	6
v. NSW	9	14	5	251*	1178	130.88	5
v. QLD	9	12	1	246	1538	139.81	8
Total	**31**	**44**	**6**	**357**	**4293**	**112.97**	**19**

Totals in all Sheffield Shield Matches	Matches	Innings	NO	HS	Runs	Average	Cent.
v. VIC	26	39	7	357	3642	113.81	14
v. NSW	9	14	5	251*	1178	130.88	5
v. SA	11	20	0	258	1269	63.45	4
v. QLD	16	23	3	452*	2837	141.85	13
Total	**62**	**96**	**15**	**452***	**8926**	**110.19**	**36**

Above statistics from B.J. Wakely's 'Bradman The Great'

Test Career Record
Sir Donald's test career batting statistics are unique

Versus	M	Inns	NO	50s	100s	HS	Runs	Ave	C
England	37	63	7	12	19	334	5028	89.79	20
India	5	6	2	1	4	201	715	178.75	6
South Africa	5	5	1	0	4	*299	806	201.50	2
West Indies	5	6	0	0	2	223	447	74.50	4
Overall	**52**	**80**	**10**	**13**	**29**	**334**	**6996**	**99.94**	**32**

Bradman's batting average exceeded 100 on five grounds: Adelaide Oval (107.77), Gabba (105.14), Melbourne Cricket Ground (128.53), Headingley (192.60), The Oval (138.25).

His batting average exceeded 100 in seven of the 13 Calendar years in which he played - and exceeded 100 in four of the 11 series in which he played - 1930 v England (139.14); 1931/32 v South Africa (201.50), 1938 v England (108.50) and 1947/48 v India (178.75).

He scored 29 centuries from 80 innings - 36.25% - the next highest was 25.00%.

He scored 12 double centuries, with the next most being nine by Brian Lara, followed by seven by Walter Hammond.

His batting average of 103.63 at No. 3 in the batting order undoubtedly makes him the best ever in that position.

His tally of 29 centuries in 52 matches is exceeded only by that of Sachin Tendulkar 39 in 147 matches, Sunil Gavaskar 34 in 125, Ricky Ponting 34 in 116 matches, Steve Waugh 32 in 168 matches, Matt Hayden 30 in 94 matches, Jacques Kallis 30 in 118 and Brian Lara 34 in 130.

He was the first player to score two triple centuries (334 & 304) and was only one run from making it a hat-trick (299* v SAF). Since he has been joined by V. Sehwag of India and Brian Lara of the West Indies with two triple centuries.

On three occasions he scored four centuries in a series: 1930 v England, 1931/32 v South Africa, and 1947/48 v India. He scored centuries in six consecutive matches from January 1, 1937, and scored centuries in four consecutive matches on two other occasions.

He has scored the most double centuries in a series - three against England in 1930.

He scored a century in each innings (132 & 127 not out) against India at the MCG in 1948 and scored a century and a duck in the same match on two occasions.

Sir Donald holds the record for the highest score for a player batting at number five in the batting order (304) as well as the record for the highest score for a player batting at number seven in the batting order (270).

He holds the record for the most runs scored in a five Test series (947 v England in 1930).

He holds the record for the highest Test inning against South Africa (299 n.o. Adelaide Oval in 1932). He has five scores exceeding 250 runs.

He holds the record for the highest Test innings at four Grounds. 299 not out Adelaide Oval ; 223 Exhibition Ground ; 226 Brisbane Cricket Ground and 334 at Headingley.

He scored the fastest 200 in Test Cricket, 214 minutes at Headingley in 1934 and has scored the most runs in a day, 309 at Headingley in 1930. He scored a century in a session on six occasions.

Two of his World Test wicket partnerships records have remained in the record books despite a flood of test matches. His records are 405 for the 5th wicket with Sid Barnes v England at Sydney 1946/47 and 346 for the 6th wicket with Jack Fingleton v England at Melbourne in 1936/37.

In addition to his two World Test records above he holds two Australian Test wicket Partnership Records: 451 for the second wicket with Bill Ponsford v England at The Oval in 1934 and 388 for the fourth wicket with Ponsford v England at Headingley in 1934.

He top scored for Australia in 24 of his 52 Tests.

He was run out only once in Test ranks, and only four times in 338 first-class innings.

Sir Donald captained Australia 24 times. His team won 15, lost three, and drew six. His win percentage of 62.5% was exceeded only recently by S. R. Waugh (71.93) 41-9-7 and Ricky Ponting (75.60 before the 2008 tour of the West Indies) 31-4-6.

Don Bradman played Test cricket against four countries - England, India, South Africa and West Indies. He did not play a Test against New Zealand (the only Australia v New Zealand Test match during his career was in 1946).

In 1932, Don Bradman played three Test innings with scores of 299 not out (v South Africa), 0 and 103 not out (v England) for an average of 402.

Don Bradman and Syd Barnes still hold the record 5th wicket partnership for any country - 405 v England at the Sydney Cricket Ground in 1946/47.

Don Bradman scored 28,067 runs in first-class cricket at an average of 95.15, with a top score of 452 not out.

Don Bradman was Wisden Cricketer of the Year in 1931.

Don Bradman played for New South Wales from 1927/28 to 1933/34, then moved to Adelaide and played for South Australia from 1935/36 to 1948/49.

The record for the highest partnership for any wicket by Australia against all countries was established by Don Bradman and Bill Ponsford at The Oval in 1934 (451 for the second wicket).

Bradman still holds the record wicket partnerships for Tests against all countries for the second, fourth, fifth and sixth wickets.

Bradman batted in 80 Test innings, being not out 10 times. Of his 70 dismissals, 39 were caught (59%) including 10 by the wicketkeeper and 23 bowled (33%). tHe was LBW six times, run out once and hit wicket once.

Don Bradman scored four centuries in five innings against South Africa, including a top score of 299 not out.

Don Bradman took 32 catches in his 52 Test matches, and took two wickets bowling leg spin (one against England, the other against West Indies).

Against India, Don Bradman averaged 178.75 in six innings. His average against all countries in 80 innings was 99.94.

Don Bradman averaged 201.50 in five Tests against South Africa compared with his overall average of 99.94 in 52 Tests against all countries.

Against India, Bradman scored four centuries and one half century in six innings.

In his Test career, Don Bradman scored 26% of the team's total runs.

Bradman scored 517 runs in three innings without losing his wicket during December and January 1933/34. His scores were 187 n.o. and 77 n.o. against Victoria and 253 against Queensland.

Bradman's average in Test matches reached 50 with his 3rd innings, and stayed above 50 for the rest of his career.

Don Bradman scored his first century (115 not out) for Bowral High School against Mittagong when he was 12 years old.

Don Bradman was originally considered for selection by NSW as a leg spinner.

Test Career: Season by Season

Year	Series	M	I	N.O.	Runs	H.S.	Ave.	100s	50s
1928-29	England	4	8	1	468	123	66.85	2	2
1930	England	5	7	0	974	334	139.14	4	0
1930-31	West Indies	5	6	0	447	223	74.50	2	0
1931-32	South Africa	5	5	1	806	299*	201.50	4	0
1932-33	England	4	8	1	396	103*	56.57	1	3
1934	England	5	8	0	758	304	94.75	2	1
1936-37	England	5	9	0	810	270	90	3	1
1938	England	4	6	2	434	144*	108.50	3	1
1946-47	England	5	8	1	680	234	97.14	2	3
1947-48	India	5	6	2	715	201	178.75	4	1
1948	England	5	9	2	508	173*	72.57	2	1
Total		**52**	**80**	**10**	**6996**	**334**	**99.94**	**29**	**13**

Most Successful Bowlers Against Bradman

Bowler	Dismissals
C. V. Grimmett	10
H. Verity	10
A. V. Bedser	8
H. Larwood	7
M. W. Tate	7
W. J. O'Reilly	6
T. W. Wall	5
W. E. Bowes	5

Bradman's Test Centuries

Score	Country	Ground	Season
112	vs England	Melbourne	1928-29
123	vs England	Melbourne	1928-29
131	vs England	Nottingham	1930
254	vs England	Lords	1930
334	vs England	Headingley	1930
232	vs England	The Oval	1930
223	vs West Indies	Brisbane	1930-31
152	vs West Indies	Melbourne	1930-31
226	vs South Africa	Brisbane	1931-32
112	vs South Africa	Sydney	1931-32
167	vs South Africa	Melbourne	1931-32
299*	vs South Africa	Adelaide	1931-32
103*	vs England	Melbourne	1932-33
304	vs England	Headingley	1934
244	vs England	The Oval	1934
270	vs England	Melbourne	1936-37
212	vs England	Adelaide	1936-37
169	vs England	Melbourne	1936-37
144*	vs England	Nottingham	1938
102*	vs England	Lords	1938
103	vs England	Headingley	1938
187	vs England	Brisbane	1946-47
234	vs England	Sydney	1946-47
185	vs India	Brisbane	1947-48
132	vs India	Melbourne	1947-48
127*	vs India	Melbourne	1947-48
201	vs India	Adelaide	1947-48
138	vs England	Nottingham	1948
173*	vs England	Headingley	1948

Bradman's Test Record Against Each Country

Country	M	I	N.O.	Runs	H.S. 1	H.S. 2	H.S. 3	Ave.	100s	50s
vs England	37	63	7	5028	334	304	270	89.78	19	12
vs India	5	6	2	715	201	185	132	178.75	4	1
vs Sth. Africa	5	5	1	806	299*	226	167	201.50	4	0
vs West Indies	5	6	0	447	223	152	43	74.50	2	0
Totals	**52**	**80**	**10**	**6996**	**334**	**304**	**299***	**99.94**	**29**	**13**

Bradman's First Class Career Season by Season

Season	M	I	N.O.	Runs	H.S.	Ave.	100s	50s
1927-28	5	10	1	416	134*	46.22	2	1
1928-29	13	24	6	1690	340*	93.88	7	5
1929-30	11	16	2	1586	452*	113.28	5	4
1930	27	36	6	2960	334	98.66	10	5
1930-31	12	18	0	1422	258	79.00	5	4
1931-32	10	13	1	1403	299*	116.91	7	0
1932-33	11	21	2	1171	238	61.63	3	7
1933-34	7	11	2	1192	253	132.44	5	4
1934	22	27	3	2020	304	84.16	7	6
1935-36	8	9	0	1173	369	130.33	4	1
1936-37	12	19	1	1552	270	86.22	6	2
1937-38	12	18	2	1437	246	89.81	7	5
1938	20	26	5	2429	278	115.66	13	5
1938-39	7	7	1	919	225	153.16	6	0
1939-40	9	15	3	1475	267	122.91	5	4
1940-41	2	4	0	18	12	4.50	0	0
1945-46	2	3	1	232	112	116.00	1	2
1946-47	9	14	1	1032	234	70.38	4	4
1947-48	9	12	2	1296	201	129.60	8	1
1948	23	31	4	2428	187	89.92	11	8
1948-49	3	4	0	216	123	54.00	1	1
Totals	**234**	**338**	**43**	**28067**	**452***	**95.14**	**117**	**69**

Bradman's First Class Record in Each Country

Country	M	I	N.O.	Runs	H.S.	Ave.	100s	50s
Australia	142	218	25	18230	452*	94.45	76	45
England	92	120	18	9837	334	96.44	41	24
Totals	**234**	**338**	**43**	**28067**	**452***	**95.14**	**117**	**69**

Bradman's First Class Record in Either Innings

	Innings	N.O.	Runs	H.S.	Ave	100s	50s
1st Innings	230	11	20403	369	93.16	88	41
2nd Innings	108	32	7664	452*	100.84	29	28
Totals	**338**	**43**	**28067**	**452***	**95.14**	**117**	**69**

How Bradman was Dismissed

Mode of Dismissal	TEST Number	% of Total	FIRST CLASS Number	% of Total
Bowled	23	32.86	78	26.44
Caught	39	55.71	174	58.98
L.B.W.	6	8.57	27	9.15
Stumped	0	0	11	3.72
Hit Wicket	1	1.43	1	0.33
Run Out	1	1.43	4	1.33

Bradman's Complete Test Record

Test No 1 at Brisbane
vs England, November 1928
1st Innings: 18
2nd Innings: 1

Test No 2 at Melbourne
vs England, Dec/Jan 1929
1st Innings: 79
2nd Innings: 112

Test No 3 at Adelaide
vs England, February 1929
1st Innings: 40
2nd Innings: 58

Test No 4 at Melbourne
vs England, March 1929
1st Innings: 123
2nd Innings: 37

Test No 5 at Nottingham
vs England, June 1930
1st Innings: 8
2nd Innings: 131

Test No 6 at Lords
vs England, June/July 1930
1st Innings: 254
2nd Innings: 1

Test No 7 at Leeds
vs England, July 1930
1st Innings: 334

Test No 8 at Manchester
vs England, July 1930
1st Innings: 14

Test No 9 at The Oval
vs England, August 1930
1st Innings: 232

Test No 10 at Adelaide
vs West Indies, December 1930
1st Innings: 4

Test No 11 at Sydney
vs West Indies, January 1931
1st Innings: 25

Test No 12 at Brisbane
vs West Indies, January 1931
1st Innings: 223

Test No 13 at Melbourne
vs West Indies, February 1931
1st Innings: 152

Test No 14 at Sydney
vs West Indies, Feb/March 1931
1st Innings: 43
2nd Innings: 0

Test No 15 at Brisbane
vs South Africa, Nov/Dec 1931
1st Innings: 226

Test No 16 at Sydney
vs South Africa, December 1931
1st Innings: 112

Test No 17 at Melbourne
vs Sth Africa, Dec/Jan 1931/32
1st Innings: 2
2nd Innings: 167

Test No 18 Adelaide
vs South Africa, Jan/Feb 1932
1st Innings: 299 n.o.

Test No 19 at Melbourne
vs South Africa, February 1932
1st Innings: Absent injured

Test No 20 at Melbourne
vs England, Dec/Jan 1932/33
1st Innings: 0
2nd Innings: 103 n.o.

Test No 21 at Adelaide
vs England, January 1933
1st Innings: 8
2nd Innings: 66

Test No 22 at Brisbane
vs England, February 1933
1st Innings: 76
2nd Innings: 24

Test No 23 at Sydney
vs England, February 1933
1st Innings: 48
2nd Innings: 71

Test No 24 at Nottingham
vs England, June 1934
1st Innings: 29
2nd Innings: 25

Test No 25 at Lords
vs England, June 1934
1st Innings: 36
2nd Innings: 13

Test No 26 at Manchester
vs England, November 1928
1st Innings: 30

Test No 27 at Leeds
vs England, July 1934
1st Innings: 304

Test No 28 at The Oval
vs England, August 1934
1st Innings: 244
2nd Innings: 77

Test No 29 at Brisbane
vs England, December 1936
1st Innings: 36
2nd Innings: 0

Test No 30 at Sydney
vs England, December 1936
1st Innings: 0
2nd Innings: 82

Test No 31 at Melbourne
vs England, January 1937
1st Innings: 13
2nd Innings: 270

Test No 32 at Adelaide
vs England, Jan/Feb 1937
1st Innings: 26
2nd Innings: 212

Test No 33 at Melbourne
vs England, Feb/Mar 1937
1st Innings: 169

Test No 34 at Nottingham
vs England, June 1938
1st Innings: 51
2nd Innings: 144 n.o.

Test No 35 at Lords
vs England, June 1938
1st Innings: 18
2nd Innings: 102 n.o.

Test No 36 at Leeds
vs England, July 1938
1st Innings: 103
2nd Innings: 16

Test No 37 at The Oval
vs England, August 1938
1st Innings: Absent injured

Test No 38 at Brisbane
vs England, Nov/Dec 1946
1st Innings: 187

Test No 39 at Sydney
vs England, December 1946
1st Innings: 234

Test No 40 at Melbourne
vs England, January 1947
1st Innings: 79
2nd Innings: 49

Test No 41 at Adelaide
vs England, Jan/Feb 1947
1st Innings: 0
2nd Innings: 56 n.o.

Test No 42 at Sydney
vs England, Feb/Mar 1947
1st Innings: 12
2nd Innings: 63

Test No 43 at Brisbane
vs India, Nov/Dec 1947
1st Innings: 185

Test No 44 at Sydney
vs India, December 1947
1st Innings: 13

Test No 45 at Melbourne
vs India, January 1948
1st Innings: 132
2nd Innings: 127 n.o.

Test No 46 at Adelaide
vs India, January 1948
1st Innings: 201

Test No 47 at Melbourne
vs India, February 1948
1st Innings: 57

Test No 48 at Nottingham
vs England, June 1948
1st Innings: 138
2nd Innings: 0

Test No 49 at Lords
vs England, June 1948
1st Innings: 38
2nd Innings: 89

Test No 50 at Manchester
vs England, July 1948
1st Innings: 7
2nd Innings: 30 n.o.

Test No 51 at Leeds
vs England, July 1948
1st Innings: 33
2nd Innings: 173 n.o.

Test No 52 at The Oval
vs England, August 1948
1st Innings: 0

Some of Bradman's greatest innings.

JACK FINGLETON

	BATSMEN		RUNS	
1	BRADMAN	1928	118	
2	BRADMAN	1928	340	NOT OUT
3	BRADMAN	1929	123	
4	BRADMAN	1930	334	
5	BRADMAN	1930	236	
6	BRADMAN	1930	452	NOT OUT
7	BRADMAN	1930	254	
8	BRADMAN	1932	299	NOT OUT
9	BRADMAN	1934	304	
10	BRADMAN	1936	270	
11	BRADMAN	1948	201	

SCOREBOARD

GROUND			
ADELAIDE	NSW	V	SA
SCG	NSW	V	VIC
MCG	AUST	V	ENGLAND
LEEDS	AUST	V	ENGLAND
WORCESTER	AUST	V	WORCESTER
SCG	NSW	V	QLD
LORDS	AUST	V	ENGLAND
ADELAIDE	AUST	V	STH AFRICA
LEEDS	AUST	V	ENGLAND
MCG	AUST	V	ENGLAND
ADELAIDE	AUST	V	INDIA

Credits

Scorecards on pg 38, 53, 58, 64, 66, 110 and 147 have been reproduced with the kind permission of Cricket NSW. Stamps on pg 251 have been reproduced with permission of the Australian Postal Corporation - the original work is held in the National Philatelic Collection. Bradman letters in 'The Administrator' chapter kindly reproduced with the permission of Cricket Australia. Arthur Mailey cartoons kindly permitted to be displayed by Arthur Mailey Jnr. Coin on pg 271 top right, kindly permitted to be displayed by the Royal Australian Mint. Cartoon on pg 248 kindly supplied by Warren Brown. Cartoon on pg 250 kindly supplied by Matt Golding. Photo of Warne, Bradman and Tenkulkar - pg 229 © Cricket South Australia. NSW Team Of The Century painting on pg 53 kindly supplied by Cricket NSW - original painting by Dave Thomas. Photo on pg 186 by Ron Berg. Poster of Bradman's death - pg 251 © The West Australian. Photo of Bill Jacobs - pg 210 © Herald & Weekly Times. The following were referenced by the Museum for the Statistics chapter: 'Bradman The Great' by B.J. Wakely, 1959 / 'The Art Of Bradman' by Richard Mulvaney & Brian Clinton, 2003 / 'Wisden Cricket Almanac' 1949 / 'Bradman, An Australian Hero' by Charles Williams, 1996.

Newspix images: pg 6 by Chris Hyde / pg 8 by Jeremy Piper / pg 10 by Wayne Ludbey / pg 27 / pg 42 top left / pg 49 bottom right / pg 54 by Nathan Edwards / pg 72 bottom right / pg 79 by Alan Pryke / pg 94 / pg 98 bottom left / pg 108 top left / pg 114 by Chris Pavlich / pg 124 top left / pg 126 top left by Phil Hillyard / pg 127 bottom right / pg 137 by James Moran / pg 138 by Neill Town / pg 141 bottom left by Wayne Ludbey / pg 142 top left / pg 148 top left / pg 152 / pg 156 bottom right / pg 158 bottom right / pg 167 top left / pg 167 top right / pg 168 / pg 172 bottom left / pg 176 / pg 193 by Stuart McEvoy / pg 200 top / pg 200 middle right /pg 201 by Jim Fenwick / pg 210 top left by Dave Schmidt / pg 213 by David Clark / pg 214 by Brett Costello / pg 216 top / pg 218 top left / pg 218 bottom left by Michael Potter / pg 220 by Sam Mooy / pg 222 top left / pg 223 main photo / pg 224 top left / pg 225 top left / pg 225 bottom left by Michael Milnes / pg 226 top left / pg 227 bottom / pg 233 top right / pg 235 bottom left by Naomi Jellicoe / pg 246 by Alan Funnell / pg 250 bottom right / pg 250 left by Brad Newman / pg 250 top right / pg 251 by Sturt Krygsman / pg 252 by Chris Crerar / pg 253 bottom by James Knowler / pg 254 by Tony Lewis / pg 256 bottom left by Brett Hartwig / pg 256 top left / pg 256 middle left by Chris Mangan / pg 256 main photo by Mark Calleja / pg 258 by James Elsby / pg 262 bottom right / pg 265 top left / pg 265 bottom left /pg 273 top right by Alan Pryke

Fairfax images: pg 190 bottom left / pg 201 top right / pg 204 top right / pg 216 bottom right / pg 241 top right / pg 244 bottom / pg 264 bottom left / pg 264 main photo / pg 288

Getty images: pg 4 by Fox Photos / pg 51 main pic by Fox Photos / pg 105 by Clive Mason / pg 120 bottom left by Keystone /pg 217 by Tom Shaw / pg 272 top left

Items kindly reproduced with the permission of the State Library of South Australia: pg 30-31: VOL01-02_019 - VOL01-02_028 - AD_VOL01-02_013 / pg 32-33: VOL01-02_016 - VOL01-02_006 - VOL01-02_029 / pg 36-37: VOL01-02_058 - VOL01-02_061 - VOL01-02_060 - VOL01-02_053 / pg 40-41: VOL01-02_076 - VOL01-02_041 / pg 42-43: 01-02_093 - VOL01-02_081 - VOL01-02_072 - VOL01-02_073 - VOL01-02_074 - VOL01-02_078 / pg 44-45: VOL01-02_108 - VOL01-02_109 - VOL01-02_100 - VOL01-02_104 / pg 48-49: VOL01-02_126 - VOL01-02_120 - VOL01-02_123 - VOL01-02_124 / pg 50-51: VOL03_167 / pg 52-53: VOL08_009 - VOL03_285 - VOL03_185 - VOL03_145 / pg 60-61: 4 bats / pg 62-63: VOL04_199 - VOL04_063 - VOL04_177 - VOL04_081 - VOL04_111 / pg 64-65: VOL04_233 - VOL05_093 - VOL05_093 - VOL05_157 / pg 68-69: VOL06_113 & bat / pg 70-71: VOL07_153 - VOL07_195 / pg 72-73: VOL09_061 - VOL09_281 - VOL09_345 - VOL09_053 / pg 74-75: VOL09_201 - VOL09_197 - VOL09_047 - VOL09_195 / pg 76-77: typewriter / pg 80-81: VOL12_007 - VOL12_053 - VOL12_075 - VOL12_051 - VOL12_009 / pg 82-83: VOL12_107 / pg 84-85: VOL11_011 - VOL11_013 - VOL11_101 / pg 86-87: VOL07_269 - VOL11_127 - VOL03_395 / pg 88-89: VOL13_215 / pg 90-91: VOL14_155 / pg 92-93: VOL15_217 - VOL15_197 / pg 102-103: VOL17_155 - AD_VOL17_111 / pg 106-107: VOL22_031 - VOL22_029 / pg 108-109: VOL18_019 - VOL18_153 - VOL21_031 / pg 112-113: VOL22_255 - VOL22_261 / pg 116-117: VOL24_011 - VOL24_049 - VOL24_239 - VOL25_233 - VOL26_103 / pg 118-119: VOL27_163 - VOL27_193/ pg 120-121: VOL33_023 / pg 122-123: VOL33_043 - VOL33_045 / pg 124-125: VOL31_139 - VOL30_103 / pg 126-127: VOL31_155 / pg 128-129: VOL32_225 - VOL32_029 - VOL32_231 / pg 130-131: VOL35_015 / pg 134-135: VOL35_047 / pg 140-141: VOL36_073 - VOL37_175 / pg 142-143: VOL39_333 / pg 144-145: VOL40_121 / PG 150-151: VOL42_009 - VOL39_303 / pg 160-161: VOL42_117 - VOL43_065 / pg 162-163: VOL48_209 / pg 166-167: VOL44_185a / pg 168-169: VOL46_137 - VOL46_017 / pg 170-171: VOL47_031 / pg 176-177: VOL47_127 / pg 178-179: VOL47_221 / pg 186-187: VOL52_145 / pg 188-189: VOL50_033 - VOL50_027 / pg 190-191: VOL49_021

This book would not have been possible without
the help of the following people and organisations:

*The 'Contributors' - whose willing and enthusiastic contributions
ensured the highest quality of acknowledgement to Sir Donald:*

*Richie Benaud - John Howard - Shane Warne - Sir Garfield Sobers - Bob Hawke - Sir Ron Brierley -
Tony Greig - Graeme Pollock - Imran Khan - Michael Clarke - Mark Taylor - Michael Hussey -
Sir Alec Bedser - Arthur Morris - Sir Richard Hadlee - Sunil Gavaskar - Neil Harvey - Bill Jacobs -
Sam Loxton - Malcolm Gray - Ranjan Madugalle - Colin Egar - Sir Michael Parkinson -
Sachin Tendulkar - James Sutherland - Richard Mulvaney - Ricky Ponting - Brett Lee -
Sir Clive Lloyd - David Wells - Rod Nicholson - Mrs Judy Gribble*

A special mention to the personal assistants of many of the contributors who worked
so diligently and effectively to ensure and enable so many important and busy people
were able to file their stories for the book.

Thanks also to Cricket Australia, Cricket New South Wales, Cricket South Australia and
Cricket Victoria for their assistance - their knowledge and contacts were invaluable.

Also thanks to the State Library of South Australia for their considerable assistance, and to News Limited,
Fairfax, the Herald & Weekly Times and Getty Images for permission to publish photographs.

The book would not have been possible without the knowledge and assistance of the executives of
the Bradman Foundation - museum curator David Wells, chief executive Rina Hore
and marketing manager Joanne Crowley and the volunteers who helped.

Michael Ball AM (Chairman - Bradman Foundation) - Cootamundra Shire Council - Andrew Munkman -
Chris Jones - Andrew Piper - Linda Emery and the Berrima District Historical & Family History Society -
Arthur Mailey Jnr. - Australia Post - David Gilbert - Pamela Tallents - James Ballaam - Mick Elsley -
Dennis & Lea Jones - Jeff Higgins - Janet Judge - Joel Fulton - Megan Hanckel - Felicity Urquhart -
Ian W. Foulsham - Matt Golding - Warren Brown - Matthew Tokley - Royal Australian Mint -
Territory Venues & Events, ACT Government - Mark Vergano - Bronwyn Alcorn -
Australian Tennis Museum - Tom Markovski - Brett Turnley - BPA Print Group

"*Now, amid ringing applause from the whole cricketing world, the greatest batsman and the most dynamic personality in the history of the game and regarded as one of the two best-known men in the Empire (Churchill being the other) finally puts away his bat...*"
(P.J.Millard on Bradman's retirement from cricket)